Alfred Lord Tennyson

SELECTED POETRY

ALFRED LORD TENNYSON

Selected Poetry

Edited with an Introduction by Herbert Marshall McLuhan

New York · *Rinehart & Company* · *Inc* · Toronto

INTRODUCTION

I. EARLY YEARS

Alfred Tennyson (1809–1892) was the fourth of twelve children of the rector of Somersby, Lincolnshire. His grandfather, George Clayton Tennyson of Bayons Manor, was a wealthy, self-made man who disinherited his eldest son in early childhood. This act toward the poet's father, so contrary to English tradition and sentiment, was to cloud the life of Alfred Tennyson with the deepest hues. The poet's father was brought up for the Church against his will and left to rear his large family in a style much below the one to which he felt them and himself to be entitled.

The recent life of Tennyson by his grandson, Sir Charles Tennyson, reveals many family circumstances that may well render Tennyson a more sympathetic figure than the stately Druid who emerged from the first official memoir by his son. Central to this new story is "the misery and heartbreak through the bitterness and humiliation of the relations with Bayons." This misery led to the gradual deterioration and dipsomania of the poet's father. From this domestic turmoil Sir Charles derives the poet's "dread of personal publicity, the exaggerated hatred of gossip, and the morbid sense of sin which haunts such early poems as the 'Supposed Confessions.' "[1]

The family story as now presented has a direct bearing on "Maud," "Locksley Hall," "Aylmer's Field," and many other poems. And the melodrama of these pieces scarcely exceeds the events in the Tennyson family. The poet's father was a gifted but nervous and unstable man whom his wealthy father always regarded as a ridiculous object. The rich old man was as rigidly conventional and humorless as he was intensely snobbish and ambitious. His disinherited son, unable to bring up his large family in a lavish or ceremonious manner, and unwilling to

---

[1] Charles Tennyson, *Alfred Tennyson* (New York: The Macmillan Company, 1949), pp. 537–538. Excerpts from this work are reprinted with the permission of The Macmillan Company.

accept the conventions of middle-class respectability, adopted the twentieth-century expedient of "progressive" or Bohemian family life. The arty, unceremonious ways of the rector's family infuriated the old martinet of Bayons. When Alfred's early volumes appeared, his uncle Charles (who had supplanted the rector of Somersby as heir of Bayons) had them scurrilously abused in print by his friend Bulwer-Lytton. And in 1850, when Alfred succeeded Wordsworth as poet laureate, Uncle Charles wrote of his nausea that "British taste and poetry should have such a representative before the nations of the Earth and Posterity."

Alfred Tennyson and his brothers and sisters grew up resentfully under the snobbish and scornful eye of their grandfather and in association with the irritable frustration of a father who was impatient of the injustice which had been done him and his children.

The poet's sweet and pious mother did not simplify the problems of her husband the rector. Gentle and indulgent to her children, she fed their vanity with endless praise of their artistic gifts but showed no ability to manage them or her household. Increasingly her husband's exasperation was directed toward her and eventually began to take a violent form. The children grew up amidst domestic horror which was only intensified by the deep affection they felt for both parents.

Unable to afford good schools for his children, the rector himself steered his precocious sons through a wide range of reading in ancient and modern languages. At fifteen, Alfred could easily write Latin, Greek, and English verses in all the conventional meters. Cut off from fashionable social life by poverty, the parents were encouraged by the rural character of the Somersby scene to give their children a sort of perpetual holiday license, so that the style of life at Somersby was nearer to the world of Huck Finn than to that of Jane Austen.² And all his life Tennyson continued to be a kind of shy but unconventional rustic. Yet his indifference to the manners and conventions of town life also

---

² *Ibid.*, pp. 34–35.

gave him a capacity for friendship with all types and classes which impressed the poet Fitzgerald.

The brooding, "black-blooded Tennysons" with their weak nerves and strong passions and constitutions were well typified in Alfred's elder brother, Frederick, whose "idealistic, passionate and unstable" personality is a factor in the formation of the Tennysonian heroes of "Locksley Hall," "Locksley Hall Sixty Years After," and "Maud." Writing of "Locksley Hall," Sir Charles says, "I have no doubt . . . that the story of cousins' love and family estrangement owes much of its form and atmosphere to the feud between Somersby and Bayons."[3]

II. THE PERSONALITY OF TENNYSON

Like the contradiction between the actualities of his home life and the saccharine image of domestic felicity in many of his poems, there is in Tennyson the contradiction between his actual dreaming, his remoteness from social existence, and his doctrinaire conviction that the way of escape from the dangers of excessive spiritual isolation was through wholehearted participation in the great stream of human experience and endeavor. There is an equally striking contradiction between his graceful lyric qualities and his giant physique. Tennyson was not only of great size but of great strength. On one occasion he amused Arthur Hallam by casually picking up a Shetland pony and carrying it around the lawn. His appearance and manner in 1840 as described in a letter of Carlyle's scarcely accords with the Druid image fostered by the photographers and painters of the later period: "A fine, large-featured, dim-eyed, bronze-coloured, shaggy-headed man is Alfred; dusty, smoky, free and easy; who swims outwardly and inwardly, with great composure in an articulate element as of tranquil chaos and tobacco smoke."[4]

And in another letter lamenting the fact that Tennyson was a poet, Carlyle calls him a "life-guardsman spoilt by making poetry." From the age of fourteen Tennyson was inseparable from a stubby

[3] *Ibid.*, p. 194.
[4] *Ibid.*, p. 177.

pipe which he stuffed with the strongest shag tobacco. And he also ate and drank with great heartiness, and customarily spoke in a broad Lincolnshire accent not far removed from that of his Northern Farmer. His personal untidiness was as notorious as his nonchalance. He replied to a friend at Cambridge who pointed to the dirtiness of his shirt: "Yours wouldn't be half so clean, Heath, if you had worn it for a fortnight." Contradictorily associated with Tennyson's shyness and rusticity was a terrifying childlike directness: "In congenial company his complete lack of self-consciousness was apt to be embarrassing, for he would ask the most awkwardly direct questions and would speak whatever was in his mind with disturbing candour and a marked Lincolnshire accent."[5] Had D. H. Lawrence been a contemporary, he would no doubt have found in Tennyson a suitable gamekeeper hero for one of his romances. Tennyson's lack of self-consciousness, together with his complete confidence in his own powers, helped to make him an excellent mimic and reader of verse. As Sir Charles writes: "His manner of reading was entirely his own, a deep-voiced swinging chant in which rhythm and vowel sounds were emphasized at the expense of the ordinary dramatic emphasis and inflection. Yet he achieved a degree of emotion and dramatic force that was often quite overwhelming."[6]

Although uninhibited habits of expression characterized Tennyson among his friends, when with strangers, as one American poet wrote after a social encounter with him, "the great American three-minute ice-cream freezer would be a red-hot stove beside him." At the funeral of his friend Sir John Simeon in 1870:

He arrived some time before the procession was due to leave the house, and asked his old friend's eldest son if he could give him a pipe of his father's and one of his cloaks and hats. "Come for me yourself," he added, "when it is time to start, and do not send a servant." When the moment arrived young Simeon went to fetch the poet. He found him stretched at full length on the ground, wearing the hat and cloak and smoking the pipe. The tears were streaming down his face, and in his hand was a scrap of paper on which he had roughly jotted down the beautiful lines "In the Garden at Swainston."[7]

This strange amalgam of uninhibited emotionalism and pathic fear of society is seen from another point of view in the undergraduate "Cambridge Conversazione Society" (derisively referred to as "The Apostles"), which left its mark on Tennyson. In the meetings and membership of this exclusive group there was a combination of intensity and naïveté, ability and bathos which is sometimes explained by describing it as representative of the new middle class. This class, nurtured in nonconformity, social inferiority, pietistic earnestness, and new wealth, could hardly be expected to exhibit eighteenth-century poise or grace. Nor did it collectively have the homogeneity which had made possible a uniform tone in prose style in the eighteenth century, and which was perhaps last heard in Jane Austen. The enormous range of tone and attitude of style between Carlyle and Pater, Macaulay and Ruskin, Newman and Arnold, is merely the index of the breakup of the reading public into dozens of noncommunicating segments. Tennyson and Browning were unable to discover a tone or attitude which would have enabled them to direct any prose to their dimly seen publics. Newman fell back on the note of private Oxford conversation. Ruskin took over the shrill emphasis of the pulpit. Arnold assumed the antiseptic note of the civil servant producing a government blue book on literary conditions. The industrial developments had set the whole society in motion so that in taste and manners there was universal uncertainty and experiment.

Alfred and two of his brothers had an extremely unpleasant time for a few years at Louth grammar school. Then from 1820 until his entry at Cambridge in 1828 Alfred was under the strenuous tuition of his father. This was the period of his devotion to the poetry of Scott and Byron, and to the Elizabethan dramatists. Wordsworth, Shelley, and Keats he seems not to have discovered before Cambridge.

---

[7] *Ibid.*, p. 389.

After the rural isolation of Somersby, Trinity College, Cambridge, was a tremendous experience, and Tennyson wrote:

> *For I could burst into a psalm of praise*
> *Seeing the heart so wondrous in her ways.*
> *Would I could pile fresh life on life and dull*
> *The sharp desire of knowledge still with knowing.*
> *Art, Science, Nature, everything is full*
> *As my own soul is full to overflowing.*[8]

Like Wordsworth he did not take kindly to the formal studies then in vogue and became a vehement critic of the traditional curriculum with its heavy mathematical bias. Arthur Hallam came up to Trinity from Eton the same year, compact of erudition, genius, gaiety, idealism, and great social gifts. Both Hallam and Tennyson were soon elected to "The Apostles," who declined on principle to spell "oxford" with a capital "o", one of them observing: "I often wonder what we have done to deserve being gifted, as we are, so much above those cursed idiotic oxford brutes."[9] Before this group, in 1831, Hallam read his essay "Theodicaea Novissima" on the problem of good and evil in creation. This Manichean tract is typical of the discussions of religion and belief which occupied much of the conversation and thoughts of Hallam and Tennyson, and which provided the typical sentiments on these subjects that appear in "In Memoriam" and the later poems.[10]

Hallam met and fell in love with Alfred's sister Emily at Christmas in 1829. He and Tennyson had projected a joint publication of their poetry, but in 1830 Hallam at the last minute modestly withdrew his work from the company of Tennyson's *Poems, Chiefly Lyrical.* Coleridge's comment on Tennyson's experiments with irregular verse forms and speech stress in this volume

---

[8] *Ibid.,* p. 57.

[9] *Ibid.,* p. 73.

[10]*Ibid.,* p. 82. For text of talk see T. H. Vail Motter, *The Writings of Arthur Hallam* (New York: Modern Language Association of America, 1943), pp. 198–212.

was that Tennyson appeared to have begun writing poetry without any clear idea of meter.

In 1830 Tennyson became the member of a mysterious military expedition to Spain whose leader, Boyd, was captured and executed. The next year the death of his father brought pressure on him and his brothers Frederick and Charles to take holy orders. Alfred came down from Cambridge without a degree. Tennyson's life now entered on two decades of misfortunes and depression which did not end until 1850: tense family relations, the hostility of critics, the death of Hallam, poor health, the frustration of his hopes to marry Emily Sellwood, and the loss of his patrimony through a bad investment. However, he worked at his poetry, and after leaving Somersby in 1837 he began to circulate in London, becoming friendly with many leading men, including Gladstone, Dickens, Carlyle, and Edward Fitzgerald. In spite of this period of misfortune, Tennyson seems never to have had to work at anything except his poetry, his private income always enabling him to eke out a living.

Still in the nineteenth century, and even today, the literary and artistic life of London had an informal clublike character which is not easily imagined by those accustomed only to the arrangements of this continent. There, people of common interests took for granted regular meetings and much conversation, so that a man did not need to have done very much in order to have regular access to the company of eminent artists and writers. The twenty years that Tennyson passed in obscurity and neglect were by our standards years of intense social and intellectual activity.

The 1842 volume, *Poems*, containing "Morte d'Arthur" and many of his best-known pieces, was brushed off by the critics, as was *The Princess* in 1847. But in 1850 everything changed very suddenly. He married Emily Sellwood; *The Princess* began to sell; he suddenly decided to publish his *Book of Elegies* ("In Memoriam") anonymously. It was an instant success, selling 60,000 copies in a few months. In their enthusiastic reception of "In Memoriam" the critics agreed that though it was a great poem it could not expect to be popular. However, Tennyson himself described it as a "Way of the Soul," which locates it in the company of the literature of spiritual quests—a record of separate moments of growth and illumination, moving from the early astonishment and confusion of grief through a gradual affirmation mediating between pain and acceptance to the finale of peace and joy.[11] This poem led Queen Victoria to offer Tennyson the laureateship.

After this, the poet became a national institution. From the sale of his verse within a few years he became a wealthy man. Part of the dynamics of this movement can be seen from Gertrude Stein's description of the influence of Victorian imperialism on writing:

> . . . in the nineteenth century . . . in order to understand, it must be understood that explaining was invented, naturally invented by those living a daily island life and owning everything else outside. They owned everything inside of course but that they had always done, but now they owned everything outside and that reinforced their owning everything inside, and that was as it was only more so but as they owned everything outside, outside and inside had to be told something about all this owning, otherwise they might not remember all this owning and so there was invented explaining and that made nineteenth century English literature what it is. And with explaining went emotional sentimental feeling because of course it had to be explained all the owning had to be told about its being owned about its owning and anybody can see that if island daily life were to continue its daily existing there must be emotional sentimental feeling.[12]

Tennyson became a voice for England and there began the Victorian myth of the "easy" Tennyson. But within the brightness of this fame and success there was hidden the obscure and minute art of a poet whose work had at first baffled the best minds of his

---

[11] Compare the treatment in A. C. Bradley, *A Commentary on Tennyson's "In Memoriam"* (London: Macmillan & Co., Ltd., 1901).

[12] Gertrude Stein, *Lectures in America* (New York: Random House, Inc., 1935), p. 40.

age. His sophisticated art has long been hidden from our eyes by the exhalation of his public Victorian aura, "epiphanized" by Joyce in the phrase "Alfred lawn Tennyson."

III. TENNYSON TODAY

The Tennyson which the twentieth century has decided to bury is now regarded as the Polonius of his age, the intoner of "self-knowledge, self-reverence, self-control." The Tennyson we have agreed to resurrect is the lyricist and landscapist. The choice has been between the Polonian and the Apollonian Tennyson. Divested of the mask of Polonius, Tennyson can be made to appear as a modern and morbid sensibility such as we have had presented by T. S. Eliot and W. H. Auden. Eliot has written: "There is no evidence in his poetry that he knew the experience of violent passion for a woman; but there is plenty of evidence of emotional intensity and violence—but of emotion so deeply suppressed even from himself, as to tend rather towards the blackest melancholia than towards dramatic action."[13]

Taking his cue from "blackest melancholia," Auden has presented Tennyson as the English Baudelaire: "Both felt themselves to be exiles from a lost paradise, desert dwellers (the barren rocks and desolate fens of Tennyson correspond to the gas-lit Paris of Baudelaire); both shared the same nostalgia for the Happy Isles, *le vert paradis des amours enfantines*, to be reached only after long voyages over water; both imagine Eden in the same Rousseauistic terms; i.e., as a place of natural innocence rather than spiritual illumination." And Tennyson's "poems deal with human emotions in their most primitive states, uncomplicated by conscious sexuality or intellectual rationalization."[14]

The twentieth century has established a view of the Romantics and Victorians as typically engaged in the elaboration of a dream world. And their practice is regarded as defeatist in an age which has sought to affirm once more the role of wit and intellect in the

---

[13] T. S. Eliot, "In Memoriam," *Essays Ancient and Modern* (London: Faber & Faber, Ltd., 1946), p. 181.
[14] W. H. Auden, "Introduction" to *Poems of Alfred Lord Tennyson* (New York: Doubleday & Company, Inc., n.d.), pp. xviii–xix.

shaping of works of art. In a chapter on Tennyson, E. D. H. Johnson concludes that Tennyson's bias was toward the inner vision and the dream life.[15] In similar fashion, Douglas Bush sees in Tennyson a poet in whom the actual world inspired "a temperamental melancholy, a brooding, a wistful sense of the past, an unappeasable desiderium . . . a cry of profound sadness and bewilderment."[16]

Tennyson's art has two major aspects which are indispensable for an understanding of the poets who preceded and followed him. These aspects are the picturesque and the little epic or "epyllion." The picturesque includes the whole range of his landscape effects; the epyllion concerns his method in ballad, narrative, and monologue. Tennyson's picturesque component is bound by technique and theory to the romantic impressionism of poetry from Thomson's *Seasons* to the work of Keats and Shelley. Tennyson's epyllia make him the erudite follower of Theocritus, Catullus, and Virgil, whose cultivation of the little epic form of the Alexandrine poetry really places him in close rapport with the art form of Joyce's *Dubliners*, Eliot's *Waste Land*, and Pound's *Cantos*.

IV. TENNYSON AND THE PICTURESQUE

The picturesque Tennyson of 1830 had an elaborate aesthetic theory and grandiose poetic ambitions which are explained in the remarkable manifesto by Arthur Hallam which introduced him to an indifferent public.[17] In 1893 W. B. Yeats found Hallam's essay an invaluable aid in the understanding of French symbolism. Although written with the flourish of a Macaulay, it is as subtle and compressed as Eliot's early prose, and there are few of Eliot's doctrines of poetry and communication which Hallam fails to pronounce. The reason is perhaps that, like Eliot, Hallam is seeking in poetry a means of the highest spiritual illumination.

---

[15] E. D. H. Johnson, *The Alien Vision of Victorian Poetry* (Princeton, N.J.: Princeton University Press, 1952), p. 63.

[16] Douglas Bush, *Mythology and the Romantic Tradition* (Minneapolis: University of Minnesota Press, 1933), p. 227.

[17] See Appendix for text.

For this reason he regards ideas and rhetoric of little avail. Hallam is confident that Tennyson's technique of the picturesque has enabled him to surpass the descriptive rhetoric of Wordsworth and Shelley in isolating those pure states of consciousness which are not of "time's covenant." He asks us to study Tennyson with a minute and exacting intensity such as we ordinarily reserve for the greatest achievements of metaphysical and scientific speculation.[18]

Hallam rightly insists on contrasting descriptive poetry and picturesque poetry, because the picturesque artist aims not just at the vivid rendering of a scene. As in Wordsworth's "Solitary Reaper" or Tennyson's "Mariana," the picturesque poet is consciously manipulating a magical formula. The external situation is employed as a magical device for eliciting a precise mental state in the reader. From Sir Philip Sidney in the sixteenth century to Alexander Pope, poetic art was typically directed to the shaping of the poetic object; from the pre-Romantics, Thomson, Gray, Collins, Akenside, and Chatterton, to the present, poetic art has consciously applied itself to the shaping of psychological effects in the reader. This could be called the Copernican revolution in poetry. It is, somewhat obscurely, the theme of Wordsworth's "Preface to the Lyrical Ballads"; it is plainly the theme of Hallam's essay on Tennyson's *Poems, Chiefly Lyrical;* it is usually the theme of Walter Pater and of T. S. Eliot. As seen by Hallam, the poet is not concerned with ideas, opinions, beliefs, except as means to an effect: "whenever the mind of the artist suffers itself to be occupied, during its periods of creation, by any other predominant motive than the desire of beauty, the result is false in art."[19]

This is the key to picturesque or symbolist theory and practice of art and communication. It is frankly a magical and "irrational" theory which envisages art as a means of exploring and charting

---

[18] For fuller discussion see H. M. McLuhan, "Tennyson and Picturesque Poetry," *Essays in Criticism,* I (July, 1951), 262–282, and H. M. McLuhan, "The Esthetic Moment in Landscape Poetry," *English Institute Essays, 1951* (ed. Alan S. Downer; New York: Columbia University Press, 1952), pp. 168–181.

[19] See Appendix for text.

exactly discriminated mental states, on one hand, and of evoking these newly discovered states in the reader, on the other hand, not indirectly, but by direct participation. Regarded in this way, Tennyson's habitual stress on a combination of music and pictures as a magical or hypnotic procedure will make sense. His experiments with varied verse forms are always linked to this predominant interest in the effect of the aesthetic moment. Moreover, poetry written to capture and elaborate a momentarily sensed dimension of emotion or feeling tends to be a small unit. Tennyson, it is recognized, is most effective in the brief flight and even in the line flash.

Between Tennyson's and T. S. Eliot's theory of art and communication there is small difference. In their practice, however, there are many distinctions which can be discovered by detailed acquaintance with their work. But in dispensing with the poetic uses of intellect and wit, Tennyson is closer to the early Yeats than to Eliot. Tennyson avoided wit for reasons as deliberate as led Eliot to bring it back to poetry. It was not a matter of temperament but of doctrinaire conviction.

V. TENNYSON AND THE LITTLE EPIC OR EPYLLION

In studying the theory and practice of the picturesque in Tennyson the student will find the comparison with and contrast of Arnold's poetry very useful. Arnold rejected the aesthetic views of Hallam, Tennyson, and the Romantics so far as they followed the magical line in poetry and art. In practice, too, he preferred description, narrative, and reflective comment to the magical evocation of the aesthetic moment or flash of illumination. In his 1853 Preface to *Poems* Arnold attacks the magical school as episodic, fragmentary, and sensational, arguing that the true business of art is not the sudden flash of insight but the gradual catharsis of emotion. Recently in *The Gate of Horn*, G. R. Levy has explained how the Greek conception of catharsis via the arts was that of character training, a preparation for "the lesser mysteries" of the Eleusinian rites. This seems to have been Arnold's point of view as well as that of the very large and articulate school of critics and educators for whom the arts are a school of ethics and moral discipline. The magical and symbolist school, on the other hand, in preferring to use the arts as a means of *gnosis* or spiritual elevation and discovery, would seem to associate the arts not with the lesser but with "the greater mysteries," as the Greeks called them. The so-called art of the little epic (the idyll and epyllion) was a late Greek form associated with magical rituals. It was especially cultivated by Theocritus, who was Tennyson's favorite poet. Theocritus and the Alexandrian school were directly responsible for "the new poetry" of Catullus, Ovid, and Virgil. The work of Theocritus, Catullus, Ovid, and Virgil, masters of the epyllion, needs to be known for any deep understanding of Tennyson's technique in narrative poetry. But the discontinuous technique of the epyllion is equally the clue to the art form of *Dubliners*, of *The Waste Land*, and of *The Cantos*.[20]

Professor Crump describes the epyllion as follows:

> . . . a short narrative poem. The length may and does vary considerably, but an epyllion seems never to have exceeded the length of a single book, and probably the average length was four to five hundred lines. The subject is sometimes merely an incident in the life of an epic hero or heroine, sometimes a complete story, the tendency of the author being to use little known stories or possibly even to invent new ones. The later Alexandrians and Romans preferred love stories and usually concentrated the interest on the heroine. . . . The dramatic form is frequently employed, and it is usual to find at least one long speech.[21]

In practice the epyllion was closely linked to the Alexandrian art of the idyll or little picture, the little epic being frequently a series of such pictures with narrative links. When these links are suppressed, the mere juxtaposition or parataxis of scenes tends (as in *The Waste Land*) to establish a dramatic mode for the

---

[20] D. F. Theall and the present writer are preparing a study of the epyllion from Ovid to the present.

[21] M. M. Crump, *The Epyllion from Theocritus to Ovid* (Oxford: Basil Blackwell & Mott, Ltd., 1931), p. 22.

poem. In the same way, simile with its linkages is nearer to narrative than dramatic metaphor, which suppresses the links between its various terms. And symbolism (as its etymology implies) is the art of juxtaposing without links. That is to say, symbolism is a gnomic, riddling art, a magical technique for casting and exorcising spells. Such was the mode of the idylls of Theocritus and the *Metamorphoses* of Ovid.

In all times and places the poet has been accorded some degree of magical power over the minds of his audience. The Romantics and the symbolists began to urge these claims in theory and in practice. They did not stop with the poet's power over the mind, but claimed, like the mathematical physicist today, that his creations had the power to influence the universe as well. This symbolic view of the poet is the theory of the culture-hero, variously developed by Carlyle, Nietzsche, and Shaw. Obviously, it is at variance with the traditions of rationalism. The student of Tennyson will find that Tennyson was never able to make up his mind about the opposing claims of the magical and rational theories of art and communication. "The Palace of Art" is a monument to his early indecision. The problem can be stated briefly in these terms: Is art a civilized *substitute* for tribal magic or is it a refined *continuation* of tribal magic? From Plato to the present, poets, critics, and philosophers have been divided over this issue. But the vogue of modern anthropology has for fifty years weighted the literary scales heavily in favor of the magical thesis.

In antiquity the cyclic epic of Homer and Hesiod moved away from primitive magic toward a rational and limited social function. This process is explained at length by G. R. Levy in *The Sword from the Rock*. The hero task of removing the sword from the rock (as performed by Arthur and many others) is figurative of the separation of man's individual spiritual life from the collective rites of the Old Stone Age culture. Nevertheless, the cyclic epic retains the structure of the solar cycle, and from this comes its twelve- (or twenty-four-) book structure. The little epic, on the other hand, was a deliberate return to religious ritual and magic. Virgil was the first to fuse the solar or cyclic epic with the magical form of the little epic. In this fusion Virgil was followed by Dante, Milton, and Tennyson. In *Four Quartets* T. S. Eliot has effected a new kind of fusion of cyclic and little epic, as have Joyce and Pound in even more complex ways.

Whereas the cyclic epic, as in Homer, moves on the single narrative plane of individual spiritual quest, the little epic as written by Ovid, Dante, Joyce, and Pound is "the tale of the tribe." That is to say, it is not so much a story of the individual quest for perfection as it is a history of collective crime and punishment, an attempt to justify the ways of God to man. From this point of view "In Memoriam," like Petrarch's *Sonnets*, is a seasonal cycle of little epics or idylls in the form of the individual quest. And the *Idylls of the King* is the collective quest, the tale of the tribe. The twelve idylls follow the cycle of the zodiac, each book corresponding faithfully to the traditional character of the twelve "houses" of the zodiac.[22] By following this traditional zodiacal track Tennyson was able over a long period to compose his twelve idylls in any order he found convenient.

The pattern of collective quest lends the prominent salvation note to the *Idylls of the King* and explains his philosophy of history. "The Coming of Arthur" is thus the coming of the culture-hero, and Arthur's struggles with the demonic earth powers are the theme of the cycle.[23] The masculine-feminine duality of most of Tennyson's *Idylls of the King* may have been suggested to him by the similar aspects of each house of the zodiac. For each planet's day home is located in a positive masculine sign and its night home in a negative or feminine sign.[24]

---

[22] See Nicholas De Vore's *Encyclopedia of Astrology* (New York: The Philosophical Library, 1947).

[23] From this point of view, Paul Tillich's chapters on the demonic in history (*The Interpretation of History* [New York: Charles Scribner's Sons, 1936], p. 98) provide a useful discussion of Tennyson's theme: "The real observation of history has to do with the phenomena which are perceptible but in which the depth can manifest itself: the battle of the divine against the demonic, the powerful coming of 'salvation.'" See also Charles Williams, *Arthurian Torso* (ed. C. S. Lewis; London: Oxford University Press, 1948).

[24] Curiously, however, as Elsdale points out in his *Studies in the Idylls* (London: Henry S. King & Co., 1878), pp. 28–29, the rational soul for Tennyson is viewed as the feminine figure in "Gareth and Lynette," for

The Romantic and Victorian conception of the lyric as expressive of some notable phase or passion of the mind is really a direct link with the Alexandrian idyll and little epic. J. W. Mackail defines the idyll as follows:

> Idyllia are cabinet pictures; small in size, highly finished, detachable, not imagined and executed as elements in any large constructive scheme of imaginative decoration, yet each holding its tiny convex mirror up to nature, each bringing art for a moment into relation with one facet or mood of life.[25]

These carefully worked pictures, each burning and brilliant with their hard, gemlike flames, called forth the whole power of Dante and of Elizabethan "conceits." In Greece and Rome this art was called "the new poetry," and it was produced in an age which had much in common with the Victorian age and our own. As Mackail describes it:

> Such was the world of Theocritus: immense, well-policed, monotonous; penetrated through and through with commercialism; pleasant for the well-to-do, . . . the great towns provided endless shows, public doles and pageants; the seat of a widespread if superficial culture among the professional classes who were continually increasing in numbers and importance.[26]

The object of the new idyllic poetry, then, was to get art back into some immediate relation with what, here and now, interested people. Like our own, this Greek and Roman world was a world where all the old boundaries had been erased and where old ideals had lost their efficacy. It is not by chance that the contemporary aims and procedures of the symbolists, and of Joyce,

---

example. Gareth is the arm of flesh assisted by the rational soul (Lynette) to deliver Lynors (the immortal spirit). When any one of body, soul, or spirit sets up as the predominant power, the viable balance is destroyed. Thus "the Holy Grail" is Tennyson's account of the destructive effect on the Table Round of mystical pursuits. The trio of body, soul, and spirit found throughout Tennyson's poems is basic in the Neoplatonic tradition.

[25] J. W. Mackail, *Lectures on Greek Poetry* (London: Longmans, Green & Co., 1910), p. 219.

[26] *Ibid.*, p. 217.

Pound, and Eliot, provide a good working view of "the new poetry" of the ancient world. The best approach to the aims and procedures of Wordsworth and Coleridge, Keats, and Tennyson may well be that of working backward from the present stage of elaboration of the forms of idyll and epyllion.

Ritualistic form, great erudition, and artistic sophistication often disguised by a folk theme or casual irony, obscurity, and concentration of allusion and expression—these are some of the most obvious features of the idyll and epyllion as practiced in antiquity and as followed by Tennyson, Joyce, and Eliot. Inseparable from these features are the omnipresent devices of discontinuity, flashback, digressions, and subplots. Dramatic parallelism, multileveled implication, and symbolic analogy, rather than linear perspective or narrative, characterize the little epic at all times. So that, if the road to modern poetry lies through Tennyson's idylls and little epics, the road to Camelot for us today is via *The Waste Land*. For example, the first lines of "The Last Tournament" at first appear as a casual encounter between Tristram and Dagonet the fool. There follows a long flashback or reconstruction of the institution of the tournament. But the juxtaposition of Tristram and his legend with The Fool of the Tarot Pack is an esoteric matter which has a complex bearing on the tournament[27] as a symbolic or mock struggle between the powers of good and evil, or order and chaos. The Tarot Pack has also obviously the greatest relevance to *The Waste Land*, whose little epic structure has so much in common with "The Last Tournament." Tennyson, it will be found, makes much the same demands as Eliot of his readers. During his long reign as laureate, however, he was gradually blurred and falsified into an easy poet. As a corrective to this conventional view of Tennyson, there is not only Hallam's essay, but also Churton Collins's *Illustrations of Tennyson* (London: Chatto & Windus, 1891) in which Collins argues that the esoteric Tennyson is pre-eminently "the poet of the cultured" and that he will never be recognized

---

[27] See Kurt Seligmann's *The History of Magic* (New York: Pantheon Books, 1948) for a discussion of The Fool and the Tarot Pack of cards.

until, like Virgil, his writings have been "submitted to the ordeal of the minutest critical investigation."

Tennyson divided his poems into "English Idyls," idylls on classical themes, and "Idylls of the King," the latter, by their reference to kingship and politics and the problem of power, having a separate character. If the student beginning with the shorter pieces will study Tennyson's idyll form as the evocation of a particular moment of consciousness, of a specialized mood or state of mind, he will find how landscape art and musical incantation are used by Tennyson to evoke and control these moments and states. Classically, and also as used by Tennyson, the idyll form may tell, as in "Maud," or merely imply a story as in "Mariana." Since the whole art is concentrated on eliciting a mental state or in directing attention to some spiritual transformation, the techniques of landscape description, narrative, monologue, or any combination of these may be employed. The traditional ballad is such a combination of pictorial flashes, discontinuous narrative and dramatic speech, being an adaptation of the Alexandrian epyllion which readers of the Middle Ages, through their devotion to Statius, Virgil, and Ovid, well understood. Tennyson's "Revenge" is only one of his interesting adaptations of the ballad form. He firmly held that the artist must adapt the traditional to the contemporary.

But the epyllion or idyll in Tennyson often takes the form of tragic lament, partly in "A Dream of Fair Women," and fully in such poems as the Wellington "Ode," "Œnone," "Tithonus," "Lucretius," and "Rizpah." In fact, the sensational realism of the modern "human interest" story strongly adumbrated in "Rizpah," and basic in so many of Hardy's poems, is precisely the quality sought by the Alexandrian idyll or epyllion. Joyce, Pound, and Eliot went much further in getting this newspaperish sensationalism of episode into their works.

In using poetry as a means of exploring the spectrum of mental states, Tennyson has been held to have fallen into the same mystic or spiritual pursuit that in "The Holy Grail" he shows to have undone the goodly fellowship of the Table Round. The correlative idyll to "The Holy Grail" is "Merlin and Vivien."

Both these idylls represent two extremes of demonic possession. "The Holy Grail" concerns the invasion of unprepared minds by "mania from above." "Merlin and Vivien," like "Lucretius," presents the struggle and fall of the merely intellectual man when invaded by "mania from below." As Paul Tillich says: "This relationship of divine and demonic ecstasy is the explanation of why in religious history the state of grace could so often change into a possessed state and why the moralistic attitude in religion denies both alike."[28] Like Arnold, Tennyson theoretically adopted the moralistic or humanistic attitude in religion, while his art moved in the "mystic" direction.

The reader of Tennyson's poems will find everywhere in his landscapes the symbolic struggle of light and darkness as the drama of the divine and the demonic. Many of his most characteristically poignant effects, as in "Tears, Idle Tears," the seventh elegy of "In Memoriam," "Morte d'Arthur," and "Crossing the Bar," are rendered by means of twilight and the poise of opposite powers. It is the inner world of the "Celtic twilight" ironically treated in Eliot's "Prufrock" but more seriously evoked in *Four Quartets*.

In that reprise of his own poetic history, "Merlin and the Gleam," Tennyson asserts the poetic role as fidelity to inner vision, to the creative moments of privileged awareness. Since these moments of vision can only be communicated by incarnation in the matter of language (Shelley's "the mind in inspiration is as a fading coal"), the paradoxical work of the artist is both to follow the gleam and also to turn that light into the darkness of the artifact or poetic work. Such at least was the tragic dilemma of the artist as seen by Tennyson. For Tennyson it is existence itself that is demonic. But the creative moments of vision of the artist are what Wordsworth called "spots in time," points where existence is suddenly irradiated with a gleam of the divine, where time is perturbed by eternity. The role of the poet is thus that of the seer. He is one who sees his time in its fullness because freed from the shackles of its material existence. But as seer the artist

---

[28] Tillich, *op. cit.*, p. 87.

is alienated, shadowed by otherness. He is Tiresias, forever hovering between two worlds.

If Tennyson is to be read today, he can only be experienced through the art and culture of the technological society which has defined itself since his time. He was not read on his own terms in the nineteenth century, and today we can only rediscover him by first sampling his quality as it comes through our mid-century ways of thought and feeling. And that means adopting a highly technical approach to his art. Since he himself was a very self-conscious and technical experimenter, he should prove much more congenial to our taste than to the taste of his own day, when deliberate technique in the arts was frowned on. The Victorians were enthusiastic about a mainly nonexistent Tennyson who had sold his artistic soul for a pot of message. We are free to discover the Tennyson who Hallam was assured had surpassed Shelley and Keats in the sophisticated art of impressionism.

CHRONOLOGY

1809: August 6, born the fourth of twelve children at Somersby in Lincolnshire to George and Elizabeth Tennyson.

1820–1822: At Louth grammar school.

1822–1824: Dr. Tennyson resumes the education of Alfred and the boys at home.

1826: *Poems by Two Brothers,* published anonymously. Alfred omits his more experimental work from the volume as "too much out of the common for the public taste."

1828–1831: Goes with Charles to Trinity College, Cambridge.

1828: Begins acquaintance with Arthur Hallam, son of the historian.

1829: Is elected to "The Apostles" club.
Alfred's *Timbuctoo* wins Chancellor's Medal.
Arthur Hallam falls in love with Alfred's sister Emily.

1830: *Poems, Chiefly Lyrical.*
Joins a revolutionary military expedition to Spain. Delighted by Spanish landscape.
First meeting with Emily Sellwood.

1831: Leaves Cambridge without obtaining a degree.
Hallam's review of *Poems, Chiefly Lyrical* in *The Englishman's Magazine* evokes violent comment from Christopher North in *Blackwood's Magazine* (1832). Tennyson classed with the "Cockney School" of Shelley and Keats.

1832: Visit to the Rhine country with Hallam.
Poems (dated 1833).

1833: Croker's virulent attack on *Poems* in *The Quarterly Review.*
Death of Hallam.

1833–1837: Tennyson rusticates at Somersby.

1837–1839: Removal of the family to High Beech and Hampstead.

1839–1840: Meets Gladstone, Rogers, Carlyle, Forster, Landor, Macready. Engagement to Emily Sellwood is broken off by her father for financial reasons.

1841–1842: Loses his patrimony in a financial venture which was to have enabled him to marry Emily Sellwood.

1842: *Poems* (2 vols.).

1845: Granted a pension of £200 by the Government of Sir Robert Peel.

1846: Friendship with Dickens and Patmore.
Visits Switzerland.

1847: *The Princess* badly received.

1848: Reconsiders his project of an Arthurian epic.
Meeting with Emerson.

1850: *In Memoriam* well received.
Marriage to Emily Sellwood.
Queen Victoria offers him the laureateship on the death of Wordsworth.

1853: Rents Farringford in the Isle of Wight.

1855: "Maud." Resumes work on the Arthurian project.

1859: *Idylls of the King.* Four idylls: "Enid," "Vivien," "Elaine," "Guinevere." Ruskin and Jowett urge him to abandon the themes of the past for those of the present.

1860: Takes his family to the Pyrenees. Profits from his poetry £4,500 in this year alone.

1861: Visits Queen Victoria at Osborne.

1862: Refuses an offer of £20,000 for a lecture tour in America.

1864: Garibaldi visits Tennyson. Close friendship with Browning and Gladstone.
Enoch Arden and Other Poems.

1865: Refuses a baronetcy.

1867–1869: Building of new home at Aldworth brings period of stagnation to an end.

1869: *The Holy Grail and Other Poems.*

1870: His poetry earns him £10,000 this year.

1874: Mrs. Tennyson becomes an invalid and Hallam Tennyson leaves Cambridge to take up the heavy task of secretary to his father.

1875: *Queen Mary,* a drama.

1876: *Harold,* a drama.

1880: *Ballads and Other Poems.* Meeting with Thomas Hardy.

1883: Becomes Baron Tennyson.

1884: *The Cup* and *The Falcon. The Falcon* had been staged in 1879; *The Cup* in 1881.
Becket.

1885: *Tiresias and Other Poems.*

1886: *Locksley Hall Sixty Years After and Other Poems.*

1889: *Demeter and Other Poems.*

1890: G. F. Watts paints two portraits of him, and his son Hallam reads Sir James Frazer's *The Golden Bough* to Watts and Tennyson during the sittings.

1892: Dies at Aldworth. Buried in Westminster Abbey.
The Death of Œnone and Other Poems.

BIBLIOGRAPHY

Auden, W. H. "Introduction" to *Poems of Alfred Lord Tennyson.* New York: Doubleday & Company, Inc., n.d., pp. xviii–xix.

Blackmur, R. P. "Lord Tennyson's Scissors," in *Language as Gesture.* London: Faber & Faber, Ltd., 1954, pp. 422–440.

Bradley, A. C. *A Commentary on Tennyson's "In Memoriam."* London: Macmillan & Co., Ltd., 1901.

Buckley, J. H. *The Victorian Temper.* Cambridge, Mass.: Harvard University Press, 1951.

Bush, Douglas. *Mythology and the Romantic Tradition.* Minneapolis: University of Minnesota Press, 1933.

Collier, John. "Tennyson," in H. J. Massingham, *The Great Victorians.* London: Penguin Books, n.d.

Collins, Churton. *Illustrations of Tennyson.* London: Chatto & Windus, Ltd., 1891.

Crump, M. M. *The Epyllion from Theocritus to Ovid.* Oxford: Basil Blackwell & Mott, Ltd., 1931.

De Vore, Nicholas. *Encyclopedia of Astrology.* New York: Philosophical Library, 1947.

Eidson, John Olin. *Tennyson in America.* Athens: University of Georgia Press, 1943.

Eliot, T. S. " 'In Memoriam,' " in *Essays Ancient and Modern.* London: Faber & Faber, Ltd., 1936.

Elsdale, Henry. *Studies in the Idylls.* London: Henry S. King & Co., 1878.

Hallam, A. H. "On Some Characteristics of Modern Poetry and on the Lyrical Poems of Alfred Tennyson," in *Literary Remains.* London: Ticknor, 1863.

Harrison, Jane Ellen. *Themis: A Study of the Social Origins of Greek Religion.* 2d ed. rev.; Cambridge: Cambridge University Press, 1927.

Irvine, William. *Apes, Angels, and Victorians.* New York: McGraw-Hill Book Company, Inc., 1955.

Johnson, E. D. H. *The Alien Vision of Victorian Poetry*. Princeton, N.J.: Princeton University Press, 1952.

Levy, G. R. *The Gate of Horn*. London: Faber & Faber, Ltd., 1947.

————. *The Sword from the Rock*. London: Faber & Faber, Ltd., 1953.

Littledale, Harold. *Essays on Lord Tennyson's "Idylls of the King."* London: Macmillan & Co., Ltd., 1893.

Mackail, J. W. *Lectures on Greek Poetry*. London: Longmans, Green & Co., 1910.

McLuhan, H. M. "The Esthetic Moment in Landscape Poetry," in *English Institute Essays, 1951*. Ed. Alan S. Downer; New York: Columbia University Press, 1952, pp. 168–181.

————. "Tennyson and Picturesque Poetry," *Essays in Criticism*, I (July, 1951), 262–282.

Motter, T. H. Vail. *The Writings of Arthur Hallam*. New York: Modern Language Association of America, 1943.

Priestley, F. E. L. "Tennyson's Idylls," *Toronto University Quarterly*, XIX (October, 1949), 35–49.

Rolfe, W. J. *Poetic and Dramatic Works of Tennyson* (Cambridge edition). Boston: Houghton Mifflin Company, 1898.

Seligmann, Kurt. *The History of Magic*. New York: Pantheon Books, 1948.

Stein, Gertrude. *Lectures in America*. New York: Random House, Inc., 1935.

Tennyson, Sir Charles. *Alfred Tennyson*. New York: The Macmillan Company, 1949.

Tennyson, Hallam. *Works of Lord Tennyson*. 9 vols.; London: Macmillan & Co., Ltd., 1908–1910.

————. *Alfred Lord Tennyson: A Memoir*. 2 vols.; New York: The Macmillan Company, 1897.

Tillich, P. *An Interpretation of History*. New York: Charles Scribner's Sons, 1936.

Williams, Charles. *Arthurian Torso*. Ed. C. S. Lewis; London: Oxford University Press, 1948.

Wolfe, Humbert. *Tennyson*. London: Faber & Faber, Ltd., 1930.

Benjamin Britten, the British composer (1913–   ), has composed a musical setting for Tennyson's song from *The Princess*, "The Splendor Falls on Castle Walls," in his *Serenade for Tenor, Horn, and Strings,* Opus 31. Britten's serenade also contains settings for poems by Blake, Keats, and Ben Jonson. It is available on long-playing records in two performances, one on London LL994 and the other on Boston 205.

Note on text:

The text used in this edition is that of W. J. Rolfe's Cambridge edition of Tennyson. The head-notes have been adapted from Rolfe's notes where they appeared to illuminate the interpretation of the poem.

CONTENTS

Alfred Lord Tennyson

SELECTED POETRY

SUPPOSED CONFESSIONS

OF A SECOND-RATE SENSITIVE MIND

O God! my God! have mercy now.
I faint, I fall. Men say that Thou
Didst die for me, for such as *me*.
Patient of ill, and death, and scorn,
And that my sin was as a thorn
Among the thorns that girt Thy brow,
Wounding Thy soul.—That even now,
In this extremest misery
Of ignorance, I should require
A sign! and if a bolt of fire   10
Would rive the slumbrous summer noon
While I do pray to Thee alone,
Think my belief would stronger grow!
Is not my human pride brought low?
The boastings of my spirit still?
The joy I had in my free-will
All cold, and dead, and corpse-like grown?
And what is left to me but Thou,
And faith in Thee? Men pass me by;
Christians with happy countenances—   20
And children all seem full of Thee!
And women smile with saint-like glances
Like Thine own mother's when she bow'd
Above Thee, on that happy morn
When angels spake to men aloud,
And Thou and peace to earth were born.
Good-will to me as well as all—
I one of them; my brothers they;
Brothers in Christ—a world of peace
And confidence, day after day;   30
And trust and hope till things should cease,
And then one Heaven receive us all.

How sweet to have a common faith!
To hold a common scorn of death!
And at a burial to hear
The creaking cords which wound and eat
Into my human heart, whene'er
Earth goes to earth, with grief, not fear,
With hopeful grief, were passing sweet!

Thrice happy state again to be   40
The trustful infant on the knee,
Who lets his rosy fingers play
About his mother's neck, and knows
Nothing beyond his mother's eyes!
They comfort him by night and day;
They light his little life alway;
He hath no thought of coming woes;
He hath no care of life or death;
Scarce outward signs of joy arise,
Because the Spirit of happiness   50
And perfect rest so inward is;
And loveth so his innocent heart,
Her temple and her place of birth,
Where she would ever wish to dwell,
Life of the fountain there, beneath
Its salient springs, and far apart,
Hating to wander out on earth,
Or breathe into the hollow air,
Whose chillness would make visible
Her subtil, warm, and golden breath,   60
Which mixing with the infant's blood,
Fulfils him with beatitude.
O, sure it is a special care
Of God, to fortify from doubt,
To arm in proof, and guard about
With triple-mailed trust, and clear
Delight, the infant's dawning year.

Would that my gloomed fancy were
As thine, my mother, when with brows
Propt on thy knees, my hands upheld   70
In thine, I listen'd to thy vows,
For me outpour'd in holiest prayer—
For me unworthy!—and beheld
Thy mild deep eyes upraised, that knew
The beauty and repose of faith,
And the clear spirit shining thro'.
O, wherefore do we grow awry
From roots which strike so deep? why dare
Paths in the desert? Could not I
Bow myself down, where thou hast knelt,   80
To the earth—until the ice would melt
Here, and I feel as thou hast felt?
What devil had the heart to scathe
Flowers thou hadst rear'd—to brush the dew
From thine own lily, when thy grave
Was deep, my mother, in the clay?
Myself? Is it thus? Myself? Had I
So little love for thee? But why
Prevail'd not thy pure prayers? Why pray
To one who heeds not, who can save   90
But will not? Great in faith, and strong
Against the grief of circumstance
Wert thou, and yet unheard. What if
Thou pleadest still, and seest me drive
Thro' utter dark a full-sail'd skiff,
Unpiloted i' the echoing dance
Of reboant whirlwinds, stooping low
Unto the death, not sunk! I know
At matins and at evensong,
That thou, if thou wert yet alive,   100
In deep and daily prayers wouldst strive
To reconcile me with thy God.
Albeit, my hope is gray, and cold

At heart, thou wouldest murmur still—
"Bring this lamb back into Thy fold,
My Lord, if so it be Thy will."
Wouldst tell me I must brook the rod
And chastisement of human pride;
That pride, the sin of devils, stood
Betwixt me and the light of God;   110
That hitherto I had defied
And had rejected God—that grace
Would drop from His o'er-brimming love,
As manna on my wilderness,
If I would pray—that God would move
And strike the hard, hard rock, and thence,
Sweet in their utmost bitterness,
Would issue tears of penitence
Which would keep green hope's life. Alas!
I think that pride hath now no place   120
Nor sojourn in me. I am void,
Dark, formless, utterly destroyed.

Why not believe then? Why not yet
Anchor thy frailty there, where man
Hath moor'd and rested? Ask the sea
At midnight, when the crisp slope waves
After a tempest rib and fret
The broad-imbased beach, why he
Slumbers not like a mountain tarn?
Wherefore his ridges are not curls   130
And ripples of an inland mere?
Wherefore he moaneth thus, nor can
Draw down into his vexed pools
All that blue heaven which hues and paves
The other? I am too forlorn,
Too shaken: my own weakness fools
My judgment, and my spirit whirls,
Moved from beneath with doubt and fear.

"Yet," said I, in my morn of youth,
The unsunn'd freshness of my strength,   140
When I went forth in quest of truth,
"It is man's privilege to doubt,
If so be that from doubt at length
Truth may stand forth unmoved of change
An image with profulgent brows
And perfect limbs, as from the storm
Of running fires and fluid range
Of lawless airs, at last stood out
This excellence and solid form
Of constant beauty. For the ox   150
Feeds in the herb, and sleeps, or fills
The horned valleys all about,
And hollows of the fringed hills
In summer heats, with placid lows
Unfearing, till his own blood flows
About his hoof. And in the flocks
The lamb rejoiceth in the year,
And raceth freely with his fere,
And answers to his mother's calls
From the flower'd furrow. In a time   160
Of which he wots not, run short pains
Thro' his warm heart; and then, from whence
He knows not, on his light there falls
A shadow; and his native slope,
Where he was wont to leap and climb,
Floats from his sick and filmed eyes,
And something in the darkness draws
His forehead earthward, and he dies.
Shall man live thus, in joy and hope
As a young lamb, who cannot dream,   170
Living, but that he shall live on?
Shall we not look into the laws
Of life and death, and things that seem,
And things that be, and analyze

Our double nature, and compare
All creeds till we have found the one,
If one there be?" Ay me! I fear
All may not doubt, but everywhere
Some must clasp idols. Yet, my God,
Whom call I idol? Let Thy dove   180
Shadow me over, and my sins
Be unremember'd, and Thy love
Enlighten me. O, teach me yet
Somewhat before the heavy clod
Weighs on me, and the busy fret
Of that sharp-headed worm begins
In the gross blackness underneath.

O weary life! O weary death!
O spirit and heart made desolate!
O damned vacillating state!   190

THE KRAKEN

Below the thunders of the upper deep,
Far, far beneath in the absymal sea,
His ancient, dreamless, uninvaded sleep
The Kraken sleepeth: faintest sunlights flee
About his shadowy sides; above him swell
Huge sponges of milennial growth and height;
And far away into the sickly light,
From many a wondrous grot and secret cell
Unnumber'd and enormous polypi
Winnow with giant arms the slumbering green.
There hath he lain for ages, and will lie
Battening upon huge sea-worms in his sleep,
Until the latter fire shall heat the deep;
Then once by man and angels to be seen,
In roaring he shall rise and on the surface die.

MARIANA

"Mariana in the moated grange."
MEASURE FOR MEASURE

With blackest moss the flower-plots
  Were thickly crusted, one and all;
The rusted nails fell from the knots
  That held the pear to the gable-wall.
The broken sheds look'd sad and strange:
  Unlifted was the clinking latch;
  Weeded and worn the ancient thatch
Upon the lonely moated grange.
      She only said, "My life is dreary,
        He cometh not," she said;   10
      She said, "I am aweary, aweary,
        I would that I were dead!"

Her tears fell with the dews at even;
  Her tears fell ere the dews were dried;
She could not look on the sweet heaven,
  Either at morn or eventide.
After the flitting of the bats,
  When thickest dark did trance the sky,
  She drew her casement-curtain by,
And glanced athwart the glooming flats.   20
      She only said, "The night is dreary,
        He cometh not," she said;
      She said, "I am aweary, aweary,
        I would that I were dead!"

Upon the middle of the night,
  Waking she heard the night-fowl crow;
The cock sung out an hour ere light;
  From the dark fen the oxen's low

Came to her; without hope of change,
  In sleep she seem'd to walk forlorn,   30
  Till cold winds woke the gray-eyed morn
About the lonely moated grange.
     She only said, "The day is dreary,
      He cometh not," she said;
     She said, "I am aweary, aweary,
      I would that I were dead!"

About a stone-cast from the wall
  A sluice with blacken'd waters slept,
And o'er it many, round and small,
  The cluster'd marish-mosses crept.   40
Hard by a poplar shook alway,
  All silver-green with gnarled bark:
  For leagues no other tree did mark
The level waste, the rounding gray.
     She only said, "My life is dreary,
      He cometh not," she said;
     She said, "I am aweary, aweary,
      I would that I were dead!"

And ever when the moon was low,
  And the shrill winds were up and away,   50
In the white curtain, to and fro,
  She saw the gusty shadow sway.
But when the moon was very low,
  And wild winds bound within their cell,
  The shadow of the poplar fell
Upon her bed, across her brow.
     She only said, "The night is dreary,
      He cometh not," she said;
     She said, "I am aweary, aweary,
      I would that I were dead!"   60

All day within the dreamy house,
  The doors upon their hinges creak'd;

The blue fly sung in the pane; the mouse
  Behind the mouldering wainscot shriek'd,
Or from the crevice peer'd about.
  Old faces glimmer'd thro' the doors,
  Old footsteps trod the upper floors,
Old voices called her from without.
    She only said, "My life is dreary,
      He cometh not," she said;   70
    She said, "I am aweary, aweary,
      I would that I were dead!"

The sparrow's chirrup on the roof,
  The slow clock ticking, and the sound
Which to the wooing wind aloof
  The poplar made, did all confound
Her sense; but most she loathed the hour
  When the thick-moted sunbeam lay
  Athwart the chambers, and the day
Was sloping toward his western bower.   80
    Then said she, "I am very dreary,
      He will not come," she said;
    She wept, "I am aweary, aweary,
      O God, that I were dead!"

RECOLLECTIONS OF THE

ARABIAN NIGHTS

When the breeze of a joyful dawn blew free
In the silken sail of infancy,
The tide of time flow'd back with me,
  The forward-flowing tide of time;
And many a sheeny summer-morn,
Adown the Tigris I was borne,
By Bagdat's shrines of fretted gold,
High-walled gardens green and old;

True Mussulman was I and sworn,
  For it was in the golden prime   10
    Of good Haroun Alraschid.

Anight my shallop, rustling thro'
The low and bloomed foliage, drove
The fragrant, glistening deeps, and clove
The citron-shadows in the blue;
By garden porches on the brim,
The costly doors flung open wide,
Gold glittering thro' lamplight dim,
And broider'd sofas on each side.
  In sooth it was a goodly time,   20
    For it was in the golden prime
      Of good Haroun Alraschid.

Often, where clear-stemm'd platans guard
The outlet, did I turn away
The boat-head down a broad canal
From the main river sluiced, where all
The sloping of the moonlit sward
Was damask-work, and deep inlay
Of braided blooms unmown, which crept
Adown to where the water slept.   30
  A goodly place, a goodly time,
    For it was in the golden prime
      Of good Haroun Alraschid.

A motion from the river won
Ridged the smooth level, bearing on
My shallop thro' the star-strown calm,
Until another night in night
I enter'd, from the clearer light,
Imbower'd vaults of pillar'd palm,
Imprisoning sweets, which, as they clomb   40
Heavenward, were stay'd beneath the dome

Of hollow boughs. A goodly time,
For it was in the golden prime
  Of good Haroun Alraschid.

Still onward; and the clear canal
Is rounded to as clear a lake.
From the green rivage many a fall
Of diamond rillets musical,
Thro' little crystal arches low
Down from the central fountain's flow   50
Fallen silver-chiming, seemed to shake
The sparkling flints beneath the prow.
  A goodly place, a goodly time,
  For it was in the golden prime
    Of good Haroun Alraschid.

Above thro' many a bowery turn
A walk with vari-colored shells
Wander'd engrain'd. On either side
All round about the fragrant marge
From fluted vase, and brazen urn   60
In order, eastern flowers large,
Some dropping low their crimson bells
Half-closed, and others studded wide
  With disks and tiars, fed the time
  With odor in the golden prime
    Of good Haroun Alraschid.

Far off, and where the lemon grove
In closest coverture upsprung,
The living airs of middle night
Died round the bulbul as he sung;   70
Not he, but something which possess'd
The darkness of the world, delight,
Life, anguish, death, immortal love,
Ceasing not, mingled, unrepress'd,

Apart from place, withholding time,
But flattering the golden prime
Of good Haroun Alraschid.

Black the garden-bowers and grots
Slumber'd; the solemn palms were ranged
Above, unwoo'd of summer wind;   80
A sudden splendor from behind
Flush'd all the leaves with rich gold-green,
And, flowing rapidly between
Their interspaces, counterchanged
The level lake with diamond-plots
    Of dark and bright. A lovely time,
    For it was in the golden prime
        Of good Haroun Alraschid.

Dark-blue the deep sphere overhead,
Distinct with vivid stars inlaid,   90
Grew darker from that under-flame;
So, leaping lightly from the boat,
With silver anchor left afloat,
In marvel whence that glory came
Upon me, as in sleep I sank
In cool soft turf upon the bank,
    Entranced with that place and time,
    So worthy of the golden prime
        Of good Haroun Alraschid.

Thence thro' the garden I was drawn—   100
A realm of pleasance, many a mound,
And many a shadow-chequer'd lawn
Full of the city's stilly sound,
And deep myrrh-thickets blowing round
The stately cedar, tamarisks,
Thick rosaries of scented thorn,
Tall orient shrubs, and obelisks

Graven with emblems of the time,
In honor of the golden prime
    Of good Haroun Alraschid.   110

With dazed vision unawares
From the long alley's latticed shade
Emerged, I came upon the great
Pavilion of the Caliphat.
Right to the carven cedarn doors,
Flung inward over spangled floors,
Broad-based flights of marble stairs
Ran up with golden balustrade,
    After the fashion of the time,
    And humor of the golden prime   120
        Of good Haroun Alraschid.

The fourscore windows all alight
As with the quintessence of flame,
A million tapers flaring bright
From twisted silvers look'd to shame
The hollow-vaulted dark, and stream'd
Upon the mooned domes aloof
In inmost Bagdat, till there seem'd
Hundreds of crescents on the roof
    Of night new-risen, that marvellous time   130
    To celebrate the golden prime
        Of good Haroun Alraschid.

Then stole I up, and trancedly
Gazed on the Persian girl alone,
Serene with argent-lidded eyes
Amorous, and lashes like to rays
Of darkness, and a brow of pearl
Tressed with redolent ebony,
In many a dark delicious curl,
Flowing beneath her rose-hued zone;   140

The sweetest lady of the time,
Well worthy of the golden prime
  Of good Haroun Alraschid.

Six columns, three on either side,
Pure silver, underpropt a rich
Throne of the massive ore, from which
Down-droop'd, in many a floating fold,
Engarlanded and diaper'd
With inwrought flowers, a cloth of gold.
Thereon, his deep eye laughter-stirr'd   150
With merriment of kingly pride,
  Sole star of all that place and time,
  I saw him—in his golden prime,
    THE GOOD HAROUN ALRASCHID.

ODE TO MEMORY

ADDRESSED TO ————

I

Thou who stealest fire,
From the fountains of the past,
To glorify the present, O, haste,
  Visit my low desire!
Strengthen me, enlighten me!
I faint in this obscurity,
Thou dewy dawn of memory.

II

Come not as thou camest of late,
  Flinging the gloom of yesternight
On the white day, but robed in soften'd light   10
    Of orient state.

Whilome thou camest with the morning mist,
    Even as a maid, whose stately brow
The dew-impearled winds of dawn have kiss'd,
            When she, as thou,
Stays on her floating locks the lovely freight
Of overflowing blooms, and earliest shoots
Of orient green, giving safe pledge of fruits,
    Which in wintertide shall star
The black earth with brilliance rare.   20

III

Whilome thou camest with the morning mist,
    And with the evening cloud,
Showering thy gleaned wealth into my open breast;
Those peerless flowers which in the rudest wind
            Never grow sere,
When rooted in the garden of the mind,
    Because they are the earliest of the year.
        Nor was the night thy shroud.
In sweet dreams softer than unbroken rest
Thou leddest by the hand thine infant Hope.   30
The eddying of her garments caught from thee
The light of thy great presence; and the cope
    Of the half-attain'd futurity,
        Tho' deep not fathomless,
Was cloven with the million stars which tremble
O'er the deep mind of dauntless infancy.
Small thought was there of life's distress;
For sure she deem'd no mist of earth could dull
Those spirit-thrilling eyes so keen and beautiful;
Sure she was nigher to heaven's spheres,   40
Listening the lordly music flowing from
        The illimitable years.
    O, strengthen me, enlighten me!
    I faint in this obscurity,
    Thou dewy dawn of memory.

IV

Come forth, I charge thee, arise,
Thou of the many tongues, the myriad eyes!
Thou comest not with shows of flaunting vines
      Unto mine inner eye,
      Divinest Memory!   50
  Thou wert not nursed by the waterfall
Which ever sounds and shines
  A pillar of white light upon the wall
Of purple cliffs, aloof descried:
Come from the woods that belt the gray hillside,
The seven elms, the poplars four
That stand beside my father's door,
And chiefly from the brook that loves
To purl o'er matted cress and ribbed sand,
Or dimple in the dark of rushy coves,   60
Drawing into his narrow earthen urn,
      In every elbow and turn,
The filter'd tribute of the rough woodland;
      O, hither lead thy feet!
Pour round mine ears the livelong bleat
Of the thick-fleeced sheep from wattled folds,
      Upon the ridged wolds,
When the first matin-song hath waken'd loud
Over the dark dewy earth forlorn,
What time the amber morn   70
Forth gushes from beneath a low-hung cloud.

V

Large dowries doth the raptured eye
  To the young spirit present
    When first she is wed,
      And like a bride of old
    In triumph led,
      With music and sweet showers
      Of festal flowers,

Unto the dwelling she must sway.
Well hast thou done, great artist Memory,   80
   In setting round thy first experiment
     With royal framework of wrought gold;
Needs must thou dearly love thy first essay,
And foremost in thy various gallery
   Place it, where sweetest sunlight falls
   Upon the storied walls;
     For the discovery
And newness of thine art so pleased thee
That all which thou hast drawn of fairest
Or boldest since but lightly weighs   90
With thee unto the love thou bearest
The first-born of thy genius. Artist-like,
Ever retiring thou dost gaze
On the prime labor of thine early days,
No matter what the sketch might be:
Whether the high field on the bushless pike,
Or even a sand-built ridge
Of heaped hills that mound the sea,
Overblown with murmurs harsh,
Or even a lowly cottage whence we see   100
Stretch'd wide and wild the waste enormous marsh,
Where from the frequent bridge,
Like emblems of infinity,
The trenched waters run from sky to sky;
Or a garden bower'd close
With plaited alleys of the trailing rose,
Long alleys falling down to twilight grots,
Or opening upon level plots
Of crowned lilies, standing near
Purple-spiked lavender: 110
Whither in after life retired
From brawling storms,
From weary wind,
With youthful fancy re-inspired,
We may hold converse with all forms

Of the many-sided mind,
And those whom passion hath not blinded,
Subtle-thoughted, myriad-minded.

My friend, with you to live alone
Were how much better than to own   120
A crown, a sceptre, and a throne!

O, strengthen me, enlighten me!
I faint in this obscurity,
Thou dewy dawn of memory.

SONG

I

A spirit haunts the year's last hours
Dwelling amid these yellowing bowers.
     To himself he talks;
For at eventide, listening earnestly,
At his work you may hear him sob and sigh
     In the walks;
  Earthward he boweth the heavy stalks
Of the mouldering flowers.
    Heavily hangs the broad sunflower
      Over its grave i' the earth so chilly;
    Heavily hangs the hollyhock,
      Heavily hangs the tiger-lily.

II

The air is damp, and hush'd, and close,
As a sick man's room when he taketh repose
     An hour before death;
My very heart faints and my whole soul grieves
At the moist rich smell of the rotting leaves,
     And the breath

Of the fading edges of box beneath,
And the year's last rose.
        Heavily hangs the broad sunflower
            Over its grave i' the earth so chilly;
        Heavily hangs the hollyhock,
            Heavily hangs the tiger-lily.

THE SEA-FAIRIES

Slow sail'd the weary mariners and saw,
Betwixt the green brink and the running foam,
Sweet faces, rounded arms, and bosoms prest
To little harps of gold; and while they mused,
Whispering to each other half in fear,
Shrill music reach'd them on the middle sea.

Whither away, whither away, whither away? fly no more.
Whither away from the high green field, and the happy
        blossoming shore?
Day and night to the billow the fountain calls;
Down shower the gambolling waterfalls   10
From wandering over the lea;
Out of the live-green heart of the dells
They freshen the silvery-crimson shells,
And thick with white bells the clover-hill swells
High over the full-toned sea.
O, hither, come hither and furl your sails,
Come hither to me and to me;
Hither, come hither and frolic and play;
Here it is only the mew that wails;
We will sing to you all the day.   20
Mariner, mariner, furl your sails,
For here are the blissful downs and dales,
And merrily, merrily carol the gales,
And the spangle dances in bight and bay,
And the rainbow forms and flies on the land

Over the islands free;
And the rainbow lives in the curve of the sand;
Hither, come hither and see;
And the rainbow hangs on the poising wave,
And sweet is the color of cove and cave,   30
And sweet shall your welcome be.
O, hither, come hither, and be our lords,
For merry brides are we.
We will kiss sweet kisses, and speak sweet words;
O, listen, listen, your eyes shall glisten
With pleasure and love and jubilee.
O, listen, listen, your eyes shall glisten
When the sharp clear twang of the golden chords
Runs up the ridged sea.
Who can light on as happy a shore   40
All the world o'er, all the world o'er?
Whither away? listen and stay; mariner, mariner, fly no more.

THE HESPERIDES

This poem is reprinted in the "Memoir" (vol. i. p. 61) with the following note:—

"Published and suppressed by my father, and republished by me here (with accents written by him) in consequence of a talk that I had with him, in which he regretted that he had done away with it from among his 'Juvenilia.'"

The author of the "Memoir" has since added "Kate" (which he does not mention) to the "Juvenilia" in the collected editions, but he has not restored this poem.

> *"Hesperus and his daughters three,*
> *That sing about the golden tree."*
>
> COMUS

The North-wind fall'n, in the new-starréd night
Zidonian Hanno, voyaging beyond
The hoary promontory of Soloë

Past Thymiaterion, in calméd bays,
Between the southern and the western Horn,
Heard neither warbling of the nightingale,
Nor melody of the Libyan lotus flute
Blown seaward from the shore; but from a slope
That ran bloom-bright into the Atlantic blue,
Beneath a highland leaning down a weight   10
Of cliffs, and zoned below with cedar shade,
Came voices, like the voices in a dream,
Continuous, till he reached the outer sea.

SONG

I

The golden apple, the golden apple, the hallowed fruit,
Guard it well, guard it warily,
Singing airily,
Standing about the charméd root.
Round about all is mute,
As the snow-field on the mountain-peaks,
As the sand-field at the mountain-foot.   20
Crocodiles in briny creeks
Sleep and stir not: all is mute.
If ye sing not, if ye make false measure,
We shall lose eternal pleasure,
Worth eternal want of rest.
Laugh not loudly: watch the treasure
Of the wisdom of the West.
In a corner wisdom whispers. Five and three
(Let it not be preached abroad) make an awful mystery.
For the blossom unto threefold music bloweth;   30
Evermore it is born anew;
And the sap to threefold music floweth,
From the root
Drawn in the dark,
Up to the fruit,

Creeping under the fragrant bark,
Liquid gold, honeysweet, thro' and thro'.
Keen-eyed Sisters, singing airily,
Looking warily
Every way,   40
Guard the apple night and day,
Lest one from the East come and take it away.

II

Father Hesper, Father Hesper, watch, watch, ever and aye,
Looking under silver hair with a silver eye.
Father, twinkle not thy steadfast sight;
Kingdoms lapse, and climates change, and races die;
Honor comes with mystery;
Hoarded wisdom brings delight.
Number, tell them over and number
How many the mystic fruit-tree holds   50
Lest the red-combed dragon slumber
Rolled together in purple folds.
Look to him, father, lest he wink, and the golden apple be
      stol'n away,
For his ancient heart is drunk with overwatchings night and
      day,
Round about the hallowed fruit-tree curled—
Sing away, sing aloud evermore in the wind, without stop,
Lest his scaléd eyelid drop,
For he is older than the world.
If he waken, we waken,
Rapidly levelling eager eyes.   60
If he sleep, we sleep,
Dropping the eyelid over the eyes.
If the golden apple be taken,
The world will be overwise.
Five links, a golden chain, are we,
Hesper, the dragon, and sisters three,
Bound about the golden tree.

III

Father Hesper, Father Hesper, watch, watch, night and day,
Lest the old wound of the world be healéd,
The glory unsealéd, 70
The golden apple stolén away,
And the ancient secret revealéd.
Look from west to east along:
Father, old Himala weakens, Caucasus is bold and strong.
Wandering waters unto wandering waters call;
Let them clash together, foam and fall.
Out of watchings, out of wiles,
Comes the bliss of secret smiles.
All things are not told to all.
Half-round the mantling night is drawn, 80
Purple fringéd with even and dawn.
Hesper hateth Phosphor, evening hateth morn.

IV

Every flower and every fruit the redolent breath
Of this warm sea-wind ripeneth,
Arching the billow in his sleep;
But the land-wind wandereth,
Broken by the highland-steep,
Two streams upon the violet deep;
For the western sun and the western star,
And the low west-wind, breathing afar, 90
The end of day and beginning of night
Make the apple holy and bright;
Holy and bright, round and full, bright and blest,
Mellowed in a land of rest;
Watch it warily day and night;
All good things are in the west.
Till mid noon the cool east light
Is shut out by the tall hillbrow;
But when the full-faced sunset yellowly
Stays on the flowering arch of the bough, 100

The luscious fruitage clustereth mellowly,
Golden-kernelled, golden-cored,
Sunset-ripened above on the tree.
The world is wasted with fire and sword,
But the apple of gold hangs over the sea
Five links, a golden chain are we,
Hesper, the dragon, and sisters three,
Daughters three,
Bound about
The gnarléd bole of the charméd tree.   110
The golden apple, the golden apple, the hallowed fruit.
Guard it well, guard it warily,
Watch it warily,
Singing airily,
Standing about the charméd root.

THE BALLAD OF ORIANA

My heart is wasted with my woe,
      Oriana.
There is no rest for me below,
      Oriana.
When the long dun wolds are ribb'd with snow,
And loud the Norland whirlwinds blow,
      Oriana,
Alone I wander to and fro,
      Oriana.

Ere the light on dark was growing,   10
      Oriana,
At midnight the cock was crowing,
      Oriana;
Winds were blowing, waters flowing,
We heard the steeds to battle going,
      Oriana,

Aloud the hollow bugle blowing,
        Oriana.

In the yew-wood black as night,
        Oriana,
Ere I rode into the fight,
        Oriana,
While blissful tears blinded my sight
By star-shine and by moonlight,
        Oriana,
I to thee my troth did plight,
        Oriana.

She stood upon the castle wall,
        Oriana;
She watch'd my crest among them all,   30
        Oriana;
She saw me fight, she heard me call,
When forth there stept a foeman tall,
        Oriana,
Atween me and the castle wall,
        Oriana.

The bitter arrow went aside,
        Oriana:
The false, false arrow went aside,
        Oriana;   40
The damned arrow glanced aside,
And pierced thy heart, my love, my bride,
        Oriana!
Thy heart, my life, my love, my bride,
        Oriana!

O, narrow, narrow was the space,
        Oriana!
Loud, loud rung out the bugle's brays,
        Oriana.

O, deathful stabs were dealt apace,   50
The battle deepen'd in its place,
    Oriana;
But I was down upon my face,
    Oriana.

They should have stabb'd me where I lay,
    Oriana!
How could I rise and come away,
    Oriana?
How could I look upon the day?
They should have stabb'd me where I lay,   60
    Oriana—
They should have trod me into clay,
    Oriana.

O breaking heart that will not break,
    Oriana!
O pale, pale face so sweet and meek,
    Oriana!
Thou smilest, but thou dost not speak,
And then the tears run down my cheek,
    Oriana.   70
What wantest thou? whom dost thou seek,
    Oriana?

I cry aloud; none hear my cries,
    Oriana.
Thou comest atween me and the skies,
    Oriana.
I feel the tears of blood arise
Up from my heart unto my eyes,
    Oriana.
Within thy heart my arrow lies,   80
    Oriana.

O cursed hand! O cursed blow!
    Oriana!

O happy thou that liest low,
        Oriana!
All night the silence seems to flow
Beside me in my utter woe,
        Oriana.
A weary, weary way I go,
        Oriana!   90

When Norland winds pipe down the sea,
        Oriana,
I walk, I dare not think of thee,
        Oriana.
Thou liest beneath the greenwood tree,
I dare not die and come to thee,
        Oriana.
I hear the roaring of the sea,
        Oriana.

ADELINE

I

Mystery of mysteries,
    Faintly smiling Adeline,
      Scarce of earth nor all divine,
Nor unhappy, nor at rest,
    But beyond expression fair
      With thy floating flaxen hair;
Thy rose-lips and full blue eyes
    Take the heart from out my breast.
      Wherefore those dim looks of thine,
Shadowy, dreaming Adeline?   10

II

Whence that aery bloom of thine,
    Like a lily which the sun

Looks thro' in his sad decline,
　　And a rose-bush leans upon,
Thou that faintly smilest still,
　　As a Naiad in a well,
　　Looking at the set of day,
Or a phantom two hours old
　　Of a maiden past away,
Ere the placid lips be cold?   20
Wherefore those faint smiles of thine,
　　Spiritual Adeline?

III

What hope or fear or joy is thine?
Who talketh with thee, Adeline?
　　For sure thou art not all alone.
　　　Do beating hearts of salient springs
　　Keep measure with thine own?
　　　Hast thou heard the butterflies
　　　What they say betwixt their wings?
　　　Or in stillest evenings   30
With what voice the violet woos
To his heart the silver dews?
　　　Or when little airs arise,
　　How the merry bluebell rings
　　To the mosses underneath?
　　Hast thou look'd upon the breath
　　　Of the lilies at sunrise?
Wherefore that faint smile of thine,
Shadowy, dreaming Adeline?

IV

Some honey-converse feeds thy mind,   40
　　Some spirit of a crimson rose
　　In love with thee forgets to close
　　His curtains, wasting odorous sighs
All night long on darkness blind.
What aileth thee? whom waitest thou

With thy soften'd, shadow'd brow,
    And those dew-lit eyes of thine,
    Thou faint smiler, Adeline?

V

Lovest thou the doleful wind
    When thou gazest at the skies?   50
Doth the low-tongued Orient
    Wander from the side of the morn,
    Dripping with Sabæan spice
On thy pillow, lowly bent
    With melodious airs lovelorn,
Breathing Light against thy face,
While his locks a-drooping twined
Round thy neck in subtle ring
Make a carcanet of rays,
    And ye talk together still,   60
In the language wherewith Spring
    Letters cowslips on the hill?
Hence that look and smile of thine,
    Spiritual Adeline.

THE LADY OF SHALOTT

PART I

On either side the river lie
Long fields of barley and of rye,
That clothe the wold and meet the sky;
And thro' the field the road runs by
    To many-tower'd Camelot;
And up and down the people go,
Gazing where the lilies blow
Round an island there below,
    The island of Shalott.

Willows whiten, aspens quiver,　　　　　　　10
Little breezes dusk and shiver
Thro' the wave that runs for ever
By the island in the river
　　　　Flowing down to Camelot.
Four gray walls, and four gray towers,
Overlook a space of flowers,
And the silent isle imbowers
　　　　The Lady of Shalott.

By the margin, willow-veil'd,
Slide the heavy barges trail'd　　　　　　　20
By slow horses; and unhail'd
The shallop flitteth silken-sail'd
　　　　Skimming down to Camelot:
But who hath seen her wave her hand?
Or at the casement seen her stand?
Or is she known in all the land,
　　　　The Lady of Shalott?

Only reapers, reaping early
In among the bearded barley,
Hear a song that echoes cheerly　　　　　　30
From the river winding clearly,
　　　　Down to tower'd Camelot;
And by the moon the reaper weary,
Piling sheaves in uplands airy,
Listening, whispers " 'T is the fairy
　　　　Lady of Shalott."

PART II

There she weaves by night and day
A magic web with colors gay.
She has heard a whisper say,

A curse is on her if she stay   40
    To look down to Camelot.
She knows not what the curse may be,
And so she weaveth steadily,
And little other care hath she,
    The Lady of Shalott.

And moving thro' a mirror clear
That hangs before her all the year,
Shadows of the world appear.
There she sees the highway near
    Winding down to Camelot;   50
There the river eddy whirls,
And there the surly village-churls,
And the red cloaks of market girls,
    Pass onward from Shalott.

Sometimes a troop of damsels glad,
An abbot on an ambling pad,
Sometimes a curly shepherd-lad,
Or long-hair'd page in crimson clad,
    Goes by to tower'd Camelot;
And sometimes thro' the mirror blue   60
The knights come riding two and two:
She hath no loyal knight and true,
    The Lady of Shalott.

But in her web she still delights
To weave the mirror's magic sights,
For often thro' the silent nights
A funeral, with plumes and lights
    And music, went to Camelot;
Or when the moon was overhead,
Came two young lovers lately wed: 70
"I am half sick of shadows," said
    The Lady of Shalott.

PART III

A bow-shot from her bower-eaves,
He rode between the barley-sheaves,
The sun came dazzling thro' the leaves,
And flamed upon the brazen greaves
    Of bold Sir Lancelot.
A red-cross knight for ever kneel'd
To a lady in his shield,
That sparkled on the yellow field,   80
    Beside remote Shalott.

The gemmy bridle glitter'd free,
Like to some branch of stars we see
Hung in the golden Galaxy.
The bridle bells rang merrily
    As he rode down to Camelot;
And from his blazon'd baldric slung
A mighty silver bugle hung,
And as he rode his armor rung,
    Beside remote Shalott.   90

All in the blue unclouded weather
Thick-jewell'd shone the saddle-leather,
The helmet and the helmet-feather
Burn'd like one burning flame together,
    As he rode down to Camelot;
As often thro' the purple night,
Below the starry clusters bright,
Some bearded meteor, trailing light,
    Moves over still Shalott.

His broad clear brow in sunlight glow'd;   100
On burnish'd hooves his war-horse trode;
From underneath his helmet flow'd
His coal-black curls as on he rode,
    As he rode down to Camelot.

From the bank and from the river
He flash'd into the crystal mirror,
"Tirra lirra," by the river
       Sang Sir Lancelot.

She left the web, she left the loom,
She made three paces thro' the room,   110
She saw the water-lily bloom,
She saw the helmet and the plume,
       She look'd down to Camelot.
Out flew the web and floated wide;
The mirror crack'd from side to side;
"The curse is come upon me," cried
       The Lady of Shalott.

PART IV

In the stormy east-wind straining,
The pale yellow woods were waning,
The broad stream in his banks complaining,   120
Heavily the low sky raining
       Over tower'd Camelot;
Down she came and found a boat
Beneath a willow left afloat,
And round about the prow she wrote
       The Lady of Shalott.

And down the river's dim expanse
Like some bold seër in a trance,
Seeing all his own mischance—
With a glassy countenance   130
       Did she look to Camelot.
And at the closing of the day
She loosed the chain, and down she lay;
The broad stream bore her far away,
       The Lady of Shalott.

Lying, robed in snowy white
That loosely flew to left and right—
The leaves upon her falling light—
Thro' the noises of the night
      She floated down to Camelot;   140
And as the boat-head wound along
The willowy hills and fields among,
They heard her singing her last song,
      The Lady of Shalott.

Heard a carol, mournful, holy,
Chanted loudly, chanted lowly,
Till her blood was frozen slowly,
And her eyes were darken'd wholly,
      Turn'd to tower'd Camelot.
For ere she reach'd upon the tide   150
The first house by the water-side,
Singing in her song she died,
      The Lady of Shalott.

Under tower and balcony,
By garden-wall and gallery,
A gleaming shape she floated by,
Dead-pale between the houses high,
      Silent into Camelot.
Out upon the wharfs they came,
Knight and burgher, lord and dame,   160
And round the prow they read her name,
      The Lady of Shalott.

Who is this? and what is here?
And in the lighted palace near
Died the sound of royal cheer;
And they cross'd themselves for fear,
      All the knights at Camelot:
But Lancelot mused a little space;
He said, "She has a lovely face;

God in his mercy lend her grace,   170
    The Lady of Shalott."

THE TWO VOICES

A still small voice spake unto me,
"Thou art so full of misery,
Were it not better not to be?"

Then to the still small voice I said:
"Let me not cast in endless shade
What is so wonderfully made."

To which the voice did urge reply:
"To-day I saw the dragon-fly
Come from the wells where he did lie.

"An inner impulse rent the veil   10
Of his old husk; from head to tail
Came out clear plates of sapphire mail.

"He dried his wings; like gauze they grew;
Thro' crofts and pastures wet with dew
A living flash of light he flew."

I said: "When first the world began,
Young Nature thro' five cycles ran,
And in the sixth she moulded man.

"She gave him mind, the lordliest
Proportion, and, above the rest,   20
Dominion in the head and breast."

Thereto the silent voice replied:
"Self-blinded are you by your pride;
Look up thro' night; the world is wide.

"This truth within thy mind rehearse,
That in a boundless universe
Is boundless better, boundless worse.

"Think you this mould of hopes and fears
Could find no statelier than his peers
In yonder hundred million spheres?"   30

It spake, moreover, in my mind:
"Tho' thou wert scatter'd to the wind,
Yet is there plenty of the kind."

Then did my response clearer fall:
"No compound of this earthly ball
Is like another, all in all."

To which he answer'd scoffingly:
"Good soul! suppose I grant it thee,
Who'll weep for thy deficiency?

"Or will one beam be less intense,   40
When thy peculiar difference
Is cancell'd in the world of sense?"

I would have said, "Thou canst not know,"
But my full heart, that work'd below,
Rain'd thro' my sight its overflow.

Again the voice spake unto me:
"Thou art so steep'd in misery,
Surely 't were better not to be.

"Thine anguish will not let thee sleep,
Nor any train of reason keep;   50
Thou canst not think, but thou wilt weep."

I said: "The years with change advance;
If I make dark my countenance,
I shut my life from happier chance.

"Some turn this sickness yet might take,
Even yet." But he: "What drug can make
A wither'd palsy cease to shake?"

I wept: "Tho' I should die, I know
That all about the thorn will blow
In tufts of rosy-tinted snow;   60

"And men, thro' novel spheres of thought
Still moving after truth long sought,
Will learn new things when I am not."

"Yet," said the secret voice, "some time,
Sooner or later, will gray prime
Make thy grass hoar with early rime.

"Not less swift souls that yearn for light,
Rapt after heaven's starry flight,
Would sweep the tracts of day and night.

"Not less the bee would range her cells,   70
The furzy prickle fire the dells,
The foxglove cluster dappled bells."

I said that "all the years invent;
Each month is various to present
The world with some development.

"Were this not well, to bide mine hour,
Tho' watching from a ruin'd tower
How grows the day of human power?"

"The highest-mounted mind," he said,
"Still sees the sacred morning spread   80
The silent summit overhead.

"Will thirty seasons render plain
Those lonely lights that still remain,
Just breaking over land and main?

"Or make that morn, from his cold crown
And crystal silence creeping down,
Flood with full daylight glebe and town?

"Forerun thy peers, thy time, and let
Thy feet, millenniums hence, be set
In midst of knowledge, dream'd not yet.   90

"Thou hast not gain'd a real height,
Nor art thou nearer to the light,
Because the scale is infinite.

" 'T were better not to breathe or speak,
Than cry for strength, remaining weak,
And seem to find, but still to seek.

"Moreover, but to seem to find
Asks what thou lackest, thought resign'd,
A healthy frame, a quiet mind."

I said: "When I am gone away,   100
'He dared not tarry,' men will say,
Doing dishonor to my clay."

"This is more vile," he made reply,
"To breathe and loathe, to live and sigh,
Than once from dread of pain to die.

"Sick art thou—a divided will
Still heaping on the fear of ill
The fear of men, a coward still.

"Do men love thee? Art thou so bound
To men that how thy name may sound   110
Will vex thee lying underground?

"The memory of the wither'd leaf
In endless time is scarce more brief
Than of the garner'd autumn-sheaf.

"Go, vexed spirit, sleep in trust;
The right ear that is fill'd with dust
Hears little of the false or just."

"Hard task, to pluck resolve," I cried,
"From emptiness and the waste wide
Of that abyss, or scornful pride!   120

"Nay—rather yet that I could raise
One hope that warm'd me in the days
While still I yearn'd for human praise.

"When, wide in soul and bold of tongue,
Among the tents I paused and sung,
The distant battle flash'd and rung.

"I sung the joyful Pæan clear,
And, sitting, burnish'd without fear
The brand, the buckler, and the spear—

"Waiting to strive a happy strife,   130
To war with falsehood to the knife,
And not to lose the good of life—

"Some hidden principle to move,
To put together, part and prove,
And mete the bounds of hate and love—

"As far as might be, to carve out
Free space for every human doubt,
That the whole mind might orb about—

"To search thro' all I felt or saw,
The springs of life, the depths of awe,   140
And reach the law within the law;

"At least, not rotting like a weed,
But, having sown some generous seed,
Fruitful of further thought and deed,

"To pass, when Life her light withdraws,
Not void of righteous self-applause,
Nor in a merely selfish cause—

"In some good cause, not in mine own,
To perish, wept for, honor'd, known,
And like a warrior overthrown;   150

"Whose eyes are dim with glorious tears,
When, soil'd with noble dust, he hears
His country's war-song thrill his ears:

"Then dying of a mortal stroke,
What time the foeman's line is broke,
And all the war is roll'd in smoke."

"Yea!" said the voice, "thy dream was good,
While thou abodest in the bud.
It was the stirring of the blood.

"If Nature put not forth her power   160
About the opening of the flower,
Who is it that could live an hour?

"Then comes the check, the change, the fall,
Pain rises up, old pleasures pall.
There is one remedy for all.

"Yet hadst thou, thro' enduring pain,
Link'd month to month with such a chain
Of knitted purport, all were vain.

"Thou hadst not between death and birth
Dissolved the riddle of the earth.   170
So were thy labor little worth.

"That men with knowledge merely play'd,
I told thee—hardly higher made,
Tho' scaling slow from grade to grade;

"Much less this dreamer, deaf and blind,
Named man, may hope some truth to find,
That bears relation to the mind.

"For every worm beneath the moon
Draws different threads, and late and soon
Spins, toiling out his own cocoon.   180

"Cry, faint not: either Truth is born
Beyond the polar gleam forlorn,
Or in the gateways of the morn.

"Cry, faint not, climb: the summits slope
Beyond the furthest flights of hope,
Wrapt in dense cloud from base to cope.

"Sometimes a little corner shines,
As over rainy mist inclines
A gleaming crag with belts of pines.

"I will go forward, sayest thou,   190
I shall not fail to find her now.
Look up, the fold is on her brow.

"If straight thy track, or if oblique,
Thou know'st not. Shadows thou dost strike,
Embracing cloud, Ixion-like;

"And owning but a little more
Than beasts, abidest lame and poor,
Calling thyself a little lower

"Than angels. Cease to wail and brawl!
Why inch by inch to darkness crawl?   200
There is one remedy for all."

"O dull, one-sided voice," said I,
"Wilt thou make everything a lie,
To flatter me that I may die?

"I know that age to age succeeds,
Blowing a noise of tongues and deeds,
A dust of systems and of creeds.

"I cannot hide that some have striven,
Achieving calm, to whom was given
The joy that mixes man with Heaven;   210

"Who, rowing hard against the stream,
Saw distant gates of Eden gleam,
And did not dream it was a dream;

"But heard, by secret transport led,
Even in the charnels of the dead,
The murmur of the fountain-head—

"Which did accomplish their desire,
Bore and forebore, and did not tire,
Like Stephen, an unquenched fire.

"He heeded not reviling tones,   220
Nor sold his heart to idle moans,
Tho' cursed and scorn'd, and bruised with stones;

"But looking upward, full of grace,
He pray'd, and from a happy place
God's glory smote him on the face."

The sullen answer slid betwixt:
"Not that the grounds of hope were fix'd,
The elements were kindlier mix'd."

I said: "I toil beneath the curse,
But, knowing not the universe,   230
I fear to slide from bad to worse;

"And that, in seeking to undo
One riddle, and to find the true,
I knit a hundred others new;

"Or that this anguish fleeting hence,
Unmanacled from bonds of sense,
Be fix'd and frozen to permanence:

"For I go, weak from suffering here;
Naked I go, and void of cheer:
What is it that I may not fear?"   240

"Consider well," the voice replied,
"His face, that two hours since hath died;
Wilt thou find passion, pain or pride?

"Will he obey when one commands?
Or answer should one press his hands?
He answers not, nor understands.

"His palms are folded on his breast;
There is no other thing express'd
But long disquiet merged in rest.

"His lips are very mild and meek;   250
Tho' one should smite him on the cheek,
And on the mouth, he will not speak.

"His little daughter, whose sweet face
He kiss'd, taking his last embrace,
Becomes dishonor to her race—

"His sons grow up that bear his name,
Some grow to honor, some to shame,—
But he is chill to praise or blame.

"He will not hear the north-wind rave,
Nor, moaning, household shelter crave   260
From winter rains that beat his grave.

"High up the vapors fold and swim;
About him broods the twilight dim;
The place he knew forgetteth him."

"If all be dark, vague voice," I said,
"These things are wrapt in doubt and dread,
Nor canst thou show the dead are dead.

"The sap dries up: the plant declines.
A deeper tale my heart divines.
Know I not death? the outward signs?   270

"I found him when my years were few;
A shadow on the graves I knew,
And darkness in the village yew.

"From grave to grave the shadow crept;
In her still place the morning wept;
Touch'd by his feet the daisy slept.

"The simple senses crown'd his head:
'Omega! thou art Lord,' they said,
'We find no motion in the dead!'

"Why, if man rot in dreamless ease,   280
Should that plain fact, as taught by these,
Not make him sure that he shall cease?

"Who forged that other influence,
That heat of inward evidence,
By which he doubts against the sense?

"He owns the fatal gift of eyes,
That read his spirit blindly wise,
Not simple as a thing that dies.

"Here sits he shaping wings to fly;
His heart forebodes a mystery;   290
He names the name Eternity.

"That type of Perfect in his mind
In Nature can he nowhere find.
He sows himself on every wind.

"He seems to hear a Heavenly Friend,
And thro' thick veils to apprehend
A labor working to an end.

"The end and the beginning vex
His reason: many things perplex,
With motions, checks, and counterchecks.   300

"He knows a baseness in his blood
At such strange war with something good,
He may not do the thing he would.

"Heaven opens inward, chasms yawn,
Vast images in glimmering dawn,
Half shown, are broken and withdrawn.

"Ah! sure within him and without,
Could his dark wisdom find it out,
There must be answer to his doubt,

"But thou canst answer not again.   310
With thine own weapon art thou slain,
Or thou wilt answer but in vain.

"The doubt would rest, I dare not solve.
In the same circle we revolve.
Assurance only breeds resolve."

As when a billow, blown against,
Falls back, the voice with which I fenced
A little ceased, but recommenced:

"Where wert thou when thy father play'd
In his free field, and pastime made,   320
A merry boy in sun and shade?

"A merry boy they call'd him then,
He sat upon the knees of men
In days that never come again;

"Before the little ducts began
To feed thy bones with lime, and ran
Their course, till thou wert also man:

"Who took a wife, who rear'd his race,
Whose wrinkles gather'd on his face,
Whose troubles number with his days;   330

"A life of nothings, nothing worth,
From that first nothing erc his birth
To that last nothing under earth!"

"These words," I said, "are like the rest;
No certain clearness, but at best
A vague suspicion of the breast:

"But if I grant, thou mightst defend
The thesis which thy words intend—
That to begin implies to end;

"Yet how should I for certain hold,   340
Because my memory is so cold,
That I first was in human mould?

"I cannot make this matter plain,
But I would shoot, howe'er in vain,
A random arrow from the brain.

"It may be that no life is found,
Which only to one engine bound
Falls off, but cycles always round.

"As old mythologies relate,
Some draught of Lethe might await 350
The slipping thro' from state to state;

"As here we find in trances, men
Forget the dream that happens then,
Until they fall in trance again;

"So might we, if our state were such
As one before, remember much,
For those two likes might meet and touch.

"But, if I lapsed from nobler place,
Some legend of a fallen race
Alone might hint of my disgrace; 360

"Some vague emotion of delight
In gazing up an Alpine height,
Some yearning toward the lamps of night;

"Or if thro' lower lives I came—
Tho' all experience past became
Consolidate in mind and frame—

"I might forget my weaker lot;
For is not our first year forgot?
The haunts of memory echo not.

"And men, whose reason long was blind,
From cells of madness unconfined, 370
Oft lose whole years of darker mind.

"Much more, if first I floated free,
As naked essence, must I be
Incompetent of memory;

"For memory dealing but with time,
And he with matter, could she climb
Beyond her own material prime?

"Moreover, something is or seems,
That touches me with mystic gleams,   380
Like glimpses of forgotten dreams—

"Of something felt, like something here;
Of something done, I know not where;
Such as no language may declare."

The still voice laugh'd. "I talk," said he,
"Not with thy dreams. Suffice it thee
Thy pain is a reality."

"But thou," said I, "hast missed thy mark,
Who sought'st to wreck my mortal ark,
By making all the horizon dark.   390

"Why not set forth, if I should do
This rashness, that which might ensue
With this old soul in organs new?

"Whatever crazy sorrow saith,
No life that breathes with human breath
Has ever truly long'd for death.

" 'T is life, whereof our nerves are scant,
O, life, not death, for which we pant;
More life, and fuller, that I want."

I ceased, and sat as one forlorn.   400
Then said the voice, in quiet scorn,
"Behold, it is the Sabbath morn."

And I arose, and I released
The casement, and the light increased
With freshness in the dawning east.

Like soften'd airs that blowing steal,
When meres begin to uncongeal,
The sweet church bells began to peal.

On to God's house the people prest;
Passing the place where each must rest,   410
Each enter'd like a welcome guest.

One walk'd between his wife and child,
With measured footfall firm and mild,
And now and then he gravely smiled.

The prudent partner of his blood
Lean'd on him, faithful, gentle, good,
Wearing the rose of womanhood.

And in their double love secure,
The little maiden walk'd demure,
Pacing with downward eyelids pure.   420

These three made unity so sweet,
My frozen heart began to beat,
Remembering its ancient heat.

I blest them, and they wander'd on;
I spoke, but answer came there none;
The dull and bitter voice was gone.

A second voice was at mine ear,
A little whisper silver-clear,
A murmur, "Be of better cheer."

As from some blissful neighborhood,   430
A notice faintly understood,
"I see the end, and know the good."

A little hint to solace woe,
A hint, a whisper breathing low,
"I may not speak of what I know."

Like an Æolian harp that wakes
No certain air, but overtakes
Far thought with music that it makes;

Such seem'd the whisper at my side:
"What is it thou knowest, sweet voice?" I cried.   440
"A hidden hope," the voice replied;

So heavenly-toned, that in that hour
From out my sullen heart a power
Broke, like the rainbow from the shower,

To feel, altho' no tongue can prove,
That every cloud, that spreads above
And veileth love, itself is love.

And forth into the fields I went,
And Nature's living motion lent
The pulse of hope to discontent.   450

I wonder'd at the bounteous hours,
The slow result of winter showers;
You scarce could see the grass for flowers.

I wonder'd, while I paced along;
The woods were fill'd so full with song,
There seem'd no room for sense of wrong;

And all so variously wrought,
I marvell'd how the mind was brought
To anchor by one gloomy thought;

And wherefore rather I made choice   460
To commune with that barren voice,
Than him that said, "Rejoice! Rejoice!"

ŒNONE

There lies a vale in Ida, lovelier
Than all the valleys of Ionian hills.
The swimming vapor slopes athwart the glen,
Puts forth an arm, and creeps from pine to pine,
And loiters, slowly drawn. On either hand
The lawns and meadow-ledges midway down
Hang rich in flowers, and far below them roars
The long brook falling thro' the cloven ravine
In cataract after cataract to the sea.
Behind the valley topmost Gargarus   10
Stands up and takes the morning; but in front
The gorges, opening wide apart, reveal
Troas and Ilion's column'd citadel,
The crown of Troas.
                    Hither came at noon
Mournful Œnone, wandering forlorn
Of Paris, once her playmate on the hills.
Her cheek had lost the rose, and round her neck
Floated her hair or seem'd to float in rest.
She, leaning on a fragment twined with vine,   20
Sang to the stillness, till the mountain-shade
Sloped downward to her seat from the upper cliff.

  "O mother Ida, many-fountain'd Ida,
Dear mother Ida, harken ere I die.
For now the noonday quiet holds the hill;

The grasshopper is silent in the grass;
The lizard, with his shadow on the stone,
Rests like a shadow, and the winds are dead.
The purple flower droops, the golden bee
Is lily-cradled; I alone awake   30
My eyes are full of tears, my heart of love,
My heart is breaking, and my eyes are dim,
And I am all aweary of my life

"O mother Ida, many-fountain'd Ida,
Dear mother Ida, harken ere I die.
Hear me, O earth, hear me, O hills, O caves
That house the cold crown'd snake! O mountain brooks,
I am the daughter of a River-God,
Hear me, for I will speak, and build up all
My sorrow with my song, as yonder walls   40
Rose slowly to a music slowly breathed,
A cloud that gather'd shape; for it may be
That, while I speak of it, a little while
My heart may wander from its deeper woe.

"O mother Ida, many-fountain'd Ida,
Dear mother Ida, harken ere I die.
I waited underneath the dawning hills;
Aloft the mountain lawn was dewy-dark,
And dewy dark aloft the mountain pine.
Beautiful Paris, evil-hearted Paris,   50
Leading a jet-black goat white-horn'd, white-hooved,
Came up from reedy Simois all alone.

"O mother Ida, harken ere I die.
Far-off the torrent call'd me from the cleft;
Far up the solitary morning smote
The streaks of virgin snow. With down-dropt eyes
I sat alone; white-breasted like a star
Fronting the dawn he moved; a leopard skin
Droop'd from his shoulder, but his sunny hair

Cluster'd about his temples like a God's;   60
And his cheek brighten'd as the foam-bow brightens
When the wind blows the foam, and all my heart
Went forth to embrace him coming ere he came.

   "Dear mother Ida, harken ere I die.
He smiled, and opening out his milk-white palm
Disclosed a fruit of pure Hesperian gold,
That smelt ambrosially, and while I look'd
And listen'd, the full-flowing river of speech
Came down upon my heart:
                " 'My own Œnone,   70
Beautiful-brow'd Œnone, my own soul,
Behold this fruit, whose gleaming rind ingraven
"For the most fair," would seem to award it thine,
As lovelier than whatever Oread haunt
The knolls of Ida, loveliest in all grace
Of movement, and the charm of married brows.'

   "Dear mother Ida, harken ere I die.
He prest the blossom of his lips to mine,
And added, 'This was cast upon the board,
When all the full-faced presence of the Gods   80
Ranged in the halls of Peleus; whereupon
Rose feud, with question unto whom 't were due;
But light-foot Iris brought it yester-eve,
Delivering, that to me, by common voice
Elected umpire, Herè comes to-day,
Pallas and Aphrodite, claiming each
This meed of fairest. Thou, within the cave
Behind yon whispering tuft of oldest pine,
Mayst well behold them unbeheld, unheard
Hear all, and see thy Paris judge of Gods.'   90

   "Dear mother Ida, harken ere I die.
It was the deep midnoon; one silvery cloud
Had lost his way between the piny sides

Of this long glen. Then to the bower they came,
Naked they came to that smooth-swarded bower,
And at their feet the crocus brake like fire,
Violet, amaracus, and asphodel,
Lotos and lilies; and a wind arose,
And overhead the wandering ivy and vine,
This way and that, in many a wild festoon   100
Ran riot, garlanding the gnarled boughs
With bunch and berry and flower thro' and thro'.

"O mother Ida, harken ere I die.
On the tree-tops a crested peacock lit,
And o'er him flow'd a golden cloud, and lean'd
Upon him, slowly dropping fragrant dew.
Then first I heard the voice of her to whom
Coming thro' heaven, like a light that grows
Larger and clearer, with one mind the Gods
Rise up for reverence. She to Paris made   110
Proffer of royal power, ample rule
Unquestion'd, overflowing revenue
Wherewith to embellish state, 'from many a vale
And river-sunder'd champaign clothed with corn,
Or labor'd mine undrainable of ore.
Honor,' she said, 'and homage, tax and toll,
From many an inland town and haven large,
Mast-throng'd beneath her shadowing citadel
In glassy bays among her tallest towers.'

"O mother Ida, harken ere I die.   120
Still she spake on and still she spake of power,
'Which in all action is the end of all;
Power fitted to the season; wisdom-bred
And throned of wisdom—from all neighbor crowns
Alliance and allegiance, till thy hand
Fail from the sceptre-staff. Such boon from me,
From me, heaven's queen, Paris, to thee king-born,
A shepherd all thy life but yet king-born,

Should come most welcome, seeing men, in power
Only, are likest Gods, who have attain'd   130
Rest in a happy place and quiet seats
Above the thunder, with undying bliss
In knowledge of their own supremacy.'

"Dear mother Ida, harken ere I die.
She ceased, and Paris held the costly fruit
Out at arm's-length, so much the thought of power
Flatter'd his spirit; but Pallas where she stood
Somewhat apart, her clear and bared limbs
O'erthwarted with the brazen-headed spear
Upon her pearly shoulder leaning cold,   140
The while, above, her full and earnest eye
Over her snow-cold breast and angry cheek
Kept watch, waiting decision, made reply:

" 'Self-reverence, self-knowledge, self-control,
These three alone lead life to sovereign power.
Yet not for power (power of herself
Would come uncall'd for) but to live by law,
Acting the law we live by without fear;
And, because right is right, to follow right
Were wisdom in the scorn of consequence.'   150

"Dear mother Ida, harken ere I die.
Again she said: 'I woo thee not with gifts.
Sequel of guerdon could not alter me
To fairer. Judge thou me by what I am,
So shalt thou find me fairest.
                              Yet, indeed,
If gazing on divinity disrobed
Thy mortal eyes are frail to judge of fair,
Unbias'd by self-profit, O, rest thee sure
That I shall love thee well and cleave to thee,   160
So that my vigor, wedded to thy blood,
Shall strike within thy pulses, like a God's,

To push thee forward thro' a life of shocks,
Dangers, and deeds, until endurance grow
Sinew'd with action, and the full-grown will,
Circled thro' all experiences, pure law,
Commeasure perfect freedom.'
                                        "Here she ceas'd,
And Paris ponder'd, and I cried, 'O Paris,
Give it to Pallas!' but he heard me not,   170
Or hearing would not hear me, woe is me!

    "O mother Ida, many-fountain'd Ida,
Dear mother Ida, harken ere I die.
Idalian Aphrodite beautiful,
Fresh as the foam, new-bathed in Paphian wells,
With rosy slender fingers backward drew
From her warm brows and bosom her deep hair
Ambrosial, golden round her lucid throat
And shoulder; from the violets her light foot
Shone rosy-white, and o'er her rounded form   180
Between the shadows of the vine-bunches
Floated the glowing sunlights, as she moved.

    "Dear mother Ida, harken ere I die.
She with a subtle smile in her mild eyes,
The herald of her triumph, drawing nigh
Half-whisper'd in his ear, 'I promise thee
The fairest and most loving wife in Greece.'
She spoke and laugh'd; I shut my sight for fear;
But when I look'd, Paris had raised his arm,
And I beheld great Herè's angry eyes,   190
As she withdrew into the golden cloud,
And I was left alone within the bower;
And from that time to this I am alone,
And I shall be alone until I die.

    "Yet, mother Ida, harken ere I die.
Fairest—why fairest wife? am I not fair?

My love hath told me so a thousand times.
Methinks I must be fair, for yesterday,
When I past by, a wild and wanton pard,
Eyed like the evening star, with playful tail   200
Crouch'd fawning in the weed. Most loving is she?
Ah me, my mountain shepherd, that my arms
Were wound about thee, and my hot lips prest
Close, close to thine in that quick-falling dew
Of fruitful kisses, thick as autumn rains
Flash in the pools of whirling Simois!

   "O mother, hear me yet before I die.
They came, they cut away my tallest pines,
My tall dark pines, that plumed the craggy ledge
High over the blue gorge, and all between   210
The snowy peak and snow-white cataract
Foster'd the callow eaglet—from beneath
Whose thick mysterious boughs in the dark morn
The panther's roar came muffled, while I sat
Low in the valley. Never, never more
Shall lone Œnone see the morning mist
Sweep thro' them; never see them overlaid
With narrow moonlit slips of silver cloud,
Between the loud stream and the trembling stars.

   "O mother, hear me yet before I die.   220
I wish that somewhere in the ruin'd folds,
Among the fragments tumbled from the glens,
Or the dry thickets, I could meet with her
The Abominable, that uninvited came
Into the fair Peleïan banquet-hall,
And cast the golden fruit upon the board,
And bred this change; that I might speak my mind,
And tell her to her face how much I hate
Her presence, hated both of Gods and men.

"O mother, hear me yet before I die.   230
Hath he not sworn his love a thousand times,
In this green valley, under this green hill,
Even on this hand, and sitting on this stone?
Seal'd it with kisses? water'd it with tears?
O happy tears, and how unlike to these!
O happy heaven, how canst thou see my face?
O happy earth, how canst thou bear my weight?
O death, death, death, thou ever-floating cloud,
There are enough unhappy on this earth,
Pass by the happy souls, that love to live;   240
I pray thee, pass before my light of life,
And shadow all my soul, that I may die.
Thou weighest heavy on the heart within,
Weigh heavy on my eyelids; let me die.

"O mother, hear me yet before I die.
I will not die alone, for fiery thoughts
Do shape themselves within me, more and more,
Whereof I catch the issue, as I hear
Dead sounds at night come from the inmost hills,
Like footsteps upon wool. I dimly see   250
My far-off doubtful purpose, as a mother
Conjectures of the features of her child
Ere it is born. Her child!—a shudder comes
Across me: never child be born of me,
Unblest, to vex me with his father's eyes!

"O mother, hear me yet before I die.
Hear me, O earth. I will not die alone,
Lest their shrill happy laughter come to me
Walking the cold and starless road of death
Uncomforted, leaving my ancient love   260
With the Greek woman. I will rise and go
Down into Troy, and ere the stars come forth
Talk with the wild Cassandra, for she says

A fire dances before her, and a sound
Rings ever in her ears of armed men.
What this may be I know not, but I know
That, wheresoe'er I am by night and day,
All earth and air seem only burning fire."

TO ———

WITH THE FOLLOWING POEM

"The Palace of Art" was printed with this introduction.

I send you here a sort of allegory—
For you will understand it—of a soul,
A sinful soul possess'd of many gifts,
A spacious garden full of flowering weeds,
A glorious devil, large in heart and brain,
That did love beauty only—beauty seen
In all varieties of mould and mind—
And knowledge for its beauty; or if good,
Good only for its beauty, seeing not
That Beauty, Good, and Knowledge are three sisters
That doat upon each other, friends to man,
Living together under the same roof,
And never can be sunder'd without tears.
And he that shuts Love out, in turn shall be
Shut out from Love, and on her threshold lie
Howling in outer darkness. Not for this
Was common clay ta'en from the common earth
Moulded by God, and temper'd with the tears
Of angels to the perfect shape of man.

THE PALACE OF ART

I built my soul a lordly pleasure-house,
    Wherein at ease for aye to dwell.

I said, "O Soul, make merry and carouse,
 Dear soul, for all is well."

A huge crag-platform, smooth as burnish'd brass,
 I chose. The ranged ramparts bright
From level meadow-bases of deep grass
 Suddenly scaled the light.

Thereon I built it firm. Of ledge or shelf
 The rock rose clear, or winding stair.   10
My soul would live alone unto herself
 In her high palace there.

And "while the world runs round and round," I said,
 "Reign thou apart, a quiet king,
Still as, while Saturn whirls, his steadfast shade
 Sleeps on his luminous ring."

To which my soul made answer readily:
 "Trust me, In bliss I shall abide
In this great mansion, that is built for me,
 So royal-rich and wide."   20

. . . .

Four courts I made, East, West and South and North,
 In each a squared lawn, wherefrom
The golden gorge of dragons spouted forth
 A flood of fountain-foam.

And round the cool green courts there ran a row
 Of cloisters, branch'd like mighty woods,
Echoing all night to that sonorous flow
 Of spouted fountain-floods;

And round the roofs a gilded gallery
 That lent broad verge to distant lands,   30
Far as the wild swan wings, to where the sky
 Dipt down to sea and sands.

From those four jets four currents in one swell
   Across the mountain stream'd below
In misty folds, that floating as they fell
    Lit up a torrent-bow.

And high on every peak a statue seem'd
   To hang on tiptoe, tossing up
A cloud of incense of all odor steam'd
    From out a golden cup.   40

So that she thought, "And who shall gaze upon
   My palace with unblinded eyes,
While this great bow will waver in the sun,
    And that sweet incense rise?"

For that sweet incense rose and never fail'd,
   And, while day sank or mounted higher,
The light aerial gallery, golden-rail'd,
    Burnt like a fringe of fire.

Likewise the deep-set windows, stain'd and traced,
   Would seem slow-flaming crimson fires   50
From shadow'd grots of arches interlaced,
    And tipt with frost-like spires.

.   .   .   .

Full of long-sounding corridors it was,
   That over-vaulted grateful gloom,
Thro' which the livelong day my soul did pass,
    Well-pleased, from room to room.

Full of great rooms and small the palace stood,
   All various, each a perfect whole
From living Nature, fit for every mood
    And change of my still soul.   60

For some were hung with arras green and blue,
   Showing a gaudy summer-morn,

Where with puff'd cheek the belted hunter blew
 His wreathed bugle-horn.

One seem'd all dark and red—a tract of sand,
 And some one pacing there alone,
Who paced for ever in a glimmering land,
 Lit with a low large moon.

One show'd an iron coast and angry waves
 You seem'd to hear them climb and fall   70
And roar rock-thwarted under bellowing caves,
 Beneath the windy wall.

And one, a full-fed river winding slow
 By herds upon an endless plain,
The ragged rims of thunder brooding low,
 With shadow-streaks of rain.

And one, the reapers at their sultry toil,
 In front they bound the sheaves. Behind
Were realms of upland, prodigal in oil,
 And hoary to the wind.   80

And one a foreground black with stones and slags;
 Beyond, a line of heights; and higher
All barr'd with long white cloud the scornful crags;
 And highest, snow and fire.

And one, an English home—gray twilight pour'd
 On dewy pastures, dewy trees,
Softer than sleep—all things in order stored,
 A haunt of ancient Peace.

Nor these alone, but every landscape fair,
 As fit for every mood of mind,   90
Or gay, or grave, or sweet, or stern, was there,
 Not less than truth design'd.

.   .   .   .

Or the maid-mother by a crucifix,
   In tracts of pasture sunny-warm,
Beneath branch-work of costly sardonyx
     Sat smiling, babe in arm.

Or in a clear-wall'd city on the sea,
   Near gilded organ-pipes, her hair
Wound with white roses, slept Saint Cecily;
     An angel look'd at her.   100

Or thronging all one porch of Paradise
   A group of Houris bow'd to see
The dying Islamite, with hands and eyes
     That said, We wait for thee.

Or mythic Uther's deeply-wounded son
   In some fair space of sloping greens
Lay, dozing in the vale of Avalon,
     And watch'd by weeping queens.

Or hollowing one hand against his ear,
   To list a foot-fall, ere he saw   110
The wood-nymph, stay'd the Ausonian king to hear
     Of wisdom and of law.

Or over hills with peaky tops engrail'd,
   And many a tract of palm and rice,
The throne of Indian Cama slowly sail'd
     A summer fann'd with spice.

Or sweet Europa's mantle blew unclasp'd,
   From off her shoulder backward borne;
From one hand droop'd a crocus; one hand grasp'd
     The mild bull's golden horn.   120

Or else flush'd Ganymede, his rosy thigh
   Half-buried in the eagle's down,
Sole as a flying star shot thro' the sky
    Above the pillar'd town.

Nor these alone; but every legend fair
   Which the supreme Caucasian mind
Carved out of Nature for itself was there,
    Not less than life design'd.

.   .   .   .

Then in the towers I placed great bells that swung,
   Moved of themselves, with silver sound;   130
And with choice paintings of wise men I hung
    The royal dais round.

For there was Milton like a seraph strong,
   Beside him Shakespeare bland and mild;
And there the world-worn Dante grasp'd his song,
    And somewhat grimly smiled.

And there the Ionian father of the rest;
   A million wrinkles carved his skin;
A hundred winters snow'd upon his breast,
    From cheek and throat and chin.   140

Above, the fair hall-ceiling stately-set
   Many an arch high up did lift,
And angels rising and descending met
    With interchange of gift.

Below was all mosaic choicely plann'd
   With cycles of the human tale
Of this wide world, the times of every land
    So wrought they will not fail.

The people here, a beast of burden slow,
   Toil'd onward, prick'd with goads and stings;   150

Here play'd, a tiger, rolling to and fro
    The heads and crowns of kings;

Here rose, an athlete, strong to break or bind
    All force in bonds that might endure,
And here once more like some sick man declined,
      And trusted any cure.

But over these she trod; and those great bells
    Began to chime. She took her throne;
She sat betwixt the shining oriels,
      To sing her songs alone.   160

And thro' the topmost oriels' colored flame
    Two godlike faces gazed below;
Plato the wise, and large-brow'd Verulam,
      The first of those who know.

And all those names that in their motion were
    Full-welling fountain-heads of change,
Betwixt the slender shafts were blazon'd fair
      In diverse raiment strange;

Thro' which the lights, rose, amber, emerald, blue,
    Flush'd in her temples and her eyes,   170
And from her lips, as morn from Memnon, drew
      Rivers of melodies.

No nightingale delighteth to prolong
    Her low preamble all alone,
More than my soul to hear her echo'd song
      Throb thro' the ribbed stone;

Singing and murmuring in her feastful mirth,
    Joying to feel herself alive,
Lord over Nature, lord of the visible earth,
      Lord of the senses five;   180

Communing with herself: "All these are mine,
   And let the world have peace or wars,
'T is one to me." She—when young night divine
     Crown'd dying day with stars,

Making sweet close of his delicious toils—
   Lit light in wreaths and anadems,
And pure quintessences of precious oils
     In hollow'd moons of gems,

To mimic heaven; and clapt her hands and cried,
   "I marvel if my still delight   190
In this great house so royal-rich and wide
     Be flatter'd to the height.

"O all things fair to sate my various eyes!
   O shapes and hues that please me well!
O silent faces of the Great and Wise,
     My Gods, with whom I dwell!

"O Godlike isolation which art mine,
   I can but count thee perfect gain,
What time I watch the darkening droves of swine
     That range on yonder plain.   200

"In filthy sloughs they roll a prurient skin,
   They graze and wallow, breed and sleep;
And oft some brainless devil enters in,
     And drives them to the deep."

Then of the moral instinct would she prate
   And of the rising from the dead,
As hers by right of full-accomplish'd Fate;
     And at the last she said:

"I take possession of man's mind and deed.
   I care not what the sects may brawl.   210

I sit as God holding no form of creed,
  But contemplating all."

    .   .   .   .

Full oft the riddle of the painful earth
  Flash'd thro' her as she sat alone,
Yet not the less held she her solemn mirth,
  And intellectual throne.

And so she throve and prosper'd; so three years
  She prosper'd; on the fourth she fell,
Like Herod, when the shout was in his ears,
  Struck thro' with pangs of hell.   220

Lest she should fail and perish utterly,
  God, before whom ever lie bare
The abysmal deeps of personality,
  Plagued her with sore despair.

When she would think, where'er she turn'd her sight
  The airy hand confusion wrought,
Wrote, "Mene, mene," and divided quite
  The kingdom of her thought.

Deep dread and loathing of her solitude
  Fell on her, from which mood was born   230
Scorn of herself; again, from out that mood
  Laughter at her self-scorn.

"What! is not this my place of strength," she said,
  "My spacious mansion built for me,
Whereof the strong foundation-stones were laid
  Since my first memory?"

But in dark corners of her palace stood
  Uncertain shapes; and unawares
On white-eyed phantasms weeping tears of blood,
  And horrible nightmares,   240

And hollow shades enclosing hearts of flame,
    And, with dim fretted foreheads all,
On corpses three-months-old at noon she came,
        That stood against the wall.

A spot of dull stagnation, without light
    Or power of movement, seem'd my soul,
Mid onward-sloping motions infinite
        Making for one sure goal;

A still salt pool, lock'd in with bars of sand,
    Left on the shore, that hears all night   250
The plunging seas draw backward from the land
        Their moon-led waters white;

A star that with the choral starry dance
    Join'd not, but stood, and standing saw
The hollow orb of moving Circumstance
        Roll'd round by one fix'd law.

Back on herself her serpent pride had curl'd
    "No voice," she shriek'd in that lone hall,
"No voice breaks thro' the stillness of this world;
        One deep, deep silence all!"   260

She, mouldering with the dull earth's mouldering sod,
    Inwrapt tenfold in slothful shame,
Lay there exiled from eternal God,
        Lost to her place and name;

And death and life she hated equally,
    And nothing saw, for her despair,
But dreadful time, dreadful eternity,
        No comfort anywhere;

Remaining utterly confused with fears,
    And ever worse with growing time,   270

And ever unrelieved by dismal tears,
    And all alone in crime.

Shut up as in a crumbling tomb, girt round
    With blackness as a solid wall,
Far off she seem'd to hear the dully sound
    Of human footsteps fall:

As in strange lands a traveller walking slow,
    In doubt and great perplexity,
A little before moonrise hears the low
    Moan of an unknown sea;   280

And knows not if it be thunder, or a sound
    Of rocks thrown down, or one deep cry
Of great wild beasts; then thinketh, "I have found
    A new land, but I die."

She howl'd aloud, "I am on fire within.
    There comes no murmur of reply.
What is it that will take away my sin,
    And save me lest I die?"

So when four years were wholly finished,
    She threw her royal robes away.   290
"Make me a cottage in the vale," she said,
    "Where I may mourn and pray.

"Yet pull not down my palace towers, that are
    So lightly, beautifully built;
Perchance I may return with others there
    When I have purged my guilt."

THE LOTOS-EATERS

"Courage!" he said, and pointed toward the land,
"This mounting wave will roll us shoreward soon."

In the afternoon they came unto a land
In which it seemed always afternoon.
All round the coast the languid air did swoon,
Breathing like one that hath a weary dream.
Full-faced above the valley stood the moon;
And, like a downward smoke, the slender stream
Along the cliff to fall and pause and fall did seem.

A land of streams! some, like a downward smoke,   10
Slow-dropping veils of thinnest lawn, did go;
And some thro' wavering lights and shadows broke,
Rolling a slumbrous sheet of foam below.
They saw the gleaming river seaward flow
From the inner land; far off, three mountain-tops,
Three silent pinnacles of aged snow,
Stood sunset-flush'd; and dew'd with showery drops,
Up-clomb the shadowy pine above the woven copse.

The charmed sunset linger'd low adown
In the red West; thro' mountain clefts the dale   20
Was seen far inland, and the yellow down
Border'd with palm, and many a winding vale
And meadow, set with slender galingale;
A land where all things always seem'd the same!
And round about the keel with faces pale,
Dark faces pale against that rosy flame,
The mild-eyed melancholy Lotos-eaters came.

Branches they bore of that enchanted stem,
Laden with flower and fruit, whereof they gave
To each, but whoso did receive of them   30
And taste, to him the gushing of the wave
Far far away did seem to mourn and rave
On alien shores; and if his fellow spake,
His voice was thin, as voices from the grave;
And deep-asleep he seem'd, yet all awake,
And music in his ears his beating heart did make.

They sat them down upon the yellow sand,
Between the sun and moon upon the shore;
And sweet it was to dream of Fatherland,
Of child, and wife, and slave; but evermore   40
Most weary seem'd the sea, weary the oar,
Weary the wandering fields of barren foam.
Then some one said, "We will return no more";
And all at once they sang, "Our island home
Is far beyond the wave; we will no longer roam."

CHORIC SONG

I

There is sweet music here that softer falls
Than petals from blown roses on the grass,
Or night-dews on still waters between walls
Of shadowy granite, in a gleaming pass;
Music that gentlier on the spirit lies,   50
Than tired eyelids upon tired eyes;
Music that brings sweet sleep down from the blissful skies.
Here are cool mosses deep,
And thro' the moss the ivies creep,
And in the stream the long-leaved flowers weep,
And from the craggy ledge the poppy hangs in sleep.

II

Why are we weigh'd upon with heaviness,
And utterly consumed with sharp distress,
While all things else have rest from weariness?
All things have rest; why should we toil alone,   60
We only toil, who are the first of things,
And make perpetual moan,
Still from one sorrow to another thrown;
Nor ever fold our wings,
And cease from wanderings,

Nor steep our brows in slumber's holy balm;
Nor harken what the inner spirit sings,
"There is no joy but calm!"—
Why should we only toil, the roof and crown of things?

III

Lo! in the middle of the wood,   70
The folded leaf is woo'd from out the bud
With winds upon the branch, and there
Grows green and broad, and takes no care,
Sun-steep'd at noon, and in the moon
Nightly dew-fed; and turning yellow
Falls, and floats adown the air.
Lo! sweeten'd with the summer light,
The full-juiced apple, waxing over-mellow,
Drops in a silent autumn night.
All its allotted length of days   80
The flower ripens in its place,
Ripens and fades, and falls, and hath no toil,
Fast-rooted in the fruitful soil.

IV

Hateful is the dark-blue sky,
Vaulted o'er the dark-blue sea.
Death is the end of life; ah, why
Should life all labor be?
Let us alone. Time driveth onward fast,
And in a little while our lips are dumb.
Let us alone. What is it that will last?   90
All things are taken from us, and become
Portions and parcels of the dreadful past.
Let us alone. What pleasure can we have
To war with evil? Is there any peace
In ever climbing up the climbing wave?
All things have rest, and ripen toward the grave
In silence—ripen, fall, and cease:
Give us long rest or death, dark death, or dreamful ease.

V

How sweet it were, hearing the downward stream,
With half-shut eyes ever to seem   100
Falling asleep in a half-dream!
To dream and dream, like yonder amber light,
Which will not leave the myrrh-bush on the height;
To hear each other's whisper'd speech;
Eating the Lotos day by day,
To watch the crisping ripples on the beach,
And tender curving lines of creamy spray;
To lend our hearts and spirits wholly
To the influence of mild-minded melancholy;
To muse and brood and live again in memory,   110
With those old faces of our infancy
Heap'd over with a mound of grass,
Two handfuls of white dust, shut in an urn of brass!

VI

Dear is the memory of our wedded lives,
And dear the last embraces of our wives
And their warm tears; but all hath suffer'd change;
For surely now our household hearths are cold,
Our sons inherit us, our looks are strange,
And we should come like ghosts to trouble joy.
Or else the island princes over-bold   120
Have eat our substance, and the minstrel sings
Before them of the ten years' war in Troy,
And our great deeds, as half-forgotten things.
Is there confusion in the little isle?
Let what is broken so remain.
The Gods are hard to reconcile;
'T is hard to settle order once again.
There *is* confusion worse than death,
Trouble on trouble, pain on pain,
Long labor unto aged breath,   130

Sore task to hearts worn out by many wars
And eyes grown dim with gazing on the pilot-stars.

VII

But, propt on beds of amaranth and moly,
How sweet—while warm airs lull us, blowing lowly—
With half-dropt eyelid still,
Beneath a heaven dark and holy,
To watch the long bright river drawing slowly
His waters from the purple hill—
To hear the dewy echoes calling
From cave to cave thro' the thick-twined vine—   140
To watch the emerald-color'd water falling
Thro' many a woven acanthus-wreath divine!
Only to hear and see the far-off sparkling brine,
Only to hear were sweet, stretch'd out beneath the pine.

VIII

The Lotos blooms below the barren peak,
The Lotos blows by every winding creek;
All day the wind breathes low with mellower tone;
Thro' every hollow cave and alley lone
Round and round the spicy downs the yellow Lotos-dust is blown.
We have had enough of action, and of motion we,   150
Roll'd to starboard, roll'd to larboard, when the surge was
    seething free,
Where the wallowing monster spouted his foam-fountains in
    the sea.
Let us swear an oath, and keep it with an equal mind,
In the hollow Lotos-land to live and lie reclined
On the hills like Gods together, careless of mankind.
For they lie beside their nectar, and the bolts are hurl'd
Far below them in the valleys, and the clouds are lightly curl'd
Round their golden houses, girdled with the gleaming world;
Where they smile in secret, looking over wasted lands,
Blight and famine, plague and earthquake, roaring deeps and
    fiery sands,   160

Clanging fights, and flaming towns, and sinking ships, and
    praying hands.
But they smile, they find a music centred in a doleful song
Steaming up, a lamentation and an ancient tale of wrong,
Like a tale of little meaning tho' the words are strong;
Chanted from an ill-used race of men that cleave the soil,
Sow the seed, and reap the harvest with enduring toil,
Storing yearly little dues of wheat, and wine and oil;
Till they perish and they suffer—some, 't is whisper'd—down in
    hell
Suffer endless anguish, others in Elysian valleys dwell,
Resting weary limbs at last on beds of asphodel.   170
Surely, surely, slumber is more sweet than toil, the shore
Than labor in the deep mid-ocean, wind and wave and oar;
O, rest ye, brother mariners, we will not wander more.

"OF OLD SAT FREEDOM ON THE HEIGHTS"

Of old sat Freedom on the heights,
    The thunders breaking at her feet;
Above her shook the starry lights;
    She heard the torrents meet.

There in her place she did rejoice,
    Self-gather'd in her prophet-mind,
But fragments of her mighty voice
    Came rolling on the wind.

Then stept she down thro' town and field
    To mingle with the human race,
And part by part to men reveal'd
    The fullness of her face—

Grave mother of majestic works,
    From her isle-altar gazing down,

Who, Godlike, grasps the triple forks,
 And, king-like, wears the crown.

Her open eyes desire the truth.
 The wisdom of a thousand years
Is in them. May perpetual youth
 Keep dry their light from tears;

That her fair form may stand and shine,
 Make bright our days and light our dreams,
Turning to scorn with lips divine
 The falsehood of extremes!

"LOVE THOU THY LAND, WITH

LOVE FAR-BROUGHT"

Love thou thy land, with love far-brought
 From out the storied past, and used
 Within the present, but transfused
Thro' future time by power of thought;

True love turn'd round on fixed poles,
 Love, that endures not sordid ends,
 For English natures, freemen, friends,
Thy brothers and immortal souls.

But pamper not a hasty time,
 Nor feed with crude imaginings   10
 The herd, wild hearts and feeble wings
That every sophister can lime.

Deliver not the tasks of might
 To weakness, neither hide the ray
 From those, not blind, who wait for day,
Tho' sitting girt with doubtful light.

Make knowledge circle with the winds;
　But let her herald, Reverence, fly
　Before her to whatever sky
Bear seed of men and growth of minds.   20

Watch what main-currents draw the years;
　Cut Prejudice against the grain.
　But gentle words are always gain;
Regard the weakness of thy peers.

Nor toil for title, place, or touch
　Of pension, neither count on praise—
　It grows to guerdon after-days.
Nor deal in watch-words overmuch;

Not clinging to some ancient saw,
　Not master'd by some modern term,   30
　Not swift nor slow to change, but firm;
And in its season bring the law,

That from Discussion's lip may fall
　With Life that, working strongly, binds—
　Set in all lights by many minds,
To close the interests of all.

For Nature also, cold and warm,
　And moist and dry, devising long,
　Thro' many agents making strong,
Matures the individual form.   40

Meet is it changes should control
　Our being, lest we rust in ease.
　We all are changed by still degrees,
All but the basis of the soul.

So let the change which comes be free
　To ingroove itself with that which flies,

And work, a joint of state, that plies
Its office, moved with sympathy.

A saying hard to shape in act;
    For all the past of Time reveals   50
    A bridal dawn of thunder-peals,
Wherever Thought hath wedded Fact.

Even now we hear with inward strife
    A motion toiling in the gloom—
    The Spirit of the years to come
Yearning to mix himself with Life.

A slow-develop'd strength awaits
    Completion in a painful school;
    Phantoms of other forms of rule,
New Majesties of mighty States—   60

The warders of the growing hour,
    But vague in vapor, hard to mark;
    And round them sea and air are dark
With great contrivances of Power.

Of many changes, aptly join'd,
    Is bodied forth the second whole.
    Regard gradation, lest the soul
Of Discord race the rising wind:

A wind to puff your idol-fires,
    And heap their ashes on the head;   70
    To shame the boast so often made,
That we are wiser than our sires.

O, yet, if Nature's evil star
    Drive men in manhood, as in youth,
    To follow flying steps of Truth
Across the brazen bridge of war—

If New and Old, disastrous feud,
 Must ever shock, like armed foes,
 And this be true, till Time shall close,
That Principles are rain'd in blood;   80

Not yet the wise of heart would cease
 To hold his hope thro' shame and guilt,
 But with his hand against the hilt,
Would pace the troubled land, like Peace;

Not less, tho' dogs of Faction bay,
 Would serve his kind in deed and word,
 Certain, if knowledge bring the sword,
That knowledge takes the sword away—

Would love the gleams of good that broke
 From either side, nor veil his eyes;   90
 And if some dreadful need should rise
Would strike, and firmly, and one stroke.

To-morrow yet would reap to-day,
 As we bear blossom of the dead;
 Earn well the thrifty months, nor wed
Raw Haste, half-sister to Delay.

WALKING TO THE MAIL

First printed in 1842, and afterwards
slightly changed in the opening lines.

 John. I'm glad I walk'd. How fresh the meadows look
Above the river, and, but a month ago,
The whole hillside was redder than a fox!
Is yon plantation where this byway joins
The turnpike?

James.   Yes.

John.   And when does this come by?

James.   The mail? At one o'clock.

John.   What is it now?

James.   A quarter to.   10

John.   Whose house is that I see?
No, not the County Member's with the vane.
Up higher with the yew-tree by it, and half
A score of gables.

James.   That? Sir Edward Head's.
But he's abroad; the place is to be sold.

John.   O, his! He was not broken.

James.   No, sir, he,
Vext with a morbid devil in his blood
That veil'd the world with jaundice, hid his face   20
From all men, and commercing with himself,
He lost the sense that handles daily life—
That keeps us all in order more or less—
And sick of home went overseas for change.

John.   And whither?

James.   Nay, who knows? he's here and there.
But let him go; his devil goes with him,
As well as with his tenant, Jocky Dawes.

John.   What's that?

James.   You saw the man—on Monday, was it? 30
There by the humpback'd willow; half stands up
And bristles, half has fallen and made a bridge;
And there he caught the younker tickling trout—
Caught *in flagrante*—what's the Latin word?—
Delicto; but his house, for so they say,
Was haunted with a jolly ghost, that shook
The curtains, whined in lobbies, tapt at doors,
And rummaged like a rat; no servant stay'd.
The farmer vext packs up his beds and chairs,
And all his household stuff; and with his boy   40
Betwixt his knees, his wife upon the tilt,
Sets out, and meets a friend who hails him, "What!

You're flitting!" "Yes, we're flitting," says the ghost—
For they had pack'd the thing among the beds.
"O, well," says he, "you flitting with us too!—
Jack, turn the horses' heads and home again."

    John.   *He* left *his* wife behind; for so I heard.

    James.   He left her, yes. I met my lady once;
A woman like a butt, and harsh as crabs.

    John.   O, yet but I remember, ten years back—   50
'T is now at least ten years—and then she was—
You could not light upon a sweeter thing;
A body slight and round, and like a pear
In growing, modest eyes, a hand, a foot
Lessening in perfect cadence, and a skin
As clean and white as privet when it flowers.

    James.   Ay, ay, the blossom fades, and they that loved
At first like dove and dove were cat and dog.
She was the daughter of a cottager,
Out of her sphere. What betwixt shame and pride,   60
New things and old, himself and her, she sour'd
To what she is; a nature never kind!
Like men, like manners; like breeds like, they say.
Kind nature is the best; those manners next
That fit us like a nature second-hand—
Which are indeed the manners of the great.

    John.   But I had heard it was this bill that past,
And fear of change at home, that drove him hence.

    James.   That was the last drop in the cup of gall.
I once was near him, when his bailiff brought   70
A Chartist pike. You should have seen him wince
As from a venomous thing; he thought himself
A mark for all, and shudder'd, lest a cry
Should break his sleep by night, and his nice eyes
Should see the raw mechanic's bloody thumbs
Sweat on his blazon'd chairs. But, sir, you know
That these two parties still divide the world—
Of those that want, and those that have; and still

The same old sore breaks out from age to age
With much the same result. Now I myself,   80
A Tory to the quick, was as a boy
Destructive, when I had not what I would.
I was at school,—a college in the South.
There lived a flayflint near; we stole his fruit,
His hens, his eggs; but there was law for *us;*
We paid in person. He had a sow, sir. She,
With meditative grunts of much content,
Lay great with pig, wallowing in sun and mud.
By night we dragg'd her to the college tower
From her warm bed, and up the corkscrew stair   90
With hand and rope we haled the groaning sow,
And on the leads we kept her till she pigg'd.
Large range of prospect had the mother sow,
And but for daily loss of one she loved
As one by one we took them—but for this—
As never sow was higher in this world—
Might have been happy; but what lot is pure?
We took them all, till she was left alone
Upon her tower, the Niobe of swine,
And so return'd unfarrow'd to her sty.   100
        John.   They found you out?
        James.   Not they.
        John.   Well—after all—
What know we of the secret of a man?
His nerves were wrong. What ails us who are sound,
That we should mimic this raw fool the world,
Which charts us all in its coarse blacks or whites,
As ruthless as a baby with a worm,
As cruel as a schoolboy ere he grows
To pity—more from ignorance than will.   110
        But put your best foot forward, or I fear
That we shall miss the mail; and here it comes
With five at top, as quaint a four-in-hand
As you shall see,—three pyebalds and a roan.

ULYSSES

It little profits that an idle king,
By this still hearth, among these barren crags,
Match'd with an aged wife, I mete and dole
Unequal laws unto a savage race,
That hoard, and sleep, and feed, and know not me.
I cannot rest from travel; I will drink
Life to the lees. All times I have enjoy'd
Greatly, have suffer'd greatly, both with those
That loved me, and alone; on shore, and when
Thro' scudding drifts the rainy Hyades   10
Vext the dim sea. I am become a name;
For always roaming with a hungry heart
Much have I seen and known,—cities of men
And manners, climates, councils, governments,
Myself not least, but honor'd of them all,—
And drunk delight of battle with my peers,
Far on the ringing plains of windy Troy.
I am a part of all that I have met;
Yet all experience is an arch wherethro'
Gleams that untravell'd world whose margin fades   20
For ever and for ever when I move.
How dull it is to pause, to make an end,
To rust unburnish'd, not to shine in use!
As tho' to breathe were life! Life piled on life
Were all too little, and of one to me
Little remains; but every hour is saved
From that eternal silence, something more,
A bringer of new things; and vile it were
For some three suns to store and hoard myself,
And this gray spirit yearning in desire   30
To follow knowledge like a sinking star,
Beyond the utmost bound of human thought.
    This is my son, mine own Telemachus,

To whom I leave the sceptre and the isle,—
Well-loved of me, discerning to fulfil
This labor, by slow prudence to make mild
A rugged people, and thro' soft degrees
Subdue them to the useful and the good.
Most blameless is he, centred in the sphere
Of common duties, decent not to fail   40
In offices of tenderness, and pay
Meet adoration to my household gods,
When I am gone. He works his work, I mine.
   There lies the port; the vessel puffs her sail;
There gloom the dark, broad seas. My mariners,
Souls that have toil'd, and wrought, and thought with me,—
That ever with a frolic welcome took
The thunder and the sunshine, and opposed
Free hearts, free foreheads,—you and I are old;
Old age hath yet his honor and his toil.   50
Death closes all; but something ere the end,
Some work of noble note, may yet be done,
Not unbecoming men that strove with Gods.
The lights begin to twinkle from the rocks;
The long day wanes; the slow moon climbs; the deep
Moans round with many voices. Come, my friends.
'T is not too late to seek a newer world.
Push off, and sitting well in order smite
The sounding furrows; for my purpose holds
To sail beyond the sunset, and the baths   60
Of all the western stars, until I die.
It may be that the gulfs will wash us down;
It may be we shall touch the Happy Isles,
And see the great Achilles, whom we knew.
Tho' much is taken, much abides; and tho'
We are not now that strength which in old days
Moved earth and heaven, that which we are, we are,—
One equal temper of heroic hearts,
Made weak by time and fate, but strong in will
To strive, to seek, to find, and not to yield.   70

TITHONUS

The woods decay, the woods decay and fall,
The vapors weep their burthen to the ground,
Man comes and tills the field and lies beneath,
And after many a summer dies the swan.
Me only cruel immortality
Consumes; I wither slowly in thine arms,
Here at the quiet limit of the world,
A white-hair'd shadow roaming like a dream
The ever-silent spaces of the East,
Far-folded mists, and gleaming halls of morn.   10
    Alas! for this gray shadow, once a man—
So glorious in his beauty and thy choice,
Who madest him thy chosen, that he seem'd
To his great heart none other than a God!
I ask'd thee, "Give me immortality."
Then didst thou grant mine asking with a smile,
Like wealthy men who care not how they give.
But thy strong Hours indignant work'd their wills,
And beat me down and marr'd and wasted me,
And tho' they could not end me, left me maim'd   20
To dwell in presence of immortal youth,
Immortal age beside immortal youth,
And all I was in ashes. Can thy love,
Thy beauty, make amends, tho' even now,
Close over us, the silver star, thy guide,
Shines in those tremulous eyes that fill with tears
To hear me? Let me go; take back thy gift.
Why should a man desire in any way
To vary from the kindly race of men,
Or pass beyond the goal of ordinance   30
Where all should pause, as is most meet for all?
    A soft air fans the cloud apart; there comes
A glimpse of that dark world where I was born.

Once more the old mysterious glimmer steals
From thy pure brows, and from thy shoulders pure,
And bosom beating with a heart renew'd.
Thy cheek begins to redden thro' the gloom,
Thy sweet eyes brighten slowly close to mine,
Ere yet they blind the stars, and the wild team
Which love thee, yearning for thy yoke, arise,   40
And shake the darkness from their loosen'd manes,
And beat the twilight into flakes of fire.

  Lo! ever thus thou growest beautiful
In silence, then before thine answer given
Departest, and thy tears are on my cheek.

  Why wilt thou ever scare me with thy tears,
And make me tremble lest a saying learnt,
In days far-off, on that dark earth, be true?
"The Gods themselves cannot recall their gifts."

  Ay me! ay me! with what another heart   50
In days far-off, and with what other eyes
I used to watch—if I be he that watch'd—
The lucid outline forming round thee; saw
The dim curls kindle into sunny rings;
Changed with thy mystic change, and felt my blood
Glow with the glow that slowly crimson'd all
Thy presence and thy portals, while I lay,
Mouth, forehead, eyelids, growing dewy-warm
With kisses balmier than half-opening buds
Of April, and could hear the lips that kiss'd   60
Whispering I knew not what of wild and sweet,
Like that strange song I heard Apollo sing,
While Ilion like a mist rose into towers.

  Yet hold me not for ever in thine East;
How can my nature longer mix with thine?
Coldly thy rosy shadows bathe me, cold
Are all thy lights, and cold my wrinkled feet
Upon thy glimmering thresholds, when the steam
Floats up from those dim fields about the homes
Of happy men that have the power to die,   70

And grassy barrows of the happier dead.
Release me, and restore me to the ground.
Thou seest all things, thou wilt see my grave;
Thou wilt renew thy beauty morn by morn,
I earth in earth forget these empty courts,
And thee returning on thy silver wheels.

LOCKSLEY HALL

Comrades, leave me here a little, while as yet 't is early morn;
Leave me here, and when you want me, sound upon the bugle-
horn.

'T is the place, and all around it, as of old, the curlews call,
Dreary gleams about the moorland flying over Locksley Hall;

Locksley Hall, that in the distance overlooks the sandy tracts,
And the hollow ocean-ridges roaring into cataracts.

Many a night from yonder ivied casement, ere I went to rest,
Did I look on great Orion sloping slowly to the west.

Many a night I saw the Pleiads, rising thro' the mellow shade,
Glitter like a swarm of fireflies tangled in a silver braid.   10

Here about the beach I wander'd, nourishing a youth sublime
With the fairy tales of science, and the long result of time;

When the centuries behind me like a fruitful land reposed;
When I clung to all the present for the promise that it closed;

When I dipt into the future far as human eye could see,
Saw the vision of the world and all the wonder that would be.—

In the spring a fuller crimson comes upon the robin's breast;
In the spring the wanton lapwing gets himself another crest;

In the spring a livelier iris changes on the burnish'd dove;   19
In the spring a young man's fancy lightly turns to thoughts of love.

Then her cheek was pale and thinner than should be for one so
        young,
And her eyes on all my motions with a mute observance hung.

And I said, "My cousin Amy, speak, and speak the truth to me,
Trust me, cousin, all the current of my being sets to thee."

On her pallid cheek and forehead came a color and a light,
As I have seen the rosy red flushing in the northern night.

And she turn'd—her bosom shaken with a sudden storm of sighs—
All the spirit deeply dawning in the dark of hazel eyes—

Saying, "I have hid my feelings, fearing they should do me
        wrong;"
Saying, "Dost thou love me, cousin?" weeping, "I have loved
        thee long."   30

Love took up the glass of Time, and turn'd it in his glowing
        hands;
Every moment, lightly shaken, ran itself in golden sands.

Love took up the harp of Life, and smote on all the chords with
        might;
Smote the chord of Self, that, trembling, past in music out of
        sight.

Many a morning on the moorland did we hear the copses ring,
And her whisper throng'd my pulses with the fulness of the
        spring.

Many an evening by the waters did we watch the stately ships,
And our spirits rush'd together at the touching of the lips.

O my cousin, shallow-hearted! O my Amy, mine no more!
O the dreary, dreary moorland! O the barren, barren shore!   40

Falser than all fancy fathoms, falser than all songs have sung,
Puppet to a father's threat, and servile to a shrewish tongue!

Is it well to wish thee happy?—having known me—to decline
On a range of lower feelings and a narrower heart than mine!

Yet it shall be; thou shalt lower to his level day by day,
What is fine within thee growing coarse to sympathize with clay.

As the husband is, the wife is; thou art mated with a clown,
And the grossness of his nature will have weight to drag thee
      down.

He will hold thee, when his passion shall have spent its novel
      force,
Something better than his dog, a little dearer than his horse.   50

What is this? his eyes are heavy; think not they are glazed with
      wine.
Go to him, it is thy duty; kiss him, take his hand in thine.

It may be my lord is weary, that his brain is overwrought;
Soothe him with thy finer fancies, touch him with thy lighter
      thought.

He will answer to the purpose, easy things to understand—
Better thou wert dead before me, tho' I slew thee with my hand!

Better thou and I were lying, hidden from the heart's disgrace,
Roll'd in one another's arms, and silent in a last embrace.

Cursed be the social wants that sin against the strength of youth!
Cursed be the social lies that warp us from the living truth!   60

Cursed be the sickly forms that err from honest Nature's rule!
Cursed be the gold that gilds the straiten'd forehead of the fool!

Well—'t is well that I should bluster!—Hadst thou less unworthy proved—
Would to God—for I had loved thee more than ever wife was
loved.

Am I mad, that I should cherish that which bears but bitter
fruit?
I will pluck it from my bosom, tho' my heart be at the root.

Never, tho' my mortal summers to such length of years should
come
As the many-winter'd crow that leads the clanging rookery home.

Where is comfort? in division of the records of the mind?   69
Can I part her from herself, and love her, as I know her, kind?

I remember one that perish'd; sweetly did she speak and move;
Such a one do I remember, whom to look at was to love.

Can I think of her as dead, and love her for the love she bore?
No—she never loved me truly; love is love for evermore.

Comfort? comfort scorn'd of devils! this is truth the poet sings,
That a sorrow's crown of sorrow is remembering happier things.

Drug thy memories, lest thou learn it, lest thy heart be put to
proof,
In the dead unhappy night, and when the rain is on the roof.

Like a dog, he hunts in dreams, and thou art staring at the wall,
Where the dying night-lamp flickers, and the shadows rise and
fall.   80

Then a hand shall pass before thee, pointing to his drunken sleep,
To thy widow'd marriage-pillows, to the tears that thou wilt weep.

Thou shalt hear the "Never, never," whisper'd by the phantom
      years,
And a song from out the distance in the ringing of thine ears;

And an eye shall vex thee, looking ancient kindness on thy pain.
Turn thee, turn thee on thy pillow; get thee to thy rest again.

Nay, but Nature brings thee solace; for a tender voice will cry.
'T is a purer life than thine, a lip to drain thy trouble dry.

Baby lips will laugh me down; my latest rival brings thee rest.
Baby fingers, waxen touches, press me from the mother's breast.

O, the child too clothes the father with a dearness not his due.   91
Half is thine and half is his; it will be worthy of the two.

O, I see thee old and formal, fitted to thy petty part,
With a little board of maxims preaching down a daughter's
      heart.

"They were dangerous guides the feelings—she herself was not
      exempt—
Truly, she herself had suffer'd"—Perish in thy self-contempt!

Overlive it—lower yet—be happy! wherefore should I care?
I myself must mix with action, lest I wither by despair.

What is that which I should turn to, lighting upon days like
      these?   99
Every door is barr'd with gold, and opens but to golden keys.

Every gate is throng'd with suitors, all the markets overflow.
I have but an angry fancy; what is that which I should do?

I had been content to perish, falling on the foeman's ground,
When the ranks are roll'd in vapor, and the winds are laid with
    sound.

But the jingling of the guinea helps the hurt that Honor feels,
And the nations do but murmur, snarling at each other's heels.

Can I but relive in sadness? I will turn that earlier page
Hide me from my deep emotion, O thou wondrous Mother-Age!

Make me feel the wild pulsation that I felt before the strife,
When I heard my days before me, and the tumult of my life;

Yearning for the large excitement that the coming years would
    yield,   111
Eager-hearted as a boy when first he leaves his father's field,

And at night along the dusky highway near and nearer drawn,
Sees in heaven the light of London flaring like a dreary dawn;

And his spirit leaps within him to be gone before him then,
Underneath the light he looks at, in among the throngs of men;

Men, my brothers, men the workers, ever reaping something
    new;
That which they have done but earnest of the things that they
    shall do.

For I dipt into the future, far as human eye could see,   119
Saw the Vision of the world, and all the wonder that would be;

Saw the heavens fill with commerce, argosies of magic sails,
Pilots of the purple twilight, dropping down with costly bales:

Heard the heavens fill with shouting, and there rain'd a ghastly
    dew
From the nations' airy navies grappling in the central blue;

Far along the world-wide whisper of the south-wind rushing
    warm,
With the standards of the peoples plunging thro' the thunder-
    storm;

Till the war-drum throbb'd no longer, and the battle-flags were
    furl'd
In the Parliament of man, the Federation of the world.

There the common sense of most shall hold a fretful realm in
    awe,
And the kindly earth shall slumber, lapt in universal law.   130

So I triumph'd ere my passion sweeping thro' me left me dry,
Left me with the palsied heart, and left me with the jaundiced eye;

Eye, to which all order festers, all things here are out of joint.
Science moves, but slowly, slowly, creeping on from point to
    point;

Slowly comes a hungry people, as a lion, creeping nigher,
Glares at one that nods and winks behind a slowly-dying fire.

Yet I doubt not thro' the ages one increasing purpose runs,
And the thoughts of men are widen'd with the process of the
    suns,

What is that to him that reaps not harvest of his youthful joys,
Tho' the deep heart of existence beat for ever like a boy's?   140

Knowledge comes, but wisdom lingers, and I linger on the shore,
And the individual withers, and the world is more and more.

Knowledge comes, but wisdom lingers, and he bears a laden
    breast,
Full of sad experience, moving toward the stillness of his rest.

Hark, my merry comrades call me, sounding on the bugle-horn,
They to whom my foolish passion were a target for their scorn.

Shall it not be scorn to me to harp on such a moulder'd string?
I am shamed thro' all my nature to have loved so slight a thing.

Weakness to be wroth with weakness! woman's pleasure, woman's
    pain—   149
Nature made them blinder motions bounded in a shallower brain.

Woman is the lesser man, and all thy passions, match'd with
    mine,
Are as moonlight unto sunlight, and as water unto wine—

Here at least, where nature sickens, nothing. Ah, for some retreat
Deep in yonder shining Orient, where my life began to beat,

Where in wild Mahratta-battle fell my father evil-starr'd;—
I was left a trampled orphan, and a selfish uncle's ward.

Or to burst all links of habit—there to wander far away,
On from island unto island at the gateways of the day.

Larger constellations burning, mellow moons and happy skies,
Breadths of tropic shade and palms in cluster, knots of Paradise.

Never comes the trader, never floats an European flag,   161
Slides the bird o'er lustrous woodland, swings the trailer from
    the crag;

Droops the heavy-blossom'd bower, hangs the heavy-fruited tree—
Summer isles of Eden lying in dark-purple spheres of sea.

There methinks would be enjoyment more than in this march of
    mind,
In the steamship, in the railway, in the thoughts that shake man-
    kind.

There the passions cramp'd no longer shall have scope and
    breathing space;
I will take some savage woman, she shall rear my dusky race.

Iron-jointed, supple-sinew'd, they shall dive, and they shall run,
Catch the wild goat by the hair, and hurl their lances in the sun;

Whistle back the parrot's call, and leap the rainbows of the
    brooks,   171
Not with blinded eyesight poring over miserable books—

Fool, again the dream, the fancy! but I *know* my words are
    wild,
But I count the gray barbarian lower than the Christian child.

I, to herd with narrow foreheads, vacant of our glorious gains,
Like a beast with lower pleasures, like a beast with lower pains!

Mated with a squalid savage—what to me were sun or clime?
I the heir of all the ages, in the foremost files of time—

I that rather held it better men should perish one by one,   179
Than that earth should stand at gaze like Joshua's moon in Ajalon!

Not in vain the distance beacons. Forward, forward let us range,
Let the great world spin for ever down the ringing grooves of
    change.

Thro' the shadow of the globe we sweep into the younger day;
Better fifty years of Europe than a cycle of Cathay.

Mother-Age,—for mine I knew not,—help me as when life begun;
Rift the hills, and roll the waters, flash the lightnings, weigh the
    sun.

O, I see the crescent promise of my spirit hath not set.
Ancient founts of inspiration well thro' all my fancy yet.

Howsoever these things be, a long farewell to Locksley Hall!
Now for me the woods may wither, now for me the roof-tree
    fall.   190

Comes a vapor from the margin, blackening over heath and holt,
Cramming all the blast before it, in its breast a thunderbolt.

Let it fall on Locksley Hall, with rain or hail, or fire or snow;
For the mighty wind arises, roaring seaward, and I go.

WILL WATERPROOF'S LYRICAL

MONOLOGUE

MADE AT THE COCK

O plump head-waiter at The Cock,
    To which I most resort,
How goes the time? 'T is five o'clock.
    Go fetch a pint of port;
But let it not be such as that
    You set before chance-comers,
But such whose father-grape grew fat
    On Lusitanian summers.

No vain libation to the Muse,
    But may she still be kind,   10
And whisper lovely words, and use
    Her influence on the mind,
To make me write my random rhymes,
    Ere they be half-forgotten;
Nor add and alter, many times,
    Till all be ripe and rotten.

I pledge her, and she comes and dips
    Her laurel in the wine,

And lays it thrice upon my lips,
   These favor'd lips of mine;   20
Until the charm have power to make
   New life-blood warm the bosom,
And barren commonplaces break
   In full and kindly blossom.

I pledge her silent at the board;
   Her gradual fingers steal
And touch upon the master-chord
   Of all I felt and feel.
Old wishes, ghosts of broken plans,
   And phantom hopes assemble;   30
And that child's heart within the man's
   Begins to move and tremble.

Thro' many an hour of summer suns,
   By many pleasant ways,
Against its fountain upward runs
   The current of my days.
I kiss the lips I once have kiss'd;
   The gaslight wavers dimmer;
And softly, thro' a vinous mist,
   My college friendships glimmer.   40

I grow in worth and wit and sense,
   Unboding critic-pen,
Or that eternal want of pence
   Which vexes public men,
Who hold their hands to all, and cry
   For that which all deny them—
Who sweep the crossings, wet or dry,
   And all the world go by them.

Ah! yet, tho' all the world forsake,
   Tho' fortune clip my wings,   50

I will not cramp my heart, nor take
  Half-views of men and things.
Let Whig and Tory stir their blood;
  There must be stormy weather;
But for some true result of good
  All parties work together.

Let there be thistles, there are grapes;
  If old things, there are new;
Ten thousand broken lights and shapes,
  Yet glimpses of the true.   60
Let raffs be rife in prose and rhyme,
  We lack not rhymes and reasons,
As on this whirligig of Time
  We circle with the seasons.

This earth is rich in man and maid,
  With fair horizons bound;
This whole wide earth of light and shade
  Comes out a perfect round.
High over roaring Temple-bar,
  And set in heaven's third story,   70
I look at all things as they are,
  But thro' a kind of glory.

———————

Head-waiter, honor'd by the guest
  Half-mused, or reeling ripe,
The pint you brought me was the best
  That ever came from pipe.
But tho' the port surpasses praise,
  My nerves have dealt with stiffer.
Is there some magic in the place?
  Or do my peptics differ?   80

For since I came to live and learn,
  No pint of white or red

Had ever half the power to turn
    This wheel within my head,
Which bears a season'd brain about,
    Unsubject to confusion,
Tho' soak'd and saturate, out and out,
    Thro' every convolution.

For I am of a numerous house,
    With many kinsmen gay,   90
Where long and largely we carouse
    As who shall say me nay?
Each month, a birthday coming on,
    We drink, defying trouble,
Or sometimes two would meet in one,
    And then we drank it double;

Whether the vintage, yet unkept,
    Had relish fiery-new,
Or elbow-deep in sawdust slept,
    As old as Waterloo,   100
Or, stow'd when classic Canning died,
    In musty bins and chambers,
Had cast upon its crusty side
    The gloom of ten Decembers.

The Muse, the jolly Muse, it is!
    She answer'd to my call;
She changes with that mood or this,
    Is all-in-all to all;
She lit the spark within my throat,
    To make my blood run quicker,   110
Used all her fiery will, and smote
    Her life into the liquor.

And hence this halo lives about
    The waiter's hands, that reach

To each his perfect pint of stout,
   His proper chop to each.
He looks not like the common breed
   That with the napkin dally;
I think he came, like Ganymede,
   From some delightful valley.   120

The Cock was of a larger egg
   Than modern poultry drop,
Stept forward on a firmer leg,
   And cramm'd a plumper crop,
Upon an ampler dunghill trod,
   Crow'd lustier late and early,
Sipt wine from silver, praising God,
   And raked in golden barley.

A private life was all his joy,
   Till in a court he saw   130
A something-pottle-bodied boy
   That knuckled at the taw.
He stoop'd and clutch'd him, fair and good,
   Flew over roof and casement:
His brothers of the weather stood
   Stock-still for sheer amazement.

But he, by farmstead, thorpe, and spire,
   And follow'd with acclaims,
A sign to many a staring shire,
   Came crowing over Thames.   140
Right down by smoky Paul's they bore,
   Till, where the street grows straiter,
One fix'd for ever at the door,
   And one became head-waiter.

———————

But whither would my fancy go?
   How out of place she makes

The violet of a legend blow
　　Among the chops and steaks!
'T is but a steward of the can,
　　One shade more plump than common;　　150
As just and mere a serving-man
　　As any born of woman.

I ranged too high: what draws me down
　　Into the common day?
Is it the weight of that half-crown
　　Which I shall have to pay?
For, something duller than at first,
　　Nor wholly comfortable,
I sit, my empty glass reversed,
　　And thrumming on the table;　　160

Half fearful that, with self at strife,
　　I take myself to task,
Lest of the fulness of my life
　　I leave an empty flask;
For I had hope, by something rare,
　　To prove myself a poet,
But, while I plan and plan, my hair
　　Is gray before I know it.

So fares it since the years began,
　　Till they be gather'd up;　　170
The truth, that flies the flowing can,
　　Will haunt the vacant cup;
And others' follies teach us not,
　　Nor much their wisdom teaches;
And most, of sterling worth, is what
　　Our own experience preaches.

Ah, let the rusty theme alone!
　　We know not what we know.

But for my pleasant hour, 't is gone;
   'T is gone, and let it go.   180
'T is gone: a thousand such have slipt
   Away from my embraces,
And fallen into the dusty crypt
   Of darken'd forms and faces.

Go, therefore, thou! thy betters went
   Long since, and came no more;
With peals of genial clamor sent
   From many a tavern-door,
With twisted quirks and happy hits,
   From misty men of letters;   190
The tavern-hours of mighty wits,—
   Thine elders and thy betters;

Hours when the Poet's words and looks
   Had yet their native glow,
Nor yet the fear of little books
   Had made him talk for show;
But, all his vast heart sherris-warm'd,
   He flash'd his random speeches,
Ere days that deal in ana swarm'd
   His literary leeches.   200

So mix for ever with the past,
   Like all good things on earth!
For should I prize thee, couldst thou last,
   At half thy real worth?
I hold it good, good things should pass;
   With time I will not quarrel;
It is but yonder empty glass
   That makes me maudlin-moral.

———————

Head-waiter of the chop-house here,
   To which I most resort,   210

I too must part; I hold thee dear
   For this good pint of port.
For this, thou shalt from all things suck
   Marrow of mirth and laughter;
And wheresoe'er thou move, good luck
   Shall fling her old shoe after.

But thou wilt never move from hence,
   The sphere thy fate allots;
Thy latter days increased with pence
   Go down among the pots;   220
Thou battenest by the greasy gleam
   In haunts of hungry sinners,
Old boxes, larded with the steam
   Of thirty thousand dinners.

We fret, we fume, would shift our skins,
   Would quarrel with our lot;
Thy care is, under polish'd tins,
   To serve the hot-and-hot;
To come and go, and come again,
   Returning like the pewit,   230
And watch'd by silent gentlemen,
   That trifle with the cruet.

Live long, ere from thy topmost head
   The thick-set hazel dies;
Long, ere the hateful crow shall tread
   The corners of thine eyes;
Live long, nor feel in head or chest
   Our changeful equinoxes,
Till mellow Death, like some late guest,
   Shall call thee from the boxes.   240

But when he calls, and thou shalt cease
   To pace the gritted floor,

And, laying down an unctuous lease
   Of life, shalt earn no more,
No carved cross-bones, the types of Death
   Shall show thee past to heaven,
But carved cross-pipes, and, underneath,
   A pint-pot neatly graven.

THE VISION OF SIN

I

I had a vision when the night was late;
A youth came riding toward a palace-gate.
He rode a horse with wings, that would have flown,
But that his heavy rider kept him down.
And from the palace came a child of sin,
And took him by the curls, and led him in,
Where sat a company with heated eyes,
Expecting when a fountain should arise.
A sleepy light upon their brows and lips—
As when the sun, a crescent of eclipse,   10
Dreams over lake and lawn, and isles and capes—
Suffused them, sitting, lying, languid shapes,
By heaps of gourds, and skins of wine, and piles of grapes.

II

Then methought I heard a mellow sound,
Gathering up from all the lower ground;
Narrowing in to where they sat assembled,
Low voluptuous music winding trembled,
Woven in circles. They that heard it sigh'd,
Panted hand-in-hand with faces pale,
Swung themselves, and in low tones replied;   20
Till the fountain spouted, showering wide
Sleet of diamond-drift and pearly hail.
Then the music touch'd the gates and died,

Rose again from where it seem'd to fail,
Storm'd in orbs of song, a growing gale;
Till thronging in and in, to where they waited,
As 't were a hundred-throated nightingale,
The strong tempestuous treble throbb'd and palpitated;
Ran into its giddiest whirl of sound,
Caught the sparkles, and in circles,   30
Purple gauzes, golden hazes, liquid mazes,
Flung the torrent rainbow round.
Then they started from their places,
Moved with violence, changed in hue,
Caught each other with wild grimaces,
Half-invisible to the view,
Wheeling with precipitate paces
To the melody, till they flew,
Hair and eyes and limbs and faces,
Twisted hard in fierce embraces,   40
Like to Furies, like to Graces,
Dash'd together in blinding dew;
Till, kill'd with some luxurious agony,
The nerve-dissolving melody
Flutter'd headlong from the sky.

III

And then I look'd up toward a mountain-tract,
That girt the region with high cliff and lawn.
I saw that every morning, far withdrawn
Beyond the darkness and the cataract,
God made Himself an awful rose of dawn,   50
Unheeded; and detaching, fold by fold,
From those still heights, and, slowly drawing near,
A vapor heavy, hueless, formless, cold,
Came floating on for many a month and year,
Unheeded; and I thought I would have spoken,
And warn'd that madman ere it grew too late,
But, as in dreams, I could not. Mine was broken,
When that cold vapor touch'd the palace-gate,

And link'd again. I saw within my head
A gray and gap-tooth'd man as lean as death,   60
Who slowly rode across a wither'd heath,
And lighted at a ruin'd inn, and said:

IV

 "Wrinkled ostler, grim and thin!
  Here is custom come your way;
Take my brute, and lead him in,
  Stuff his ribs with mouldy hay.

 "Bitter barmaid, waning fast!
  See that sheets are on my bed.
What! the flower of life is past;
  It is long before you wed.   70

 "Slip-shod waiter, lank and sour,
  At the Dragon on the heath!
Let us have a quiet hour,
  Let us hob-and-nob with Death.

 "I am old, but let me drink;
  Bring me spices, bring me wine;
I remember, when I think,
  That my youth was half divine.

 "Wine is good for shrivell'd lips,
  When a blanket wraps the day,   80
When the rotten woodland drips,
  And the leaf is stamp'd in clay.

 "Sit thee down, and have no shame,
  Cheek by jowl, and knee by knee;
What care I for any name?
  What for order or degree?

"Let me screw thee up a peg;
　Let me loose thy tongue with wine;
Callest thou that thing a leg?
　Which is thinnest? thine or mine?　　　　90

"Thou shalt not be saved by works,
　Thou hast been a sinner too;
Ruin'd trunks on wither'd forks,
　Empty scarecrows, I and you!

"Fill the cup and fill the can,
　Have a rouse before the morn;
Every moment dies a man,
　Every moment one is born.

"We are men of ruin'd blood;
　Therefore comes it we are wise.　　　　100
Fish are we that love the mud,
　Rising to no fancy-flies.

"Name and fame! to fly sublime
　Thro' the courts, the camps, the schools,
Is to be the ball of Time,
　Bandied by the hands of fools.

"Friendship!—to be two in one—
　Let the canting liar pack!
Well I know, when I am gone,
　How she mouths behind my back.　　　　110

"Virtue!—to be good and just—
　Every heart, when sifted well,
Is a clot of warmer dust,
　Mix'd with cunning sparks of hell.

"O, we two as well can look
　Whited thought and cleanly life

As the priest, above his book
  Leering at his neighbor's wife.

"Fill the cup and fill the can,
  Have a rouse before the morn: 120
Every moment dies a man,
  Every moment one is born.

"Drink, and let the parties rave;
  They are fill'd with idle spleen,
Rising, falling, like a wave,
  For they know not what they mean.

"He that roars for liberty
  Faster binds a tyrant's power,
And the tyrant's cruel glee
  Forces on the freer hour.   130

"Fill the can and fill the cup;
  All the windy ways of men
Are but dust that rises up,
  And is lightly laid again.

"Greet her with applausive breath,
  Freedom, gaily doth she tread;
In her right a civic wreath,
  In her left a human head.

"No, I love not what is new;
  She is of an ancient house,   140
And I think we know the hue
  Of that cap upon her brows.

"Let her go! her thirst she slakes
  Where the bloody conduit runs,
Then her sweetest meal she makes
  On the first-born of her sons.

"Drink to lofty hopes that cool,—
 Visions of a perfect State;
Drink we, last, the public fool,
 Frantic love and frantic hate.   150

"Chant me now some wicked stave,
 Till thy drooping courage rise,
And the glow-worm of the grave
 Glimmer in thy rheumy eyes.

"Fear not thou to loose thy tongue,
 Set thy hoary fancies free;
What is loathsome to the young
 Savors well to thee and me.

"Change, reverting to the years,
 When thy nerves could understand 160
What there is in loving tears,
 And the warmth of hand in hand.

"Tell me tales of thy first love—
 April hopes, the fools of chance—
Till the graves begin to move,
 And the dead begin to dance.

"Fill the can and fill the cup;
 All the windy ways of men
Are but dust that rises up,
 And is lightly laid again.   170

"Trooping from their mouldy dens
 The chap-fallen circle spreads—
Welcome, fellow-citizens,
 Hollow hearts and empty heads!

"You are bones, and what of that?
 Every face, however full,

Padded round with flesh and fat,
  Is but modell'd on a skull.

"Death is king, and Vivat Rex!
  Tread a measure on the stones,   180
Madam—if I know your sex
  From the fashion of your bones.

"No, I cannot praise the fire
  In your eye—nor yet your lip;
All the more do I admire
  Joints of cunning workmanship.

"Lo! God's likeness—the ground-plan—
  Neither modell'd, glazed, nor framed;
Buss me, thou rough sketch of man,
  Far too naked to be shamed!   190

"Drink to Fortune, drink to Chance,
  While we keep a little breath!
Drink to heavy Ignorance!
  Hob-and-nob with brother Death!

"Thou art mazed, the night is long,
  And the longer night is near—
What! I am not all as wrong
  As a bitter jest is dear.

"Youthful hopes, by scores, to all,
  When the locks are crisp and curl'd;   200
Unto me my maudlin gall
  And my mockeries of the world.

"Fill the cup and fill the can;
  Mingle madness, mingle scorn!
Dregs of life, and lees of man;
  Yet we will not die forlorn."

V

The voice grew faint; there came a further change;
Once more uprose the mystic mountain-range.
Below were men and horses pierced with worms,
And slowly quickening into lower forms;   210
By shards and scurf of salt, and scum of dross,
Old plash of rains, and refuse patch'd with moss.
Then some one spake: "Behold! it was a crime
Of sense avenged by sense that wore with time."
Another said: "The crime of sense became
The crime of malice, and is equal blame."
And one: "He had not wholly quench'd his power;
A little grain of conscience made him sour."
At last I heard a voice upon the slope
Cry to the summit, "Is there any hope?"   220
To which an answer peal'd from that high land,
But in a tongue no man could understand;
And on the glimmering limit far withdrawn
God made Himself an awful rose of dawn.

"BREAK, BREAK, BREAK"

Break, break, break,
   On thy cold gray stones, O Sea!
And I would that my tongue could utter
   The thoughts that arise in me.

O, well for the fisherman's boy,
   That he shouts with his sister at play!
O, well for the sailor lad,
   That he sings in his boat on the bay!

And the stately ships go on
   To their haven under the hill;

But O for the touch of a vanish'd hand,
  And the sound of a voice that is still!

Break, break, break,
  At the foot of thy crags, O Sea!
But the tender grace of a day that is dead
  Will never come back to me.

SONGS FROM

THE PRINCESS; A MEDLEY

"Tears, idle tears, I know not what they mean,
Tears from the depth of some divine despair
Rise in the heart, and gather to the eyes,
In looking on the happy autumn-fields,
And thinking of the days that are no more.

"Fresh as the first beam glittering on a sail,
That brings our friends up from the underworld,
Sad as the last which reddens over one
That sinks with all we love below the verge;
So sad, so fresh, the days that are no more.

"Ah, sad and strange as in dark summer dawns
The earliest pipe of half-awaken'd birds
To dying ears, when unto dying eyes
The casement slowly grows a glimmering square;
So sad, so strange, the days that are no more.

"Dear as remember'd kisses after death,
And sweet as those by hopeless fancy feign'd
On lips that are for others; deep as love,
Deep as first love, and wild with all regret;
O Death in Life, the days that are no more!"

"O Swallow, Swallow, flying, flying south,
Fly to her, and fall upon her gilded eaves,
And tell her, tell her, what I tell to thee.

"O, tell her, Swallow, thou that knowest each,
That bright and fierce and fickle is the South,
And dark and true and tender is the North.

"O Swallow, Swallow, if I could follow, and light
Upon her lattice, I would pipe and trill,
And cheep and twitter twenty million loves.

"O, were I thou that she might take me in,
And lay me on her bosom, and her heart
Would rock the snowy cradle till I died!

"Why lingereth she to clothe her heart with love,
Delaying as the tender ash delays
To clothe herself, when all the woods are green?

"O, tell her, Swallow, that thy brood is flown;
Say to her, I do but wanton in the South,
But in the North long since my nest is made.

"O, tell her, brief is life but love is long,
And brief the sun of summer in the North,
And brief the moon of beauty in the South.

"O Swallow, flying from the golden woods,
Fly to her, and pipe and woo her, and make her mine,
And tell her, tell her, that I follow thee."

"Now sleeps the crimson petal, now the white;
Nor waves the cypress in the palace walk;
Nor winks the gold fin in the porphyry font.
The fire-fly wakens; waken thou with me.

"Now droops the milk-white peacock like a ghost,
And like a ghost she glimmers on to me.

"Now lies the Earth all Danaë to the stars,
And all thy heart lies open unto me.

"Now slides the silent meteor on, and leaves
A shining furrow, as thy thoughts in me.

"Now folds the lily all her sweetness up,
And slips into the bosom of the lake.
So fold thyself, my dearest, thou, and slip
Into my bosom and be lost in me."

"Come down, O maid, from yonder mountain height.
What pleasure lives in height (the shepherd sang),
In height and cold, the splendor of the hills?
But cease to move so near the heavens, and cease
To glide a sunbeam by the blasted pine,
To sit a star upon the sparkling spire;
And come, for Love is of the valley, come,
For Love is of the valley, come thou down
And find him; by the happy threshold, he,
Or hand in hand with Plenty in the maize,   10
Or red with spirted purple of the vats,
Or foxlike in the vine; nor cares to walk
With Death and Morning on the Silver Horns,
Nor wilt thou snare him in the white ravine,
Nor find him dropt upon the firths of ice,
That huddling slant in furrow-cloven falls
To roll the torrent out of dusky doors.
But follow; let the torrent dance thee down
To find him in the valley; let the wild
Lean-headed eagles yelp alone, and leave   20
The monstrous ledges there to slope, and spill
Their thousand wreaths of dangling water-smoke,

That like a broken purpose waste in air.
So waste not thou, but come; for all the vales
Await thee; azure pillars of the hearth
Arise to thee; the children call, and I
Thy shepherd pipe, and sweet is every sound,
Sweeter thy voice, but every sound is sweet;
Myriads of rivulets hurrying thro' the lawn,
The moan of doves in immemorial elms,   30
And murmuring of innumerable bees."

Sweet and low, sweet and low,
    Wind of the western sea,
Low, low, breathe and blow,
    Wind of the western sea!
Over the rolling waters go,
Come from the dying moon, and blow,
    Blow him again to me;
While my little one, while my pretty one sleeps.

Sleep and rest, sleep and rest,
    Father will come to thee soon;
Rest, rest, on mother's breast,
    Father will come to thee soon;
Father will come to his babe in the nest,
Silver sails all out of the west
    Under the silver moon;
Sleep, my little one, sleep, my pretty one, sleep.

The splendor falls on castle walls
    And snowy summits old in story;
The long light shakes across the lakes,
    And the wild cataract leaps in glory.
Blow, bugle, blow, set the wild echoes flying,
Blow, bugle; answer, echoes, dying, dying, dying.

O, hark, O hear! how thin and clear,
    And thinner, clearer, farther going!
O, sweet and far from cliff and scar
    The horns of Elfland faintly blowing!
Blow, let us hear the purple glens replying,
Blow, bugle; answer, echoes, dying, dying, dying.

O love, they die in yon rich sky,
    They faint on hill or field or river;
Our echoes roll from soul to soul,
    And grow for ever and for ever.
Blow, bugle, blow, set the wild echoes flying,
And answer, echoes, answer, dying, dying, dying.

IN MEMORIAM A. H. H.

OBIIT MDCCCXXXIII

First published in 1850, "In Memoriam" was a tribute to Arthur Henry Hallam, whose friendship with the poet is discussed at length in the Introduction. For Hallam's critical appreciation of Tennyson's early poems, see the Appendix. The present fifty-ninth section was added in 1851 and the present thirty-ninth section in 1871.

Strong Son of God, immortal Love,
   Whom we, that have not seen thy face,
   By faith, and faith alone, embrace,
Believing where we cannot prove;

Thine are these orbs of light and shade;
   Thou madest Life in man and brute;
   Thou madest Death; and lo, thy foot
Is on the skull which thou hast made.

Thou wilt not leave us in the dust:
   Thou madest man, he knows not why,   10
   He thinks he was not made to die;
And thou hast made him: thou art just.

Thou seemest human and divine,
   The highest, holiest manhood, thou.
   Our wills are ours, we know not how;
Our wills are ours, to make them thine.

Our little systems have their day;
   They have their day and cease to be;
   They are but broken lights of thee,
And thou, O Lord, art more than they.   20

We have but faith: we cannot know,
    For knowledge is of things we see;
    And yet we trust it comes from thee,
A beam in darkness: let it grow.

Let knowledge grow from more to more,
    But more of reverence in us dwell;
    That mind and soul, according well,
May make one music as before,

But vaster. We are fools and slight;
    We mock thee when we do not fear: 30
    But help thy foolish ones to bear;
Help thy vain worlds to bear thy light.

Forgive what seem'd my sin in me,
    What seem'd my worth since I began;
    For merit lives from man to man,
And not from man, O Lord, to thee.

Forgive my grief for one removed,
    Thy creature, whom I found so fair.
    I trust he lives in thee, and there
I find him worthier to be loved.   40

Forgive these wild and wandering cries,
    Confusions of a wasted youth;
    Forgive them where they fail in truth,
And in thy wisdom make me wise.
    1849.

I

I held it truth, with him who sings
    To one clear harp in divers tones,

That men may rise on stepping-stones
Of their dead selves to higher things.

But who shall so forecast the years
   And find in loss a gain to match?
   Or reach a hand thro' time to catch
The far-off interest of tears?

Let Love clasp Grief lest both be drown'd,
   Let darkness keep her raven gloss.   10
   Ah, sweeter to be drunk with loss,
To dance with Death, to beat the ground,

Than that the victor Hours should scorn
   The long result of love, and boast,
   "Behold the man that loved and lost,
But all he was is overworn."

II

Old yew, which graspest at the stones
   That name the underlying dead,
   Thy fibres net the dreamless head,
Thy roots are wrapt about the bones.   20

The seasons bring the flower again,
   And bring the firstling to the flock;
   And in the dusk of thee the clock
Beats out the little lives of men.

O, not for thee the glow, the bloom,
   Who changest not in any gale,
   Nor branding summer suns avail
To touch thy thousand years of gloom;

And gazing on thee, sullen tree,
   Sick for thy stubborn hardihood,   30

I seem to fail from out my blood
And grow incorporate into thee.

III

O Sorrow, cruel fellowship,
　　O Priestess in the vaults of Death,
　　O sweet and bitter in a breath,
What whispers from thy lying lip?

"The stars," she whispers, "blindly run;
　　A web is woven across the sky;
　　From out waste places comes a cry,
And murmurs from the dying sun;　　　　　40

"And all the phantom, Nature, stands—
　　With all the music in her tone,
　　A hollow echo of my own,—
A hollow form with empty hands."

And shall I take a thing so blind,
　　Embrace her as my natural good;
　　Or crush her, like a vice of blood,
Upon the threshold of the mind?

IV

To Sleep I give my powers away;
　　My will is bondsman to the dark;　　　　50
　　I sit within a helmless bark,
And with my heart I muse and say:

O heart, how fares it with thee now,
　　That thou shouldst fail from thy desire,
　　Who scarcely darest to inquire,
"What is it makes me beat so low?"

Something it is which thou hast lost,
　　Some pleasure from thine early years.

Break, thou deep vase of chilling tears,
That grief hath shaken into frost!　　　　　　　60

Such clouds of nameless trouble cross
　　All night below the darken'd eyes;
　　With morning wakes the will, and cries,
"Thou shalt not be the fool of loss."

V

I sometimes hold it half a sin
　　To put in words the grief I feel;
　　For words, like Nature, half reveal
And half conceal the Soul within.

But, for the unquiet heart and brain,
　　A use in measured language lies;　　　　　　70
　　The sad mechanic exercise,
Like dull narcotics, numbing pain.

In words, like weeds, I'll wrap me o'er,
　　Like coarsest clothes against the cold;
　　But that large grief which these enfold
Is given in outline and no more.

VI

One writes, that "other friends remain,"
　　That "loss is common to the race"—
　　And common is the commonplace,
And vacant chaff well meant for grain.　　　　　80

That loss is common would not make
　　My own less bitter, rather more.
　　Too common! Never morning wore
To evening, but some heart did break.

O father, wheresoe'er thou be,
　　Who pledgest now thy gallant son,

A shot, ere half thy draught be done,
Hath still'd the life that beat from thee.

O mother, praying God will save
  Thy sailor,—while thy head is bow'd,   90
  His heavy-shotted hammock-shroud
Drops in his vast and wandering grave.

Ye know no more than I who wrought
  At that last hour to please him well;
  Who mused on all I had to tell,
And something written, something thought;

Expecting still his advent home;
  And ever met him on his way
  With wishes, thinking, "here to-day,"
Or "here to-morrow will he come."   100

O, somewhere, meek, unconscious dove,
  That sittest ranging golden hair;
  And glad to find thyself so fair,
Poor child, that waitest for thy love!

For now her father's chimney glows
  In expectation of a guest;
  And thinking "this will please him best,"
She takes a riband or a rose;

For he will see them on to-night;
  And with the thought her color burns;   110
  And, having left the glass, she turns
Once more to set a ringlet right;

And, even when she turn'd, the curse
  Had fallen, and her future lord
  Was drown'd in passing thro' the ford,
Or kill'd in falling from his horse.

O, what to her shall be the end?
   And what to me remains of good?
   To her perpetual maidenhood,
And unto me no second friend.   120

VII

Dark house, by which once more I stand
   Here in the long unlovely street,
   Doors, where my heart was used to beat
So quickly, waiting for a hand,

A hand that can be clasp'd no more—
   Behold me, for I cannot sleep,
   And like a guilty thing I creep
At earliest morning to the door.

He is not here; but far away
   The noise of life begins again,   130
   And ghastly thro' the drizzling rain
On the bald street breaks the blank day.

VIII

A happy lover who has come
   To look on her that loves him well,
   Who 'lights and rings the gateway bell,
And learns her gone and far from home;

He saddens, all the magic light
   Dies off at once from bower and hall,
   And all the place is dark, and all
The chambers emptied of delight: 140

So find I every pleasant spot
   In which we two were wont to meet,
   The field, the chamber, and the street,
For all is dark where thou art not.

Yet as that other, wandering there
  In those deserted walks, may find
  A flower beat with rain and wind,
Which once she foster'd up with care;

So seems it in my deep regret,
  O my forsaken heart, with thee   150
  And this poor flower of poesy
Which, little cared for, fades not yet.

But since it pleased a vanish'd eye,
  I go to plant it on his tomb,
  That if it can it there may bloom,
Or, dying, there at least may die.

IX

Fair ship, that from the Italian shore
  Sailest the placid ocean-plains
  With my lost Arthur's loved remains,
Spread thy full wings, and waft him o'er.   160

So draw him home to those that mourn
  In vain; a favorable speed
  Ruffle thy mirror'd mast, and lead
Thro' prosperous floods his holy urn.

All night no ruder air perplex
  Thy sliding keel, till Phosphor, bright
  As our pure love, thro' early light
Shall glimmer on the dewy decks.

Sphere all your lights around, above;
  Sleep, gentle heavens, before the prow;   170
  Sleep, gentle winds, as he sleeps now,
My friend, the brother of my love;

My Arthur, whom I shall not see
   Till all my widow'd race be run;
   Dear as the mother to the son,
More than my brothers are to me.

X

I hear the noise about thy keel;
   I hear the bell struck in the night;
   I see the cabin-window bright;
I see the sailor at the wheel.   180

Thou bring'st the sailor to his wife,
   And travell'd men from foreign lands;
   And letters unto trembling hands;
And, thy dark freight, a vanish'd life.

So bring him; we have idle dreams;
   This look of quiet flatters thus
   Our home-bred fancies. O, to us,
The fools of habit, sweeter seems

To rest beneath the clover sod,
   That takes the sunshine and the rains,   190
   Or where the kneeling hamlet drains
The chalice of the grapes of God;

Than if with thee the roaring wells
   Should gulf him fathom-deep in brine,
   And hands so often clasp'd in mine,
Should toss with tangle and with shells.

XI

Calm is the morn without a sound,
   Calm as to suit a calmer grief,
   And only thro' the faded leaf
The chestnut pattering to the ground;   200

Calm and deep peace on this high wold,
   And on these dews that drench the furze,
   And all the silvery gossamers
That twinkle into green and gold;

Calm and still light on yon great plain
   That sweeps with all its autumn bowers,
   And crowded farms and lessening towers,
To mingle with the bounding main;

Calm and deep peace in this wide air,
   These leaves that redden to the fall,   210
   And in my heart, if calm at all,
If any calm, a calm despair;

Calm on the seas, and silver sleep,
   And waves that sway themselves in rest,
   And dead calm in that noble breast
Which heaves but with the heaving deep.

XII

Lo, as a dove when up she springs
   To bear thro' heaven a tale of woe,
   Some dolorous message knit below
The wild pulsation of her wings;   220

Like her I go, I cannot stay;
   I leave this mortal ark behind,
   A weight of nerves without a mind,
And leave the cliffs, and haste away

O'er ocean-mirrors rounded large,
   And reach the glow of southern skies,
   And see the sails at distance rise,
And linger weeping on the marge,

And saying, "Comes he thus, my friend?
　　Is this the end of all my care?"   230
　　And circle moaning in the air,
"Is this the end? Is this the end?"

And forward dart again, and play
　　About the prow, and back return
　　To where the body sits, and learn
That I have been an hour away.

XIII

Tears of the widower, when he sees
　　A late-lost form that sleep reveals,
　　And moves his doubtful arms, and feels
Her place is empty, fall like these;   240

Which weep a loss for ever new,
　　A void where heart on heart reposed;
　　And, where warm hands have prest and closed,
Silence, till I be silent too;

Which weep the comrade of my choice,
　　An awful thought, a life removed,
　　The human-hearted man I loved,
A Spirit, not a breathing voice.

Come, Time, and teach me, many years,
　　I do not suffer in a dream;   250
　　For now so strange do these things seem,
Mine eyes have leisure for their tears,

My fancies time to rise on wing,
　　And glance about the approaching sails,
　　As tho' they brought but merchants' bales,
And not the burthen that they bring.

XIV

If one should bring me this report,
  That thou hadst touch'd the land to-day,
  And I went down unto the quay,
And found thee lying in the port;   260

And standing, muffled round with woe,
  Should see thy passengers in rank
  Come stepping lightly down the plank
And beckoning unto those they know;

And if along with these should come
  The man I held as half-divine,
  Should strike a sudden hand in mine,
And ask a thousand things of home;

And I should tell him all my pain,
  And how my life had droop'd of late,   270
  And he should sorrow o'er my state
And marvel what possess'd my brain;

And I perceived no touch of change,
  No hint of death in all his frame,
  But found him all in all the same,
I should not feel it to be strange.

XV

To-night the winds begin to rise
  And roar from yonder dropping day;
  The last red leaf is whirl'd away,
The rooks are blown about the skies;   280

The forest crack'd, the waters curl'd,
  The cattle huddled on the lea;
  And wildly dash'd on tower and tree
The sunbeam strikes along the world:

And but for fancies, which aver
   That all thy motions gently pass
   Athwart a plane of molten glass,
I scarce could brook the strain and stir

That makes the barren branches loud;
   And but for fear it is not so,   290
   The wild unrest that lives in woe
Would dote and pore on yonder cloud

That rises upward always higher,
   And onward drags a laboring breast,
   And topples round the dreary west,
A looming bastion fringed with fire.

XVI

What words are these have fallen from me?
   Can calm despair and wild unrest
   Be tenants of a single breast,
Or Sorrow such a changeling be?   300

Or doth she only seem to take
   The touch of change in calm or storm,
   But knows no more of transient form
In her deep self, than some dead lake

That holds the shadow of a lark
   Hung in the shadow of a heaven?
   Or has the shock, so harshly given,
Confused me like the unhappy bark

That strikes by night a craggy shelf,
   And staggers blindly ere she sink?   310
   And stunn'd me from my power to think
And all my knowledge of myself;

And made me that delirious man
    Whose fancy fuses old and new,
    And flashes into false and true,
And mingles all without a plan?

XVII

Thou comest, much wept for; such a breeze
    Compell'd thy canvas, and my prayer
    Was as the whisper of an air
To breathe thee over lonely seas.   320

For I in spirit saw thee move
    Thro' circles of the bounding sky,
    Week after week; the days go by;
Come quick, thou bringest all I love.

Henceforth, wherever thou mayst roam,
    My blessing, like a line of light,
    Is on the waters day and night,
And like a beacon guards thee home.

So may whatever tempest mars
    Mid-ocean spare thee, sacred bark,   330
    And balmy drops in summer dark
Slide from the bosom of the stars;

So kind an office hath been done,
    Such precious relics brought by thee,
    The dust of him I shall not see
Till all my widow'd race be run.

XVIII

'T is well; 't is something; we may stand
    Where he in English earth is laid,
    And from his ashes may be made
The violet of his native land.   340

'T is little; but it looks in truth
    As if the quiet bones were blest
    Among familiar names to rest
And in the places of his youth.

Come then, pure hands, and bear the head
    That sleeps or wears the mask of sleep,
    And come, whatever loves to weep,
And hear the ritual of the dead.

Ah yet, even yet, if this might be,
    I, falling on his faithful heart,   350
    Would breathing thro' his lips impart
The life that almost dies in me;

That dies not, but endures with pain,
    And slowly forms the firmer mind,
    Treasuring the look it cannot find,
The words that are not heard again.

XIX

The Danube to the Severn gave
    The darken'd heart that beat no more;
    They laid him by the pleasant shore,
And in the hearing of the wave.   360

There twice a day the Severn fills;
    The salt sea-water passes by,
    And hushes half the babbling Wye,
And makes a silence in the hills.

The Wye is hush'd nor moved along,
    And hush'd my deepest grief of all,
    When fill'd with tears that cannot fall,
I brim with sorrow drowning song.

The tide flows down, the wave again
    Is vocal in its wooded walls;   370
    My deeper anguish also falls,
And I can speak a little then.

XX

The lesser griefs that may be said,
    That breathe a thousand tender vows,
    Are but as servants in a house
Where lies the master newly dead;

Who speak their feeling as it is,
    And weep the fulness from the mind.
    "It will be hard," they say, "to find
Another service such as this."   380

My lighter moods are like to these,
    That out of words a comfort win;
    But there are other griefs within,
And tears that at their fountain freeze;

For by the hearth the children sit
    Cold in that atmosphere of death,
    And scarce endure to draw the breath,
Or like to noiseless phantoms flit;

But open converse is there none,
    So much the vital spirits sink   390
    To see the vacant chair, and think,
"How good! how kind! and he is gone."

XXI

I sing to him that rests below,
    And, since the grasses round me wave,
    I take the grasses of the grave,
And make them pipes whereon to blow.

The traveller hears me now and then,
   And sometimes harshly will he speak:
   "This fellow would make weakness weak,
And melt the waxen hearts of men."   400

Another answers: "Let him be,
   He loves to make parade of pain,
   That with his piping he may gain
The praise that comes to constancy."

A third is wroth: "Is this an hour
   For private sorrow's barren song,
   When more and more the people throng
The chairs and thrones of civil power?

"A time to sicken and to swoon,
   When Science reaches forth her arms   410
   To feel from world to world, and charms
Her secret from the latest moon?"

Behold, ye speak an idle thing;
   Ye never knew the sacred dust.
   I do but sing because I must,
And pipe but as the linnets sing;

And one is glad; her note is gay,
   For now her little ones have ranged;
   And one is sad; her note is changed,
Because her brood is stolen away.   420

XXII

The path by which we twain did go,
   Which led by tracts that pleased us well,
   Thro' four sweet years arose and fell,
From flower to flower, from snow to snow;

And we with singing cheer'd the way,
 And, crown'd with all the season lent,
 From April on to April went,
And glad at heart from May to May.

But where the path we walk'd began
 To slant the fifth autumnal slope,   430
 As we descended following Hope,
There sat the Shadow fear'd of man;

Who broke our fair companionship,
 And spread his mantle dark and cold,
 And wrapt thee formless in the fold,
And dull'd the murmur on thy lip,

And bore thee where I could not see
 Nor follow, tho' I walk in haste,
 And think that somewhere in the waste
The Shadow sits and waits for me.   440

XXIII

Now, sometimes in my sorrow shut,
 Or breaking into song by fits,
 Alone, alone, to where he sits,
The Shadow cloak'd from head to foot,

Who keeps the keys of all the creeds,
 I wander, often falling lame,
 And looking back to whence I came,
Or on to where the pathway leads;

And crying, How changed from where it ran
 Thro' lands where not a leaf was dumb, 450
 But all the lavish hills would hum
The murmur of a happy Pan;

When each by turns was guide to each,
   And Fancy light from Fancy caught,
   And Thought leapt out to wed with Thought
Ere Thought could wed itself with Speech;

And all we met was fair and good,
   And all was good that Time could bring,
   And all the secret of the Spring
Moved in the chambers of the blood;   460

And many an old philosophy
   On Argive heights divinely sang,
   And round us all the thicket rang
To many a flute of Arcady.

XXIV

And was the day of my delight
   As pure and perfect as I say?
   The very source and fount of day
Is dash'd with wandering isles of night.

If all was good and fair we met,
   This earth had been the Paradise   470
   It never look'd to human eyes
Since our first sun arose and set.

And is it that the haze of grief
   Makes former gladness loom so great?
   The lowness of the present state,
That sets the past in this relief?

Or that the past will always win
   A glory from its being far,
   And orb into the perfect star
We saw not when we moved therein?   480

XXV

I know that this was Life,—the track
   Whereon with equal feet we fared;
   And then, as now, the day prepared
The daily burden for the back.

But this it was that made me move
   As light as carrier-birds in air;
   I loved the weight I had to bear,
Because it needed help of Love;

Nor could I weary, heart or limb,
   When mighty Love would cleave in twain   490
   The lading of a single pain,
And part it, giving half to him.

XXVI

Still onward winds the dreary way;
   I with it, for I long to prove
   No lapse of moons can canker Love,
Whatever fickle tongues may say.

And if that eye which watches guilt
   And goodness, and hath power to see
   Within the green the moulder'd tree,
And towers fallen as soon as built—   500

O, if indeed that eye foresee
   Or see—in Him is no before—
   In more of life true life no more
And Love the indifference to be,

Then might I find, ere yet the morn
   Breaks hither over Indian seas,
   That Shadow waiting with the keys,
To shroud me from my proper scorn.

XXVII

I envy not in any moods
　　The captive void of noble rage,　　　　　510
　　The linnet born within the cage,
That never knew the summer woods;

I envy not the beast that takes
　　His license in the field of time,
　　Unfetter'd by the sense of crime,
To whom a conscience never wakes;

Nor, what may count itself as blest,
　　The heart that never plighted troth
　　But stagnates in the weeds of sloth;
Nor any want-begotten rest.　　　　　　　520

I hold it true, whate'er befall;
　　I feel it, when I sorrow most;
　　'T is better to have loved and lost
Than never to have loved at all.

XXVIII

The time draws near the birth of Christ.
　　The moon is hid, the night is still;
　　The Christmas bells from hill to hill
Answer each other in the mist.

Four voices of four hamlets round,
　　From far and near, on mead and moor,　　530
　　Swell out and fail, as if a door
Were shut between me and the sound;

Each voice four changes on the wind,
　　That now dilate, and now decrease,
　　Peace and goodwill, goodwill and peace,
Peace and goodwill, to all mankind.

This year I slept and woke with pain,
  I almost wish'd no more to wake,
  And that my hold on life would break
Before I heard those bells again;   540

But they my troubled spirit rule,
  For they controll'd me when a boy;
  They bring me sorrow touch'd with joy,
The merry, merry bells of Yule.

XXIX

With such compelling cause to grieve
  As daily vexes household peace,
  And chains regret to his decease,
How dare we keep our Christmas-eve,

Which brings no more a welcome guest
  To enrich the threshold of the night   550
  With shower'd largess of delight
In dance and song and game and jest?

Yet go, and while the holly boughs
  Entwine the cold baptismal font,
  Make one wreath more for Use and Wont,
That guard the portals of the house;

Old sisters of a day gone by,
  Gray nurses, loving nothing new—
  Why should they miss their yearly due
Before their time? They too will die.   560

XXX

With trembling fingers did we weave
  The holly round the Christmas hearth;
  A rainy cloud possess'd the earth,
And sadly fell our Christmas-eve.

At our old pastimes in the hall
   We gamboll'd, making vain pretence
   Of gladness, with an awful sense
Of one mute Shadow watching all.

We paused: the winds were in the beech;
   We heard them sweep the winter land;   570
   And in a circle hand-in-hand
Sat silent, looking each at each.

Then echo-like our voices rang;
   We sung, tho' every eye was dim,
   A merry song we sang with him
Last year; impetuously we sang.

We ceased; a gentler feeling crept
   Upon us: surely rest is meet.
   "They rest," we said, "their sleep is sweet,"
And silence follow'd, and we wept.   580

Our voices took a higher range;
   Once more we sang: "They do not die
   Nor lose their mortal sympathy,
Nor change to us, although they change;

"Rapt from the fickle and the frail
   With gather'd power, yet the same,
   Pierces the keen seraphic flame
From orb to orb, from veil to veil."

Rise, happy morn, rise, holy morn,
   Draw forth the cheerful day from night: 590
   O Father, touch the east, and light
The light that shone when Hope was born.

XXXI

When Lazarus left his charnel-cave,
   And home to Mary's house return'd,
   Was this demanded—if he yearn'd
To hear her weeping by his grave?

"Where wert thou, brother, those four days?"
   There lives no record of reply,
   Which telling what it is to die
Had surely added praise to praise.   600

From every house the neighbors met,
   The streets were fill'd with joyful sound,
   A solemn gladness even crown'd
The purple brows of Olivet.

Behold a man raised up by Christ!
   The rest remaineth unreveal'd;
   He told it not, or something seal'd
The lips of that Evangelist.

XXXII

Her eyes are homes of silent prayer,
   Nor other thought her mind admits   610
   But, he was dead, and there he sits,
And he that brought him back is there.

Then one deep love doth supersede
   All other, when her ardent gaze
   Roves from the living brother's face,
And rests upon the Life indeed.

All subtle thought, all curious fears,
   Borne down by gladness so complete,
   She bows, she bathes the Saviour's feet
With costly spikenard and with tears.   620

Thrice blest whose lives are faithful prayers,
 Whose loves in higher love endure;
 What souls possess themselves so pure,
Or is there blessedness like theirs?

XXXIII

O thou that after toil and storm
 Mayst seem to have reach'd a purer air,
 Whose faith has centre everywhere,
Nor cares to fix itself to form,

Leave thou thy sister when she prays
 Her early heaven, her happy views;   630
 Nor thou with shadow'd hint confuse
A life that leads melodious days.

Her faith thro' form is pure as thine,
 Her hands are quicker unto good.
 O, sacred be the flesh and blood
To which she links a truth divine!

See thou, that countest reason ripe
 In holding by the law within,
 Thou fail not in a world of sin,
And even for want of such a type.   640

XXXIV

My own dim life should teach me this,
 That life shall live for evermore,
 Else earth is darkness at the core,
And dust and ashes all that is;

This round of green, this orb of flame,
 Fantastic beauty; such as lurks
 In some wild poet, when he works
Without a conscience or an aim.

What then were God to such as I?
     'T were hardly worth my while to choose   650
     Of things all mortal, or to use
A little patience ere I die;

'T were best at once to sink to peace,
     Like birds the charming serpent draws,
     To drop head-foremost in the jaws
Of vacant darkness and to cease.

XXXV

Yet if some voice that man could trust
     Should murmur from the narrow house,
     "The cheeks drop in, the body bows;
Man dies, nor is there hope in dust;"   660

Might I not say? "Yet even here,
     But for one hour, O Love, I strive
     To keep so sweet a thing alive."
But I should turn mine ears and hear

The moanings of the homeless sea,
     The sound of streams that swift or slow
     Draw down Æonian hills, and sow
The dust of continents to be;

And Love would answer with a sigh,
     "The sound of that forgetful shore   670
     Will change my sweetness more and more,
Half-dead to know that I shall die."

O me, what profits it to put
     An idle case? If Death were seen
     At first as Death, Love had not been,
Or been in narrowest working shut,

Mere fellowship of sluggish moods,
   Or in his coarsest Satyr-shape
   Had bruised the herb and crush'd the grape,
And bask'd and batten'd in the woods.   680

XXXVI

Tho' truths in manhood darkly join,
   Deep-seated in our mystic frame,
   We yield all blessing to the name
Of Him that made them current coin;

For Wisdom dealt with mortal powers,
   Where truth in closest words shall fail,
   When truth embodied in a tale
Shall enter in at lowly doors.

And so the Word had breath, and wrought
   With human hands the creed of creeds   690
   In loveliness of perfect deeds,
More strong than all poetic thought;

Which he may read that binds the sheaf,
   Or builds the house, or digs the grave,
   And those wild eyes that watch the wave
In roarings round the coral reef.

XXXVII

Urania speaks with darken'd brow:
   "Thou pratest here where thou art least;
   This faith has many a purer priest,
And many an abler voice than thou.   700

"Go down beside thy native rill,
   On thy Parnassus set thy feet,
   And hear thy laurel whisper sweet
About the ledges of the hill."

And my Melpomene replies,
    A touch of shame upon her cheek:
    "I am not worthy even to speak
Of thy prevailing mysteries;

"For I am but an earthly Muse,
    And owning but a little art   710
    To lull with song an aching heart,
And render human love his dues;

"But brooding on the dear one dead,
    And all he said of things divine,—
    And dear to me as sacred wine
To dying lips is all he said,—

"I murmur'd, as I came along,
    Of comfort clasp'd in truth reveal'd,
    And loiter'd in the master's field,
And darken'd sanctities with song."   720

XXXVIII

With weary steps I loiter on,
    Tho' always under alter'd skies
    The purple from the distance dies,
My prospect and horizon gone.

No joy the blowing season gives,
    The herald melodies of spring,
    But in the songs I love to sing
A doubtful gleam of solace lives.

If any care for what is here
    Survive in spirits render'd free,   730
    Then are these songs I sing of thee
Not all ungrateful to thine ear.

XXXIX

Old warder of these buried bones,
　And answering now my random stroke
　With fruitful cloud and living smoke,
Dark yew, that graspest at the stones

And dippest toward the dreamless head,
　To thee too comes the golden hour
　When flower is feeling after flower;
But Sorrow,—fixt upon the dead,　　　　　　740

And darkening the dark graves of men,—
　What whisper'd from her lying lips?
　Thy gloom is kindled at the tips,
And passes into gloom again.

XL

Could we forget the widow'd hour
　And look on Spirits breathed away,
　As on a maiden in the day
When first she wears her orange-flower!

When crown'd with blessing she doth rise
　To take her latest leave of home,　　　　　750
　And hopes and light regrets that come
Make April of her tender eyes;

And doubtful joys the father move,
　And tears are on the mother's face,
　As parting with a long embrace
She enters other realms of love;

Her office there to rear, to teach,
　Becoming as is meet and fit
　A link among the days, to knit
The generations each with each;　　　　　　760

And, doubtless, unto thee is given
  A life that bears immortal fruit
  In those great offices that suit
The full-grown energies of heaven.

Ay me, the difference I discern!
  How often shall her old fireside
  Be cheer'd with tidings of the bride,
How often she herself return,

And tell them all they would have told,
  And bring her babe, and make her boast,   770
  Till even those that miss'd her most
Shall count new things as dear as old;

But thou and I have shaken hands,
  Till growing winters lay me low;
  My paths are in the fields I know,
And thine in undiscover'd lands.

XLI

Thy spirit ere our fatal loss
  Did ever rise from high to higher,
  As mounts the heavenward altar-fire,
As flies the lighter thro' the gross.   780

But thou art turn'd to something strange,
  And I have lost the links that bound
  Thy changes; here upon the ground,
No more partaker of thy change.

Deep folly! yet that this could be—
  That I could wing my will with might
  To leap the grades of life and light,
And flash at once, my friend, to thee!

For tho' my nature rarely yields
   To that vague fear implied in death,   790
   Nor shudders at the gulfs beneath,
The howlings from forgotten fields;

Yet oft when sundown skirts the moor
   An inner trouble I behold,
   A spectral doubt which makes me cold,
That I shall be thy mate no more,

Tho' following with an upward mind
   The wonders that have come to thee,
   Thro' all the secular to-be,
But evermore a life behind.   800

XLII

I vex my heart with fancies dim.
   He still outstript me in the race;
   It was but unity of place
That made me dream I rank'd with him.

And so may Place retain us still,
   And he the much-beloved again,
   A lord of large experience, train
To riper growth the mind and will;

And what delights can equal those
   That stir the spirit's inner deeps,   810
   When one that loves, but knows not, reaps
A truth from one that loves and knows?

XLIII

If Sleep and Death be truly one,
   And every spirit's folded bloom
   Thro' all its intervital gloom
In some long trance should slumber on;

Unconscious of the sliding hour,
   Bare of the body, might it last,
   And silent traces of the past
Be all the color of the flower: 820

So then were nothing lost to man;
   So that still garden of the souls
   In many a figured leaf enrolls
The total world since life began;

And love will last as pure and whole
   As when he loved me here in Time,
   And at the spiritual prime
Rewaken with the dawning soul.

XLIV

How fares it with the happy dead?
   For here the man is more and more,   830
   But he forgets the days before
God shut the doorways of his head.

The days have vanish'd, tone and tint,
   And yet perhaps the hoarding sense
   Gives out at times—he knows not whence—
A little flash, a mystic hint;

And in the long harmonious years—
   If Death so taste Lethean springs—
   May some dim touch of earthly things
Surprise thee ranging with thy peers.   840

If such a dreamy touch should fall,
   O, turn thee round, resolve the doubt;
   My guardian angel will speak out
In that high place, and tell thee all.

XLV

The baby new to earth and sky,
   What time his tender palm is prest
   Against the circle of the breast,
Has never thought that "this is I;"

But as he grows he gathers much,
   And learns the use of "I" and "me,"   850
   And finds "I am not what I see,
And other than the things I touch."

So rounds he to a separate mind
   From whence clear memory may begin,
   As thro' the frame that binds him in
His isolation grows defined.

This use may lie in blood and breath,
   Which else were fruitless of their due,
   Had man to learn himself anew
Beyond the second birth of death.   860

XLVI

We ranging down this lower track,
   The path we came by, thorn and flower,
   Is shadow'd by the growing hour,
Lest life should fail in looking back.

So be it: there no shade can last
   In that deep dawn behind the tomb,
   But clear from marge to marge shall bloom
The eternal landscape of the past;

A lifelong tract of time reveal'd,
   The fruitful hours of still increase;   870
   Days order'd in a wealthy peace,
And those five years its richest field.

O Love, thy province were not large,
  A bounded field, nor stretching far;
  Look also, Love, a brooding star,
A rosy warmth from marge to marge.

XLVII

That each, who seems a separate whole,
  Should move his rounds, and fusing all
  The skirts of self again, should fall
Remerging in the general Soul,   880

Is faith as vague as all unsweet.
  Eternal form shall still divide
  The eternal soul from all beside;
And I shall know him when we meet;

And we shall sit at endless feast,
  Enjoying each the other's good.
  What vaster dream can hit the mood
Of Love on earth? He seeks at least

Upon the last and sharpest height,
  Before the spirits fade away,   890
  Some landing-place, to clasp and say,
"Farewell! We lose ourselves in light."

XLVIII

If these brief lays, of Sorrow born,
  Were taken to be such as closed
  Grave doubts and answers here proposed,
Then these were such as men might scorn.

Her care is not to part and prove;
  She takes, when harsher moods remit,
  What slender shade of doubt may flit,
And makes it vassal unto love;   900

And hence, indeed, she sports with words,
    But better serves a wholesome law,
    And holds it sin and shame to draw
The deepest measure from the chords;

Nor dare she trust a larger lay,
    But rather loosens from the lip
    Short swallow-flights of song, that dip
Their wings in tears, and skim away.

XLIX

From art, from nature, from the schools,
    Let random influences glance,   910
    Like light in many a shiver'd lance
That breaks about the dappled pools.

The lightest wave of thought shall lisp,
    The fancy's tenderest eddy wreathe,
    The slightest air of song shall breathe
To make the sullen surface crisp.

And look thy look, and go thy way,
    But blame not thou the winds that make
    The seeming-wanton ripple break,
The tender-pencill'd shadow play.   920

Beneath all fancied hopes and fears
    Ay me, the sorrow deepens down,
    Whose muffled motions blindly drown
The bases of my life in tears.

L

Be near me when my light is low,
    When the blood creeps, and the nerves prick
    And tingle; and the heart is sick,
And all the wheels of being slow.

Be near me when the sensuous frame
 Is rack'd with pangs that conquer trust; 930
 And Time, a maniac scattering dust,
And Life, a Fury slinging flame.

Be near me when my faith is dry,
 And men the flies of latter spring,
 That lay their eggs, and sting and sing
And weave their petty cells and die.

Be near me when I fade away,
 To point the term of human strife,
 And on the low dark verge of life
The twilight of eternal day. 940

LI

Do we indeed desire the dead
 Should still be near us at our side?
 Is there no baseness we would hide?
No inner vileness that we dread?

Shall he for whose applause I strove,
 I had such reverence for his blame,
 See with clear eye some hidden shame
And I be lessen'd in his love?

I wrong the grave with fears untrue.
 Shall love be blamed for want of faith? 950
 There must be wisdom with great Death;
The dead shall look me thro' and thro'.

Be near us when we climb or fall;
 Ye watch, like God, the rolling hours
 With larger other eyes than ours,
To make allowance for us all.

LII

I cannot love thee as I ought,
   For love reflects the thing beloved;
   My words are only words, and moved
Upon the topmost froth of thought.   960

"Yet blame not thou thy plaintive song,"
   The Spirit of true love replied;
   "Thou canst not move me from thy side,
Nor human frailty do me wrong.

"What keeps a spirit wholly true
   To that ideal which he bears?
   What record? not the sinless years
That breathed beneath the Syrian blue;

"So fret not, like an idle girl,
   That life is dash'd with flecks of sin.   970
   Abide; thy wealth is gather'd in,
When Time hath sunder'd shell from pearl."

LIII

How many a father have I seen,
   A sober man, among his boys,
   Whose youth was full of foolish noise,
Who wears his manhood hale and green;

And dare we to this fancy give,
   That had the wild oat not been sown,
   The soil, left barren, scarce had grown
The grain by which a man may live?   980

Or, if we held the doctrine sound
   For life outliving heats of youth,
   Yet who would preach it as a truth
To those that eddy round and round?

Hold thou the good, define it well;
　　For fear divine Philosophy
　　Should push beyond her mark, and be
Procuress to the Lords of Hell.

LIV

O, yet we trust that somehow good
　　Will be the final goal of ill,   990
　　To pangs of nature, sins of will,
Deflects of doubt, and taints of blood;

That nothing walks with aimless feet;
　　That not one life shall be destroy'd,
　　Or cast as rubbish to the void,
When God hath made the pile complete;

That not a worm is cloven in vain;
　　That not a moth with vain desire
　　Is shrivell'd in a fruitless fire,
Or but subserves another's gain.   1000

Behold, we know not anything;
　　I can but trust that good shall fall
　　At last—far off—at last, to all,
And every winter change to spring.

So runs my dream; but what am I?
　　An infant crying in the night;
　　An infant crying for the light,
And with no language but a cry.

LV

The wish, that of the living whole
　　No life may fail beyond the grave,   1010
　　Derives it not from what we have
The likest God within the soul?

Are God and Nature then at strife,
  That Nature lends such evil dreams?
  So careful of the type she seems,
So careless of the single life,

That I, considering everywhere
  Her secret meaning in her deeds,
  And finding that of fifty seeds
She often brings but one to bear,   1020

I falter where I firmly trod,
  And falling with my weight of cares
  Upon the great world's altar-stairs
That slope thro' darkness up to God,

I stretch lame hands of faith, and grope,
  And gather dust and chaff, and call
  To what I feel is Lord of all,
And faintly trust the larger hope.

LVI

"So careful of the type?" but no.
  From scarped cliff and quarried stone   1030
  She cries, "A thousand types are gone;
I care for nothing, all shall go.

"Thou makest thine appeal to me.
  I bring to life, I bring to death;
  The spirit does but mean the breath:
I know no more." And he, shall he,

Man, her last work, who seem'd so fair,
  Such splendid purpose in his eyes,
  Who roll'd the psalm to wintry skies,
Who built him fanes of fruitless prayer,   1040

Who trusted God was love indeed
    And love Creation's final law—
    Tho' Nature, red in tooth and claw
With ravine, shriek'd against his creed—

Who loved, who suffer'd countless ills,
    Who battled for the True, the Just,
    Be blown about the desert dust,
Or seal'd within the iron hills?

No more? A monster then, a dream,
    A discord. Dragons of the prime,   1050
    That tare each other in their slime,
Were mellow music match'd with him.

O life as futile, then, as frail!
    O for thy voice to soothe and bless!
    What hope of answer, or redress?
Behind the veil, behind the veil.

LVII

Peace; come away: the song of woe
    Is after all an earthly song.
    Peace; come away: we do him wrong
To sing so wildly: let us go.   1060

Come; let us go: your cheeks are pale;
    But half my life I leave behind.
    Methinks my friend is richly shrined;
But I shall pass, my work will fail.

Yet in these ears, till hearing dies,
    One set slow bell will seem to toll
    The passing of the sweetest soul
That ever look'd with human eyes.

I hear it now, and o'er and o'er,
 Eternal greetings to the dead;   1070
 And "Ave, Ave, Ave," said,
"Adieu, adieu," for evermore.

LVIII

In those sad words I took farewell.
 Like echoes in sepulchral halls,
 As drop by drop the water falls
In vaults and catacombs, they fell;

And, falling, idly broke the peace
 Of hearts that beat from day to day,
 Half-conscious of their dying clay,
And those cold crypts where they shall cease.   1080

The high Muse answer'd: "Wherefore grieve
 Thy brethren with a fruitless tear?
 Abide a little longer here,
And thou shalt take a nobler leave."

LIX

O Sorrow, wilt thou live with me
 No casual mistress, but a wife,
 My bosom-friend and half of life;
As I confess it needs must be?

O Sorrow, wilt thou rule my blood,
 Be sometimes lovely like a bride,   1090
 And put thy harsher moods aside,
If thou wilt have me wise and good?

My centred passion cannot move,
 Nor will it lessen from to-day;
 But I'll have leave at times to play
As with the creature of my love;

And set thee forth, for thou art mine,
　　With so much hope for years to come,
　　That, howsoe'er I know thee, some
Could hardly tell what name were thine.   1100

LX

He past, a soul of nobler tone;
　　My spirit loved and loves him yet,
　　Like some poor girl whose heart is set
On one whose rank exceeds her own.

He mixing with his proper sphere,
　　She finds the baseness of her lot,
　　Half jealous of she knows not what,
And envying all that meet him there.

The little village looks forlorn;
　　She sighs amid her narrow days,   1110
　　Moving about the household ways,
In that dark house where she was born.

The foolish neighbors come and go,
　　And tease her till the day draws by;
　　At night she weeps, "How vain am I!
How should he love a thing so low?"

LXI

If, in thy second state sublime,
　　Thy ransom'd reason change replied
　　With all the circle of the wise,
The perfect flower of human time;   1120

And if thou cast thine eyes below,
　　How dimly character'd and slight,
　　How dwarf'd a growth of cold and night,
How blanch'd with darkness must I grow!

Yet turn thee to the doubtful shore,
>Where thy first form was made a man;
>I loved thee, Spirit, and love, nor can
The soul of Shakespeare love thee more.

LXII

Tho' if an eye that 's downward cast
>Could make thee somewhat blench or fail,   1130
>Then be my love an idle tale
And fading legend of the past;

And thou, as one that once declined,
>When he was little more than boy,
>On some unworthy heart with joy,
But lives to wed an equal mind,

And breathes a novel world, the while
>His other passion wholly dies,
>Or in the light of deeper eyes
Is matter for a flying smile.   1140

LXIII

Yet pity for a horse o'er-driven,
>And love in which my hound has part
>Can hang no weight upon my heart
In its assumptions up to heaven;

And I am so much more than these,
>As thou, perchance, art more than I,
>And yet I spare them sympathy,
And I would set their pains at ease.

So mayst thou watch me where I weep,
>As, unto vaster motions bound,   1150
>The circuits of thine orbit round
A higher height, a deeper deep.

LXIV

Dost thou look back on what hath been,
   As some divinely gifted man,
   Whose life in low estate began
And on a simple village green;

Who breaks his birth's invidious bar,
   And grasps the skirts of happy chance,
   And breasts the blows of circumstance,
And grapples with his evil star;   1160

Who makes by force his merit known
   And lives to clutch the golden keys,
   To mould a mighty state's decrees,
And shape the whisper of the throne;

And moving up from high to higher,
   Becomes on Fortune's crowning slope
   The pillar of a people's hope,
The centre of a world's desire;

Yet feels, as in a pensive dream,
   When all his active powers are still,   1170
   A distant dearness in the hill,
A secret sweetness in the stream,

The limit of his narrower fate,
   While yet beside its vocal springs
   He play'd at counsellors and kings,
With one that was his earliest mate;

Who ploughs with pain his native lea
   And reaps the labor of his hands,
   Or in the furrow musing stands:
"Does my old friend remember me?"   1180

LXV

Sweet soul, do with me as thou wilt;
   I lull a fancy trouble-tost
   With "Love 's too precious to be lost,
A little grain shall not be spilt."

And in that solace can I sing,
   Till out of painful phases wrought
   There flutters up a happy thought,
Self-balanced on a lightsome wing;

Since we deserved the name of friends,
   And thine effect so lives in me,   1190
   A part of mine may live in thee
And move thee on to noble ends.

LXVI

You thought my heart too far diseased;
   You wonder when my fancies play
   To find me gay among the gay,
Like one with any trifle pleased.

The shade by which my life was crost,
   Which makes a desert in the mind,
   Has made me kindly with my kind,
And like to him whose sight is lost;   1200

Whose feet are guided thro' the land,
   Whose jest among his friends is free,
   Who takes the children on his knee,
And winds their curls about his hand.

He plays with threads, he beats his chair
   For pastime, dreaming of the sky;
   His inner day can never die,
His night of loss is always there.

LXVII

When on my bed the moonlight falls,
　　I know that in thy place of rest   1210
　　By that broad water of the west
There comes a glory on the walls:

Thy marble bright in dark appears,
　　As slowly steals a silver flame
　　Along the letters of thy name,
And o'er the number of thy years.

The mystic glory swims away,
　　From off my bed the moonlight dies;
　　And closing eaves of wearied eyes
I sleep till dusk is dipt in gray;   1220

And then I know the mist is drawn
　　A lucid veil from coast to coast,
　　And in the dark church like a ghost
Thy tablet glimmers in the dawn.

LXVIII

When in the down I sink my head,
　　Sleep, Death's twin-brother, times my breath;
　　Sleep, Death's twin-brother, knows not Death,
Nor can I dream of thee as dead.

I walk as ere I walk'd forlorn,
　　When all our path was fresh with dew,   1230
　　And all the bugle breezes blew
Reveillée to the breaking morn.

But what is this? I turn about,
　　I find a trouble in thine eye,
　　Which makes me sad I know not why,
Nor can my dream resolve the doubt;

But ere the lark hath left the lea
 I wake, and I discern the truth;
 It is the trouble of my youth
That foolish sleep transfers to thee.   1240

LXIX

I dream'd there would be Spring no more,
 That Nature's ancient power was lost;
 The streets were black with smoke and frost,
They chatter'd trifles at the door;

I wander'd from the noisy town,
 I found a wood with thorny boughs;
 I took the thorns to bind my brows,
I wore them like a civic crown;

I met with scoffs, I met with scorns
 From youth and babe and hoary hairs: 1250
 They call'd me in the public squares
The fool that wears a crown of thorns.

They call'd me fool, they call'd me child:
 I found an angel of the night;
 The voice was low, the look was bright;
He look'd upon my crown and smiled.

He reach'd the glory of a hand,
 That seem'd to touch it into leaf;
 The voice was not the voice of grief,
The words were hard to understand.   1260

LXX

I cannot see the features right,
 When on the gloom I strive to paint
 The face I know; the hues are faint
And mix with hollow masks of night;

Cloud-towers by ghostly masons wrought,
   A gulf that ever shuts and gapes,
   A hand that points, and palled shapes
In shadowy thoroughfares of thought;

And crowds that stream from yawning doors,
   And shoals of pucker'd faces drive;   1270
   Dark bulks that tumble half alive,
And lazy lengths on boundless shores;

Till all at once beyond the will
   I hear a wizard music roll,
   And thro' a lattice on the soul
Looks thy fair face and makes it still.

LXXI

Sleep, kinsman thou to death and trance
   And madness, thou hast forged at last
   A night-long present of the past
In which we went thro' summer France.   1280

Hadst thou such credit with the soul?
   Then bring an opiate trebly strong,
   Drug down the blindfold sense of wrong,
That so my pleasure may be whole;

While now we talk as once we talk'd
   Of men and minds, the dust of change,
   The days that grow to something strange,
In walking as of old we walk'd

Beside the river's wooded reach,
   The fortress, and the mountain ridge,   1290
   The cataract flashing from the bridge,
The breaker breaking on the beach.

LXXII

Risest thou thus, dim dawn, again,
　　And howlest, issuing out of night,
　　With blasts that blow the poplar white,
And lash with storm the streaming pane?

Day, when my crown'd estate begun
　　To pine in that reverse of doom,
　　Which sicken'd every living bloom,
And blurr'd the splendor of the sun;　　　　1300

Who usherest in the dolorous hour
　　With thy quick tears that make the rose
　　Pull sideways, and the daisy close
Her crimson fringes to the shower;

Who mightst have heaved a windless flame
　　Up the deep East, or, whispering, play'd
　　A chequer-work of beam and shade
Along the hills, yet look'd the same,

As wan, as chill, as wild as now;
　　Day, mark'd as with some hideous crime,　　1310
　　When the dark hand struck down thro' time,
And cancell'd nature's best: but thou,

Lift as thou mayst thy burthen'd brows
　　Thro' clouds that drench the morning star,
　　And whirl the ungarner'd sheaf afar,
And sow the sky with flying boughs,

And up thy vault with roaring sound
　　Climb thy thick noon, disastrous day;
　　Touch thy dull goal of joyless gray,
And hide thy shame beneath the ground.　　　1320

LXXIII

So many worlds, so much to do,
   So little done, such things to be,
   How know I what had need of thee,
For thou wert strong as thou wert true?

The fame is quench'd that I foresaw,
   The head hath miss'd an earthly wreath:
   I curse not Nature, no, nor Death;
For nothing is that errs from law.

We pass; the path that each man trod
   Is dim, or will be dim, with weeds.   1330
   What fame is left for human deeds
In endless age? It rests with God.

O hollow wraith of dying fame,
   Fade wholly, while the soul exults,
   And self-infolds the large results
Of force that would have forged a name.

LXXIV

As sometimes in a dead man's face,
   To those that watch it more and more,
   A likeness, hardly seen before,
Comes out—to some one of his race;   1340

So, dearest, now thy brows are cold,
   I see thee what thou art, and know
   Thy likeness to the wise below,
Thy kindred with the great of old.

But there is more than I can see,
   And what I see I leave unsaid,
   Nor speak it, knowing Death has made
His darkness beautiful with thee.

LXXV

I leave thy praises unexpress'd
　In verse that brings myself relief,　　　　1350
　And by the measure of my grief
I leave thy greatness to be guess'd.

What practice howsoe'er expert
　In fitting aptest words to things,
　Or voice the richest-toned that sings,
Hath power to give thee as thou wert?

I care not in these fading days
　To raise a cry that lasts not long,
　And round thee with the breeze of song
To stir a little dust of praise.　　　　1360

Thy leaf has perish'd in the green,
　And, while we breathe beneath the sun,
　The world which credits what is done
Is cold to all that might have been.

So here shall silence guard thy fame;
　But somewhere, out of human view,
　Whate'er thy hands are set to do
Is wrought with tumult of acclaim.

LXXVI

Take wings of fancy, and ascend,
　And in a moment set thy face　　　　1370
　Where all the starry heavens of space
Are sharpen'd to a needle's end;

Take wings of foresight; lighten thro'
　The secular abyss to come,
　And lo, thy deepest lays are dumb
Before the mouldering of a yew;

And if the matin songs, that woke
   The darkness of our planet, last,
   Thine own shall wither in the vast,
Ere half the lifetime of an oak.   1380

Ere these have clothed their branchy bowers
   With fifty Mays, thy songs are vain;
   And what are they when these remain
The ruin'd shells of hollow towers?

LXXVII

What hope is here for modern rhyme
   To him who turns a musing eye
   On songs, and deeds, and lives, that lie
Foreshorten'd in the tract of time?

These mortal lullabies of pain
   May bind a book, may line a box,   1390
   May serve to curl a maiden's locks;
Or when a thousand moons shall wane

A man upon a stall may find,
   And, passing, turn the page that tells
   A grief, then changed to something else,
Sung by a long-forgotten mind.

But what of that? My darken'd ways
   Shall ring with music all the same;
   To breathe my loss is more than fame,
To utter love more sweet than praise.   1400

LXXVIII

Again at Christmas did we weave
   The holly round the Christmas hearth;
   The silent snow possess'd the earth,
And calmly fell our Christmas-eve.

The yule-clog sparkled keen with frost,
  No wing of wind the region swept,
  But over all things brooding slept
The quiet sense of something lost.

As in the winters left behind,
  Again our ancient games had place,   1410
  The mimic picture's breathing grace,
And dance and song and hoodman-blind.

Who show'd a token of distress?
  No single tear, no mark of pain—
  O sorrow, then can sorrow wane?
O grief, can grief be changed to less?

O last regret, regret can die!
  No—mixt with all this mystic frame,
  Her deep relations are the same,
But with long use her tears are dry.   1420

LXXIX

"More than my brothers are to me,"—
  Let this not vex thee, noble heart!
  I know thee of what force thou art
To hold the costliest love in fee.

But thou and I are one in kind,
  As moulded like in Nature's mint;
  And hill and wood and field did print
The same sweet forms in either mind.

For us the same cold streamlet curl'd
  Thro' all his eddying coves, the same   1430
  All winds that roam the twilight came
In whispers of the beauteous world.

At one dear knee we proffer'd vows,
   One lesson from one book we learn'd,
   Ere childhood's flaxen ringlet turn'd
To black and brown on kindred brows.

And so my wealth resembles thine,
   But he was rich where I was poor,
   And he supplied my want the more
As his unlikeness fitted mine.   1440

LXXX

If any vague desire should rise,
   That holy Death ere Arthur died
   Had moved me kindly from his side,
And dropt the dust on tearless eyes;

Then fancy shapes, as fancy can,
   The grief my loss in him had wrought,
   A grief as deep as life or thought,
But stay'd in peace with God and man.

I make a picture in the brain;
   I hear the sentence that he speaks;   1450
   He bears the burthen of the weeks,
But turns his burthen into gain.

His credit thus shall set me free;
   And, influence-rich to soothe and save,
   Unused example from the grave
Reach out dead hands to comfort me.

LXXXI

Could I have said while he was here,
   "My love shall now no further range;
   There cannot come a mellower change,
For now is love mature in ear"?   1460

Love, then, had hope of richer store:
   What end is here to my complaint?
   This haunting whisper makes me faint,
"More years had made me love thee more."

But Death returns an answer sweet:
   "My sudden frost was sudden gain,
   And gave all ripeness to the grain
It might have drawn from after-heat."

LXXXII

I wage not any feud with Death
   For changes wrought on form and face;   1470
   No lower life that earth's embrace
May breed with him can fright my faith.

Eternal process moving on,
   From state to state the spirit walks;
   And these are but the shatter'd stalks,
Or ruin'd chrysalis of one.

Nor blame I Death, because he bare
   The use of virtue out of earth;
   I know transplanted human worth
Will bloom to profit, otherwhere.   1480

For this alone on Death I wreak
   The wrath that garners in my heart:
   He put our lives so far apart
We cannot hear each other speak.

LXXXIII

Dip down upon the northern shore,
   O sweet new-year delaying long;
   Thou doest expectant Nature wrong;
Delaying long, delay no more.

What stays thee from the clouded noons,
   Thy sweetness from its proper place?   1490
   Can trouble live with April days,
Or sadness in the summer moons?

Bring orchis, bring the foxglove spire,
   The little speedwell's darling blue,
   Deep tulips dash'd with fiery dew,
Laburnums, dropping-wells of fire.

O thou, new-year, delaying long,
   Delayest the sorrow in my blood,
   That longs to burst a frozen bud
And flood a fresher throat with song.   1500

LXXXIV

When I contemplate all alone
   The life that had been thine below,
   And fix my thoughts on all the glow
To which thy crescent would have grown,

I see thee sitting crown'd with good,
   A central warmth diffusing bliss
   In glance and smile, and clasp and kiss,
On all the branches of thy blood;

Thy blood, my friend, and partly mine;
   For now the day was drawing on,   1510
   When thou shouldst link thy life with one
Of mine own house, and boys of thine

Had babbled "Uncle" on my knee;
   But that remorseless iron hour
   Made cypress of her orange flower,
Despair of hope, and earth of thee.

I seem to meet their least desire,
   To clap their cheeks, to call them mine.
   I see their unborn faces shine
Beside the never-lighted fire.   1520

I see myself an honor'd guest,
   Thy partner in the flowery walk
   Of letters, genial table-talk,
Or deep dispute, and graceful jest;

While now thy prosperous labor fills
   The lips of men with honest praise,
   And sun by sun the happy days
Descend below the golden hills

With promise of a morn as fair;
   And all the train of bounteous hours   1530
   Conduct, by paths of growing powers,
To reverence and the silver hair;

Till slowly worn her earthly robe,
   Her lavish mission richly wrought,
   Leaving great legacies of thought,
Thy spirit should fail from off the globe;

What time mine own might also flee,
   As link'd with thine in love and fate,
   And, hovering o'er the dolorous strait
To the other shore, involved in thee,   1540

Arrive at last the blessed goal,
   And He that died in Holy Land
   Would reach us out the shining hand,
And take us as a single soul.

What reed was that on which I leant?
   Ah, backward fancy, wherefore wake

The old bitterness again, and break
The low beginnings of content?

LXXXV

This truth came borne with bier and pall,
   I felt it, when I sorrow'd most,   1550
    'T is better to have loved and lost,
Than never to have loved at all—

O true in word, and tried in deed,
   Demanding, so to bring relief
    To this which is our common grief,
What kind of life is that I lead;

And whether trust in things above
   Be dimm'd of sorrow, or sustain'd;
    And whether love for him have drain'd
My capabilities of love;   1560

Your words have virtue such as draws
   A faithful answer from the breast,
    Thro' light reproaches, half exprest,
And loyal unto kindly laws.

My blood an even tenor kept,
   Till on mine ear this message falls,
    That in Vienna's fatal walls
God's finger touch'd him, and he slept.

The great Intelligences fair
   That range above our mortal state,   1570
    In circle round the blessed gate,
Received and gave him welcome there;

And led him thro' the blissful climes,
   And show'd him in the fountain fresh

All knowledge that the sons of flesh
Shall gather in the cycled times.

But I remain'd, whose hopes were dim,
   Whose life, whose thoughts were little worth,
   To wander on a darken'd earth,
Where all things round me breathed of him.   1580

O friendship, equal-poised control,
   O heart, with kindliest motion warm,
   O sacred essence, other form,
O solemn ghost, O crowned soul!

Yet none could better know than I,
   How much of act at human hands
   The sense of human will demands
By which we dare to live or die.

Whatever way my days decline,
   I felt and feel, tho' left alone,   1590
   His being working in mine own,
The footsteps of his life in mine;

A life that all the Muses deck'd
   With gifts of grace, that might express
   All-comprehensive tenderness,
All-subtilizing intellect:

And so my passion hath not swerved
   To works of weakness, but I find
   An image comforting the mind,
And in my grief a strength reserved.   1600

Likewise the imaginative woe,
   That loved to handle spiritual strife,
   Diffused the shock thro' all my life,
But in the present broke the blow.

My pulses therefore beat again
   For other friends that once I met;
   Nor can it suit me to forget
The mighty hopes that make us men.

I woo your love: I count it crime
   To mourn for any overmuch;   1610
   I, the divided half of such
A friendship as had master'd Time;

Which masters Time indeed, and is
   Eternal, separate from fears.
   The all-assuming months and years
Can take no part away from this;

But Summer on the steaming floods,
   And Spring that swells the narrow brooks,
   And Autumn, with a noise of rooks,
That gather in the waning woods,   1620

And every pulse of wind and wave
   Recalls, in change of light or gloom,
   My old affection of the tomb,
And my prime passion in the grave.

My old affection of the tomb,
   A part of stillness, yearns to speak:
   "Arise, and get thee forth and seek
A friendship for the years to come.

"I watch thee from the quiet shore;
   Thy spirit up to mine can reach;   1630
   But in dear words of human speech
We two communicate no more."

And I, "Can clouds of nature stain
   The starry clearness of the free?

How is it? Canst thou feel for me
Some painless sympathy with pain?"

And lightly does the whisper fall:
  " 'T is hard for thee to fathom this;
  I triumph in conclusive bliss,
And that serene result of all."   1640

So hold I commerce with the dead;
  Or so methinks the dead would say;
  O so shall grief with symbols play
And pining life be fancy-fed.

Now looking to some settled end,
  That these things pass, and I shall prove
  A meeting somewhere, love with love,
I crave your pardon, O my friend;

If not so fresh, with love as true,
  I, clasping brother-hands, aver   1650
  I could not, if I would, transfer
The whole I felt for him to you.

For which be they that hold apart
  The promise of the golden hours?
  First love, first friendship, equal powers,
That marry with the virgin heart.

Still mine, that cannot but deplore,
  That beats within a lonely place,
  That yet remembers his embrace,
But at his footstep leaps no more,   1660

My heart, tho' widow'd, may not rest
  Quite in the love of what is gone,
  But seeks to beat in time with one
That warms another living breast.

Ah, take the imperfect gift I bring,
 Knowing the primrose yet is dear,
 The primrose of the later year,
As not unlike to that of Spring.

LXXXVI

Sweet after showers, ambrosial air,
 That rollest from the gorgeous gloom   1670
 Of evening over brake and bloom
And meadow, slowly breathing bare

The round of space, and rapt below
 Thro' all the dewy tassell'd wood,
 And shadowing down the horned flood
In ripples, fan my brows and blow

The fever from my cheek, and sigh
 The full new life that feeds thy breath
 Throughout my frame, till Doubt and Death,
Ill brethren, let the fancy fly   1680

From belt to belt of crimson seas
 On leagues of odor streaming far,
 To where in yonder orient star
A hundred spirits whisper "Peace."

LXXXVII

I past beside the reverend walls
 In which of old I wore the gown;
 I roved at random thro' the town,
And saw the tumult of the halls;

And heard once more in college fanes
 The storm their high-built organs make,   1690
 And thunder-music, rolling, shake
The prophet blazon'd on the panes;

And caught once more the distant shout,
  The measured pulse of racing oars
  Among the willows; paced the shores
And many a bridge, and all about

The same gray flats again, and felt
  The same, but not the same; and last
  Up that long walk of limes I past
To see the rooms in which he dwelt.   1700

Another name was on the door.
  I linger'd; all within was noise
  Of songs, and clapping hands, and boys
That crash'd the glass and beat the floor;

Where once we held debate, a band
  Of youthful friends, on mind and art,
  And labor, and the changing mart,
And all the framework of the land;

When one would aim an arrow fair,
  But send it slackly from the string;   1710
  And one would pierce an outer ring,
And one an inner, here and there;

And last the master-bowman, he,
  Would cleave the mark. A willing ear
  We lent him. Who but hung to hear
The rapt oration flowing free

From point to point, with power and grace
  And music in the bounds of law,
  To those conclusions when we saw
The God within him light his face,   1720

And seem to lift the form, and glow
  In azure orbits heavenly-wise;

And over those ethereal eyes
The bar of Michael Angelo?

LXXXVIII

Wild bird, whose warble, liquid sweet,
   Rings Eden thro' the budded quicks,
   O, tell me where the senses mix,
O, tell me where the passions meet,

Whence radiate: fierce extremes employ
   Thy spirits in the darkening leaf,   1730
   And in the midmost heart of grief
Thy passion clasps a secret joy;

And I—my harp would prelude woe—
   I cannot all command the strings;
   The glory of the sum of things
Will flash along the chords and go.

LXXXIX

Witch-elms that counterchange the floor
   Of this flat lawn with dusk and bright;
   And thou, with all thy breadth and height
Of foliage, towering sycamore;   1740

How often, hither wandering down,
   My Arthur found your shadows fair,
   And shook to all the liberal air
The dust and din and steam of town!

He brought an eye for all he saw;
   He mixt in all our simple sports;
   They pleased him, fresh from brawling courts
And dusty purlieus of the law.

O joy to him in this retreat,
   Immantled in ambrosial dark,   1750

To drink the cooler air, and mark
The landscape winking thro' the heat!

O sound to rout the brood of cares,
   The sweep of scythe in morning dew,
   The gust that round the garden flew,
And tumbled half the mellowing pears!

O bliss, when all in circle drawn
   About him, heart and ear were fed
   To hear him, as he lay and read
The Tuscan poets on the lawn!   1760

Or in the all-golden afternoon
   A guest, or happy sister, sung,
   Or here she brought the harp and flung
A ballad to the brightening moon.

Nor less it pleased in livelier moods,
   Beyond the bounding hill to stray,
   And break the livelong summer day
With banquet in the distant woods;

Whereat we glanced from theme to theme,
   Discuss'd the books to love or hate,   1770
   Or touch'd the changes of the state,
Or threaded some Socratic dream;

But if I praised the busy town,
   He loved to rail against it still,
   For "ground in yonder social mill
We rub each other's angles down,

"And merge," he said, "in form and gloss
   The picturesque of man and man."
   We talk'd: the stream beneath us ran,
The wine-flask lying couch'd in moss,   1780

Or cool'd within the glooming wave;
　　And last, returning from afar,
　　Before the crimson-circled star
Had fallen into her father's grave,

And brushing ankle-deep in flowers,
　　We heard behind the woodbine veil
　　The milk that bubbled in the pail,
And buzzings of the honeyed hours.

XC

He tasted love with half his mind,
　　Nor ever drank the inviolate spring   1790
　　Where nighest heaven, who first could fling
This bitter seed among mankind:

That could the dead, whose dying eyes
　　Were closed with wail, resume their life,
　　They would but find in child and wife
An iron welcome when they rise.

'T was well, indeed, when warm with wine,
　　To pledge them with a kindly tear,
　　To talk them o'er, to wish them here,
To count their memories half divine;   1800

But if they came who past away,
　　Behold their brides in other hands;
　　The hard heir strides about their lands,
And will not yield them for a day.

Yea, tho' their sons were none of these,
　　Not less the yet-loved sire would make
　　Confusion worse than death, and shake
The pillars of domestic peace.

Ah, dear, but come thou back to me!
   Whatever change the years have wrought,   1810
   I find not yet one lonely thought
That cries against my wish for thee.

XCI

When rosy plumelets tuft the larch,
   And rarely pipes the mounted thrush,
   Or underneath the barren bush
Flits by the sea-blue bird of March;

Come, wear the form by which I know
   Thy spirit in time among thy peers;
   The hope of unaccomplish'd years
Be large and lucid round thy brow.   1820

When summer's hourly-mellowing change
   May breathe, with many roses sweet,
   Upon the thousand waves of wheat
That ripple round the lowly grange,

Come; not in watches of the night,
   But where the sunbeam broodeth warm,
   Come, beauteous in thine after form,
And like a finer light in light.

XCII

If any vision should reveal
   Thy likeness, I might count it vain   1830
   As but the canker of the brain;
Yea, tho' it spake and made appeal

To chances where our lots were cast
   Together in the days behind,
   I might but say, I hear a wind
Of memory murmuring the past.

Yea, tho' it spake and bared to view
   A fact within the coming year;
   And tho' the months, revolving near,
Should prove the phantom-warning true,   1840

They might not seem thy prophecies,
   But spiritual presentiments,
   And such refraction of events
As often rises ere they rise.

XCIII

I shall not see thee. Dare I say
   No spirit ever brake the band
   That stays him from the native land
Where first he walk'd when claspt in clay?

No visual shade of some one lost,
   But he, the Spirit himself, may come   1850
   Where all the nerve of sense is numb,
Spirit to Spirit, Ghost to Ghost.

O, therefore from thy sightless range
   With gods in unconjectured bliss,
   O, from the distance of the abyss
Of tenfold-complicated change,

Descend, and touch, and enter; hear
   The wish too strong for words to name,
   That in this blindness of the frame
My Ghost may feel that thine is near.   1860

XCIV

How pure at heart and sound in head,
   With what divine affections bold
   Should be the man whose thought would hold
An hour's communion with the dead.

In vain shalt thou, or any, call
 The spirits from their golden day,
  Except, like them, thou too canst say,
My spirit is at peace with all.

They haunt the silence of the breast,
 Imaginations calm and fair,   1870
  The memory like a cloudless air,
The conscience as a sea at rest;

But when the heart is full of din,
 And doubt beside the portal waits,
  They can but listen at the gates,
And hear the household jar within.

XCV

By night we linger'd on the lawn,
 For underfoot the herb was dry;
  And genial warmth; and o'er the sky
The silvery haze of summer drawn;   1880

And calm that let the tapers burn
 Unwavering: not a cricket chirr'd;
  The brook alone far-off was heard,
And on the board the fluttering urn.

And bats went round in fragrant skies,
 And wheel'd or lit the filmy shapes
  That haunt the dusk, with ermine capes
And woolly breasts and beaded eyes;

While now we sang old songs that peal'd
 From knoll to knoll, where, couch'd at ease, 1890
  The white kine glimmer'd, and the trees
Laid their dark arms about the field.

But when those others, one by one,
   Withdrew themselves from me and night,
   And in the house light after light
Went out, and I was all alone,

A hunger seized my heart; I read
   Of that glad year which once had been,
   In those fallen leaves which kept their green,
The noble letters of the dead.   1900

And strangely on the silence broke
   The silent-speaking words, and strange
   Was love's dumb cry defying change
To test his worth; and strangely spoke

The faith, the vigor, bold to dwell
   On doubts that drive the coward back,
   And keen thro' wordy snares to track
Suggestion to her inmost cell.

So word by word, and line by line,
   The dead man touch'd me from the past,   1910
   And all at once it seem'd at last
The living soul was flash'd on mine,

And mine in this was wound, and whirl'd
   About empyreal heights of thought,
   And came on that which is, and caught
The deep pulsations of the world,

Æonian music measuring out
   The steps of Time—the shocks of Chance—
   The blows of Death. At length my trance
Was cancell'd, stricken thro' with doubt.   1920

Vague words! but ah, how hard to frame
   In matter-moulded forms of speech,

Or even for intellect to reach
Thro' memory that which I became;

Till now the doubtful dusk reveal'd
　　The knolls once more where, couch'd at ease,
　　The white kine glimmer'd, and the trees
Laid their dark arms about the field;

And suck'd from out the distant gloom
　　A breeze began to tremble o'er   1930
　　The large leaves of the sycamore,
And fluctuate all the still perfume,

And gathering freshlier overhead,
　　Rock'd the full-foliaged elms, and swung
　　The heavy-folded rose, and flung
The lilies to and fro, and said,

"The dawn, the dawn," and died away;
　　And East and West, without a breath,
　　Mixt their dim lights, like life and death,
To broaden into boundless day.   1940

XCVI

You say, but with no touch of scorn,
　　Sweet-hearted, you, whose light-blue eyes
　　Are tender over drowning flies,
You tell me, doubt is Devil-born.

I know not: one indeed I knew
　　In many a subtle question versed,
　　Who touch'd a jarring lyre at first,
But ever strove to make it true;

Perplext in faith, but pure in deeds,
　　At last he beat his music out.   1950

There lives more faith in honest doubt,
Believe me, than in half the creeds.

He fought his doubts and gather'd strength,
   He would not make his judgment blind,
   He faced the spectres of the mind
And laid them; thus he came at length

To find a stronger faith his own,
   And Power was with him in the night,
   Which makes the darkness and the light,
And dwells not in the light alone,   1960

But in the darkness and the cloud,
   As over Sinaï's peaks of old,
   While Israel made their gods of gold,
Altho' the trumpet blew so loud.

XCVII

My love has talk'd with rocks and trees;
   He finds on misty mountain-ground
   His own vast shadow glory-crown'd;
He sees himself in all he sees.

Two partners of a married life—
   I look'd on these and thought of thee   1970
   In vastness and in mystery,
And of my spirit as of a wife.

These two—they dwelt with eye on eye,
   Their hearts of old have beat in tune,
   Their meetings made December June,
Their every parting was to die.

Their love has never past away;
   The days she never can forget

Are earnest that he loves her yet,
Whate'er the faithless people say.   1980

Her life is lone, he sits apart;
    He loves her yet, she will not weep,
    Tho' rapt in matters dark and deep
He seems to slight her simple heart.

He thrids the labyrinth of the mind,
    He reads the secret of the star,
    He seems so near and yet so far,
He looks so cold: she thinks him kind.

She keeps the gift of years before,
    A wither'd violet is her bliss;   1990
    She knows not what his greatness is,
For that, for all, she loves him more.

For him she plays, to him she sings
    Of early faith and plighted vows;
    She knows but matters of the house,
And he, he knows a thousand things.

Her faith is fixt and cannot move,
    She darkly feels him great and wise,
    She dwells on him with faithful eyes,
"I cannot understand; I love."   2000

XCVIII

You leave us: you will see the Rhine,
    And those fair hills I sail'd below,
    When I was there with him; and go
By summer belts of wheat and vine

To where he breathed his latest breath,
    That city. All her splendor seems

No livelier than the wisp that gleams
On Lethe in the eyes of Death.

Let her great Danube rolling fair
    Enwind her isles, unmark'd of me;   2010
    I have not seen, I will not see
Vienna; rather dream that there,

A treble darkness, Evil haunts
    The birth, the bridal; friend from friend
    Is oftener parted, fathers bend
Above more graves, a thousand wants

Gnarr at the heels of men, and prey
    By each cold hearth, and sadness flings
    Her shadow on the blaze of kings.
And yet myself have heard him say,   2020

That not in any mother town
    With statelier progress to and fro
    The double tides of chariots flow
By park and suburb under brown

Of lustier leaves; nor more content,
    He told me, lives in any crowd,
    When all is gay with lamps, and loud
With sport and song, in booth and tent,

Imperial halls, or open plain;
    And wheels the circled dance, and breaks   2030
    The rocket molten into flakes
Of crimson or in emerald rain.

XCIX

Risest thou thus, dim dawn, again,
    So loud with voices of the birds,

So thick with lowings of the herds,
Day, when I lost the flower of men;

Who tremblest thro' thy darkling red
  On yon swollen brook that bubbles fast
  By meadows breathing of the past,
And woodlands holy to the dead;   2040

Who murmurest in the foliaged eaves
  A song that slights the coming care,
  And Autumn laying here and there
A fiery finger on the leaves;

Who wakenest with thy balmy breath
  To myriads on the genial earth,
  Memories of bridal, or of birth,
And unto myriads more, of death.

O, wheresoever those may be,
  Betwixt the slumber of the poles,   2050
  To-day they count as kindred souls;
They know me not, but mourn with me.

C

I climb the hill: from end to end
  Of all the landscape underneath,
  I find no place that does not breathe
Some gracious memory of my friend;

No gray old grange, or lonely fold,
  Or low morass and whispering reed,
  Or simple stile from mead to mead,
Or sheepwalk up the windy wold;   2060

Nor hoary knoll of ash and haw
  That hears the latest linnet trill,

Nor quarry trench'd along the hill
And haunted by the wrangling daw;

Nor runlet tinkling from the rock;
    Nor pastoral rivulet that swerves
    To left and right thro' meadowy curves,
That feed the mothers of the flock;

But each has pleased a kindred eye,
    And each reflects a kindlier day;   2070
    And, leaving these, to pass away,
I think once more he seems to die.

CI

Unwatch'd, the garden bough shall sway,
    The tender blossom flutter down,
    Unloved, that beech will gather brown,
This maple burn itself away;

Unloved, the sunflower, shining fair,
    Ray round with flames her disk of seed,
    And many a rose-carnation feed
With summer spice the humming air;   2080

Unloved, by many a sandy bar,
    The brook shall babble down the plain,
    At noon or when the Lesser Wain
Is twisting round the polar star;

Uncared for, gird the windy grove,
    And flood the haunts of hern and crake,
    Or into silver arrows break
The sailing moon in creek and cove;

Till from the garden and the wild
    A fresh association blow,   2090

And year by year the landscape grow
Familiar to the stranger's child;

As year by year the laborer tills
   His wonted glebe, or lops the glades,
   And year by year our memory fades
From all the circle of the hills.

CII

We leave the well-beloved place
   Where first we gazed upon the sky;
   The roofs that heard our earliest cry
Will shelter one of stranger race.   2100

We go, but ere we go from home,
   As down the garden-walks I move,
   Two spirits of a diverse love
Contend for loving masterdom.

One whispers, "Here thy boyhood sung
   Long since its matin song, and heard
   The low love-language of the bird
In native hazels tassel-hung."

The other answers, "Yea, but here
   Thy feet have stray'd in after hours   2110
   With thy lost friend among the bowers,
And this hath made them trebly dear."

These two have striven half the day,
   And each prefers his separate claim,
   Poor rivals in a losing game,
That will not yield each other way.

I turn to go; my feet are set
   To leave the pleasant fields and farms;

They mix in one another's arms
To one pure image of regret.   2120

CIII

On that last night before we went
    From out the doors where I was bred,
    I dream'd a vision of the dead,
Which left my after-morn content.

Methought I dwelt within a hall,
    And maidens with me; distant hills
    From hidden summits fed with rills
A river sliding by the wall.

The hall with harp and carol rang.
    They sang of what is wise and good   2130
    And graceful. In the centre stood
A statue veil'd, to which they sang;

And which, tho' veil'd, was known to me,
    The shape of him I loved, and love
    For ever. Then flew in a dove
And brought a summons from the sea;

And when they learnt that I must go,
    They wept and wail'd, but led the way
    To where a little shallop lay
At anchor in the flood below;   2140

And on by many a level mead,
    And shadowing bluff that made the banks,
    We glided winding under ranks
Of iris and the golden reed;

And still as vaster grew the shore
    And roll'd the floods in grander space,

The maidens gather'd strength and grace
And presence, lordlier than before;

And I myself, who sat apart
  And watch'd them, wax'd in every limb;   2150
  I felt the thews of Anakim,
The pulses of a Titan's heart;

As one would sing the death of war,
  And one would chant the history
  Of that great race which is to be,
And one the shaping of a star;

Until the forward-creeping tides
  Began to foam, and we to draw
  From deep to deep, to where we saw
A great ship lift her shining sides.   2160

The man we loved was there on deck,
  But thrice as large as man he bent
  To greet us. Up the side I went,
And fell in silence on his neck;

Whereat those maidens with one mind
  Bewail'd their lot; I did them wrong:
  "We served thee here," they said, "so long,
And wilt thou leave us now behind?"

So rapt I was, they could not win
  An answer from my lips, but he   2170
  Replying, "Enter likewise ye
And go with us:" they enter'd in.

And while the wind began to sweep
  A music out of sheet and shroud,
  We steer'd her toward a crimson cloud
That landlike slept along the deep.

CIV

The time draws near the birth of Christ;
  The moon is hid, the night is still;
  A single church below the hill
Is pealing, folded in the mist.   2180

A single peal of bells below,
  That wakens at this hour of rest
  A single murmur in the breast,
That these are not the bells I know.

Like strangers' voices here they sound,
  In lands where not a memory strays,
  Nor landmark breathes of other days,
But all is new unhallow'd ground.

CV

To-night ungather'd let us leave
  This laurel, let this holly stand: 2190
  We live within the stranger's land,
And strangely falls our Christmas-eve.

Our father's dust is left alone
  And silent under other snows:
  There in due time the woodbine blows,
The violet comes, but we are gone.

No more shall wayward grief abuse
  The genial hour with mask and mime;
  For change of place, like growth of time,
Has broke the bond of dying use.   2200

Let cares that petty shadows cast,
  By which our lives are chiefly proved,
  A little spare the night I loved,
And hold it solemn to the past.

But let no footstep beat the floor,
 Nor bowl of wassail mantle warm;
 For who would keep an ancient form
Thro' which the spirit breathes no more?

Be neither song, nor game, nor feast;
 Nor harp be touch'd, nor flute be blown; 2210
 No dance, no motion, save alone
What lightens in the lucid East

Of rising worlds by yonder wood.
 Long sleeps the summer in the seed;
 Run out your measured arcs, and lead
The closing cycle rich in good.

CVI

Ring out, wild bells, to the wild sky,
 The flying cloud, the frosty light:
 The year is dying in the night;
Ring out, wild bells, and let him die. 2220

Ring out the old, ring in the new,
 Ring, happy bells, across the snow:
 The year is going, let him go;
Ring out the false, ring in the true.

Ring out the grief that saps the mind,
 For those that here we see no more;
 Ring out the feud of rich and poor,
Ring in redress to all mankind.

Ring out a slowly dying cause,
 And ancient forms of party strife; 2230
 Ring in the nobler modes of life,
With sweeter manners, purer laws.

Ring out the want, the care, the sin,
   The faithless coldness of the times;
   Ring out, ring out my mournful rhymes,
But ring the fuller minstrel in.

Ring out false pride in place and blood,
   The civic slander and the spite;
   Ring in the love of truth and right,
Ring in the common love of good.   2240

Ring out old shapes of foul disease;
   Ring out the narrowing lust of gold;
   Ring out the thousand wars of old,
Ring in the thousand years of peace.

Ring in the valiant man and free,
   The larger heart, the kindlier hand;
   Ring out the darkness of the land,
Ring in the Christ that is to be.

CVII

It is the day when he was born,
   A bitter day that early sank   2250
   Behind a purple-frosty bank
Of vapor, leaving night forlorn.

The time admits not flowers or leaves
   To deck the banquet. Fiercely flies
   The blast of North and East, and ice
Makes daggers at the sharpen'd eaves,

And bristles all the brakes and thorns
   To yon hard crescent, as she hangs
   Above the wood which grides and clangs
Its leafless ribs and iron horns   2260

Together, in the drifts that pass
　　To darken on the rolling brine
　　That breaks the coast. But fetch the wine,
Arrange the board and brim the glass;

Bring in great logs and let them lie,
　　To make a solid core of heat;
　　Be cheerful-minded, talk and treat
Of all things even as he were by;

We keep the day. With festal cheer,
　　With books and music, surely we 　　　　　　　2270
　　Will drink to him, whate'er he be,
And sing the songs he loved to hear.

CVIII

I will not shut me from my kind,
　　And, lest I stiffen into stone,
　　I will not eat my heart alone,
Nor feed with sighs a passing wind:

What profit lies in barren faith,
　　And vacant yearning, tho' with might
　　To scale the heaven's highest height,
Or dive below the wells of death? 　　　　　　　2280

What find I in the highest place,
　　But mine own phantom chanting hymns?
　　And on the depths of death there swims
The reflex of a human face.

I 'll rather take what fruit may be
　　Of sorrow under human skies:
　　'T is held that sorrow makes us wise,
Whatever wisdom sleep with thee.

CIX

Heart-affluence in discursive talk
   From household fountains never dry;   2290
   The critic clearness of an eye
That saw thro' all the Muses' walk;

Seraphic intellect and force
   To seize and throw the doubts of man;
   Impassion'd logic, which outran
The hearer in its fiery course;

High nature amorous of the good,
   But touch'd with no ascetic gloom;
   And passion pure in snowy bloom
Thro' all the years of April blood;   2300

A love of freedom rarely felt,
   Of freedom in her regal seat
   Of England; not the schoolboy heat,
The blind hysterics of the Celt;

And manhood fused with female grace
   In such a sort, the child would twine
   A trustful hand, unask'd, in thine,
And find his comfort in thy face;

All these have been, and thee mine eyes
   Have look'd on: if they look'd in vain,   2310
   My shame is greater who remain,
Nor let thy wisdom make me wise.

CX

Thy converse drew us with delight,
   The men of rathe and riper years;
   The feeble soul, a haunt of fears,
Forgot his weakness in thy sight.

On thee the loyal-hearted hung,
　　The proud was half disarm'd of pride,
　　Nor cared the serpent at thy side
To flicker with his double tongue.　　　　　　2320

The stern were mild when thou wert by,
　　The flippant put himself to school
　　And heard thee, and the brazen fool
Was soften'd, and he knew not why;

While I, thy nearest, sat apart,
　　And felt thy triumph was as mine;
　　And loved them more, that they were thine,
The graceful tact, the Christian art;

Nor mine the sweetness or the skill,
　　But mine the love that will not tire,　　　　2330
　　And, born of love, the vague desire
That spurs an imitative will.

CXI

The churl in spirit, up or down
　　Along the scale of ranks, thro' all,
　　To him who grasps a golden ball,
By blood a king, at heart a clown,—

The churl in spirit, howe'er he veil
　　His want in forms for fashion's sake,
　　Will let his coltish nature break
At seasons thro' the gilded pale;　　　　　　2340

For who can always act? but he,
　　To whom a thousand memories call,
　　Not being less but more than all
The gentleness he seem'd to be,

Best seem'd the thing he was, and join'd
    Each office of the social hour
    To noble manners, as the flower
And native growth of noble mind;

Nor ever narrowness or spite,
    Or villain fancy fleeting by,   2350
    Drew in the expression of an eye
Where God and Nature met in light;

And thus he bore without abuse
    The grand old name of gentleman,
    Defamed by every charlatan,
And soil'd with all ignoble use.

CXII

High wisdom holds my wisdom less,
    That I, who gaze with temperate eyes
    On glorious insufficiencies,
Set light by narrower perfectness.   2360

But thou, that fillest all the room
    Of all my love, art reason why
    I seem to cast a careless eye
On souls, the lesser lords of doom.

For what wert thou? some novel power
    Sprang up for ever at a touch,
    And hope could never hope too much,
In watching thee from hour to hour,

Large elements in order brought,
    And tracts of calm from tempest made,   2370
    And world-wide fluctuation sway'd
In vassal tides that follow'd thought.

CXIII

'T is held that sorrow makes us wise;
 Yet how much wisdom sleeps with thee
 Which not alone had guided me,
But served the seasons that may rise;

For can I doubt, who knew thee keen
 In intellect, with force and skill
 To strive, to fashion, to fulfil—
I doubt not what thou wouldst have been: 2380

A life in civic action warm,
 A soul on highest mission sent,
 A potent voice of Parliament,
A pillar steadfast in the storm,

Should licensed boldness gather force,
 Becoming, when the time has birth,
 A lever to uplift the earth
And roll it in another course,

With thousand shocks that come and go,
 With agonies, with energies,   2390
 With overthrowings, and with cries,
And undulations to and fro.

CXIV

Who loves not Knowledge? Who shall rail
 Against her beauty? May she mix
 With men and prosper! Who shall fix
Her pillars? Let her work prevail.

But on her forehead sits a fire;
 She sets her forward countenance
 And leaps into the future chance,
Submitting all things to desire.   2400

Half-grown as yet, a child, and vain—
 She cannot fight the fear of death.
 What is she, cut from love and faith,
But some wild Pallas from the brain

Of demons? fiery-hot to burst
 All barriers in her onward race
 For power. Let her know her place;
She is the second, not the first.

A higher hand must make her mild,
 If all be not in vain, and guide   2410
 Her footsteps, moving side by side
With Wisdom, like the younger child;

For she is earthly of the mind,
 But Wisdom heavenly of the soul.
 O friend, who camest to thy goal
So early, leaving me behind,

I would the great world grew like thee,
 Who grewest not alone in power
 And knowledge, but by year and hour
In reverence and in charity.   2420

CXV

Now fades the last long streak of snow,
 Now burgeons every maze of quick
 About the flowering squares, and thick
By ashen roots the violets blow.

Now rings the woodland loud and long,
 The distance takes a lovelier hue,
 And drown'd in yonder living blue
The lark becomes a sightless song.

Now dance the lights on lawn and lea,
   The flocks are whiter down the vale,   2430
   And milkier every milky sail
On winding stream or distant sea;

Where now the seamew pipes, or dives
   In yonder greening gleam, and fly
   The happy birds, that change their sky
To build and brood, that live their lives

From land to land; and in my breast
   Spring wakens too, and my regret
   Becomes an April violet,
And buds and blossoms like the rest.   2440

CXVI

Is it, then, regret for buried time
   That keenlier in sweet April wakes,
   And meets the year, and gives and takes
The colors of the crescent prime?

Not all: the songs, the stirring air,
   The life re-orient out of dust,
   Cry thro' the sense to hearten trust
In that which made the world so fair.

Not all regret: the face will shine
   Upon me, while I muse alone,   2450
   And that dear voice, I once have known,
Still speak to me of me and mine.

Yet less of sorrow lives in me
   For days of happy commune dead,
   Less yearning for the friendship fled
Than some strong bond which is to be.

CXVII

O days and hours, your work is this,
  To hold me from my proper place,
  A little while from his embrace,
For fuller gain of after bliss;   2460

That out of distance might ensue
  Desire of nearness doubly sweet,
  And unto meeting, when we meet,
Delight a hundredfold accrue,

For every grain of sand that runs,
  And every span of shade that steals,
  And every kiss of toothed wheels,
And all the courses of the suns.

CXVIII

Contemplate all this work of Time,
  The giant laboring in his youth;   2470
  Nor dream of human love and truth,
As dying Nature's earth and lime;

But trust that those we call the dead
  Are breathers of an ampler day
  For ever nobler ends. They say,
The solid earth whereon we tread

In tracts of fluent heat began,
  And grew to seeming-random forms,
  The seeming prey of cyclic storms,
Till at the last arose the man;   2480

Who throve and branch'd from clime to clime,
  The herald of a higher race,
  And of himself in higher place,
If so he type this work of time

Within himself, from more to more;
　　Or, crown'd with attributes of woe
　　Like glories, move his course, and show
That life is not as idle ore,

But iron dug from central gloom,
　　And heated hot with burning fears,　　　2490
　　And dipt in baths of hissing tears,
And batter'd with the shocks of doom

To shape and use. Arise and fly
　　The reeling Faun, the sensual feast;
　　Move upward, working out the beast,
And let the ape and tiger die.

CXIX

Doors, where my heart was used to beat
　　So quickly, not as one that weeps
　　I come once more; the city sleeps;
I smell the meadow in the street;　　　　2500

I hear a chirp of birds; I see
　　Betwixt the black fronts long-withdrawn
　　A light-blue lane of early dawn,
And think of early days and thee,

And bless thee, for thy lips are bland,
　　And bright the friendship of thine eye;
　　And in my thoughts with scarce a sigh
I take the pressure of thine hand.

CXX

I trust I have not wasted breath:
　　I think we are not wholly brain,　　　　2510
　　Magnetic mockeries; not in vain,
Like Paul with beasts, I fought with Death;

Not only cunning casts in clay:
   Let Science prove we are, and then
   What matters Science unto men,
At least to me? I would not stay.

Let him, the wiser man who springs
   Hereafter, up from childhood shape
   His action like the greater ape,
But I was *born* to other things.   2520

CXXI

Sad Hesper o'er the buried sun
   And ready, thou, to die with him,
   Thou watchest all things ever dim
And dimmer, and a glory done.

The team is loosen'd from the wain,
   The boat is drawn upon the shore;
   Thou listenest to the closing door,
And life is darken'd in the brain.

Bright Phosphor, fresher for the night,
   By thee the world's great work is heard   2530
   Beginning, and the wakeful bird;
Behind thee comes the greater light.

The market boat is on the stream,
   And voices hail it from the brink;
   Thou hear'st the village hammer clink,
And see'st the moving of the team.

Sweet Hesper-Phosphor, double name
   For what is one, the first, the last,
   Thou, like my present and my past,
Thy place is changed; thou art the same.   2540

CXXII

O, wast thou with me, dearest, then,
　　While I rose up against my doom,
　　And yearn'd to burst the folded gloom,
To bare the eternal heavens again,

To feel once more, in placid awe,
　　The strong imagination roll
　　A sphere of stars about my soul,
In all her motion one with law?

If thou wert with me, and the grave
　　Divide us not, be with me now,　　　　　　2550
　　And enter in at breast and brow,
Till all my blood, a fuller wave,

Be quicken'd with a livelier breath,
　　And like an inconsiderate boy,
　　As in the former flash of joy,
I slip the thoughts of life and death;

And all the breeze of Fancy blows,
　　And every dewdrop paints a bow,
　　The wizard lightnings deeply glow,
And every thought breaks out a rose.　　　　2560

CXXIII

There rolls the deep where grew the tree.
　　O earth, what changes hast thou seen!
　　There where the long street roars hath been
The stillness of the central sea.

The hills are shadows, and they flow
　　From form to form, and nothing stands;
　　They melt like mist, the solid lands,
Like clouds they shape themselves and go.

But in my spirit will I dwell,
   And dream my dream, and hold it true;   2570
   For tho' my lips may breathe adieu,
I cannot think the thing farewell.

CXXIV

That which we dare invoke to bless;
   Our dearest faith; our ghastliest doubt;
   He, They, One, All; within, without;
The Power in darkness whom we guess,—

I found Him not in world or sun,
   Or eagle's wing, or insect's eye,
   Nor thro' the questions men may try,
The petty cobwebs we have spun.   2580

If e'er when faith had fallen asleep,
   I heard a voice, "believe no more,"
   And heard an ever-breaking shore
That tumbled in the Godless deep,

A warmth within the breast would melt
   The freezing reason's colder part,
   And like a man in wrath the heart
Stood up and answer'd, "I have felt."

No, like a child in doubt and fear:
   But that blind clamor made me wise;   2590
   Then was I as a child that cries,
But, crying, knows his father near;

And what I am beheld again
   What is, and no man understands;
   And out of darkness came the hands
That reach thro' nature, moulding men.

CXXV

Whatever I have said or sung,
  Some bitter notes my harp would give,
  Yea, tho' there often seem'd to live
A contradiction on the tongue,   2600

Yet Hope had never lost her youth,
  She did but look through dimmer eyes;
  Or Love but play'd with gracious lies,
Because he felt so fix'd in truth;

And if the song were full of care,
  He breathed the spirit of the song;
  And if the words were sweet and strong
He set his royal signet there;

Abiding with me till I sail
  To seek thee on the mystic deeps,
  And this electric force, that keeps   2610
A thousand pulses dancing, fail.

CXXVI

Love is and was my lord and king,
  And in his presence I attend
  To hear the tidings of my friend,
Which every hour his couriers bring.

Love is and was my king and lord,
  And will be, tho' as yet I keep
  Within the court on earth, and sleep
Encompass'd by his faithful guard,   2620

And hear at times a sentinel
  Who moves about from place to place,
  And whispers to the worlds of space,
In the deep night, that all is well.

CXXVII

And all is well, tho' faith and form
   Be sunder'd in the night of fear;
   Well roars the storm to those that hear
A deeper voice across the storm,

Proclaiming social truth shall spread,
   And justice, even tho' thrice again   2630
   The red fool-fury of the Seine
Should pile her barricades with dead.

But ill for him that wears a crown,
   And him, the lazar, in his rags!
   They tremble, the sustaining crags;
The spires of ice are toppled down,

And molten up, and roar in flood;
   The fortress crashes from on high,
   The brute earth lightens to the sky,
And the great Æon sinks in blood,   2640

And compass'd by the fires of hell;
   While thou, dear spirit, happy star,
   O'erlook'st the tumult from afar,
And smilest, knowing all is well.

CXXVIII

The love that rose on stronger wings,
   Unpalsied when he met with Death,
   Is comrade of the lesser faith
That sees the course of human things.

No doubt vast eddies in the flood
   Of onward time shall yet be made,   2650
   And throned races may degrade;
Yet, O ye mysteries of good,

Wild Hours that fly with Hope and Fear,
　　If all your office had to do
　　With old results that look like new—
If this were all your mission here,

To draw, to sheathe a useless sword,
　　To fool the crowd with glorious lies,
　　To cleave a creed in sects and cries,
To change the bearing of a word,　　　　　　　2660

To shift an arbitrary power,
　　To cramp the student at his desk,
　　To make old bareness picturesque
And tuft with grass a feudal tower,

Why, then my scorn might well descend
　　On you and yours. I see in part
　　That all, as in some piece of art,
Is toil coöperant to an end.

CXXIX

Dear friend, far off, my lost desire,
　　So far, so near in woe and weal,　　　　　　　2670
　　O loved the most, when most I feel
There is a lower and a higher;

Known and unknown, human, divine;
　　Sweet human hand and lips and eye;
　　Dear heavenly friend that canst not die,
Mine, mine, for ever, ever mine;

Strange friend, past, present, and to be;
　　Loved deeplier, darklier understood;
　　Behold, I dream a dream of good,
And mingle all the world with thee.　　　　　　　2680

CXXX

Thy voice is on the rolling air;
 I hear thee where the waters run;
 Thou standest in the rising sun,
And in the setting thou art fair.

What art thou then? I cannot guess;
 But tho' I seem in star and flower
 To feel thee some diffusive power,
I do not therefore love thee less.

My love involves the love before;
 My love is vaster passion now;   2690
 Tho' mix'd with God and Nature thou,
I seem to love thee more and more.

Far off thou art, but ever nigh;
 I have thee still, and I rejoice;
 I prosper, circled with thy voice;
I shall not lose thee tho' I die.

CXXXI

O living will that shalt endure
 When all that seems shall suffer shock,
 Rise in the spiritual rock,
Flow thro' our deeds and make them pure,   2700

That we may lift from out of dust
 A voice as unto him that hears,
 A cry above the conquer'd years
To one that with us works, and trust,

With faith that comes of self-control,
 The truths that never can be proved
 Until we close with all we loved,
And all we flow from, soul in soul.

———————

O true and tried, so well and long,
   Demand not thou a marriage lay;   2710
   In that it is thy marriage day
Is music more than any song.

Nor have I felt so much of bliss
   Since first he told me that he loved
   A daughter of our house, nor proved
Since that dark day a day like this;

Tho' I since then have number'd o'er
   Some thrice three years; they went and came,
   Remade the blood and changed the frame,
And yet is love not less, but more;   2720

No longer caring to embalm
   In dying songs a dead regret,
   But like a statue solid-set,
And moulded in colossal calm.

Regret is dead, but love is more
   Than in the summers that are flown,
   For I myself with these have grown
To something greater than before;

Which makes appear the songs I made
   As echoes out of weaker times,   2730
   As half but idle brawling rhymes,
The sport of random sun and shade.

But where is she, the bridal flower,
   That must be made a wife ere noon?
   She enters, glowing like the moon
Of Eden on its bridal bower.

On me she bends her blissful eyes
   And then on thee; they meet thy look
   And brighten like the star that shook
Betwixt the palms of Paradise.   2740

O, when her life was yet in bud,
   He too foretold the perfect rose.
   For thee she grew, for thee she grows
For ever, and as fair as good.

And thou art worthy, full of power;
   As gentle; liberal-minded, great,
   Consistent; wearing all that weight
Of learning lightly like a flower.

But now set out: the noon is near,
   And I must give away the bride;   2750
   She fears not, or with thee beside
And me behind her, will not fear.

For I that danced her on my knee,
   That watch'd her on her nurse's arm,
   That shielded all her life from harm,
At last must part with her to thee;

Now waiting to be made a wife,
   Her feet, my darling, on the dead;
   Their pensive tablets round her head,
And the most living words of life   2760

Breathed in her ear. The ring is on,
   The "Wilt thou?" answer'd, and again
   The "Wilt thou?" ask'd, till out of twain
Her sweet "I will" has made you one.

Now sign your names, which shall be read,
   Mute symbols of a joyful morn,

By village eyes as yet unborn.
The names are sign'd, and overhead

Begins the clash and clang that tells
 The joy to every wandering breeze;   2770
 The blind wall rocks, and on the trees
The dead leaf trembles to the bells.

O happy hour, and happier hours
 Await them. Many a merry face
 Salutes them—maidens of the place,
That pelt us in the porch with flowers.

O happy hour, behold the bride
 With him to whom her hand I gave.
 They leave the porch, they pass the grave
That has to-day its sunny side.   2780

To-day the grave is bright for me,
 For them the light of life increased,
 Who stay to share the morning feast,
Who rest to-night beside the sea.

Let all my genial spirits advance
 To meet and greet a whiter sun;
 My drooping memory will not shun
The foaming grape of eastern France.

It circles round, and fancy plays,
 And hearts are warm'd and faces bloom,   2790
 As drinking health to bride and groom
We wish them store of happy days.

Nor count me all to blame if I
 Conjecture of a stiller guest,
 Perchance, perchance, among the rest,
And, tho' in silence, wishing joy.

But they must go, the time draws on,
   And those white-favor'd horses wait;
   They rise, but linger; it is late;
Farewell, we kiss, and they are gone.   2800

A shade falls on us like the dark
   From little cloudlets on the grass,
   But sweeps away as out we pass
To range the woods, to roam the park,

Discussing how their courtship grew,
   And talk of others that are wed,
   And how she look'd, and what he said,
And back we come at fall of dew.

Again the feast, the speech, the glee,
   The shade of passing thought, the wealth   2810
   Of words and wit, the double health,
The crowning cup, the three-times-three,

And last the dance;—till I retire.
   Dumb is that tower which spake so loud,
   And high in heaven the streaming cloud,
And on the downs a rising fire:

And rise, O moon, from yonder down,
   Till over down and over dale
   All night the shining vapor sail
And pass the silent-lighted town,   2820

The white-faced halls, the glancing rills,
   And catch at every mountain head,
   And o'er the friths that branch and spread
Their sleeping silver thro' the hills;

And touch with shade the bridal doors,
   With tender gloom the roof, the wall

And breaking let the splendor fall
To spangle all the happy shores

By which they rest, and ocean sounds,
   And, star and system rolling past,   2830
   A soul shall draw from out the vast
And strike his being into bounds,

And, moved thro' life of lower phase,
   Result in man, be born and think,
   And act and love, a closer link
Betwixt us and the crowning race

Of those that, eye to eye, shall look
   On knowledge; under whose command
   Is Earth and Earth's, and in their hand
Is Nature like an open book;   2840

No longer half-akin to brute,
   For all we thought and loved and did,
   And hoped, and suffer'd, is but seed
Of what in them is flower and fruit;

Whereof the man that with me trod
   This planet was a noble type
   Appearing ere the times were ripe,
That friend of mine who lives in God,

That God, which ever lives and loves,
   One God, one law, one element,   2850
   And one far-off divine event,
To which the whole creation moves.

MAUD; A MONODRAMA

The earlier critics of the poem failed to recognize its dramatic character. They ascribed to the author the thoughts and sentiments which he puts into the mouth of the morbid young man who is the *dramatis persona*; for, as in recent editions it has been designated, the poem is a "monodrama," and, in that respect, unique. Tennyson, when reading it to Mr. Knowles, said (as in substance he said when reading it to me) : "It should be called 'Maud, or the Madness.' It is slightly akin to 'Hamlet.' No other poem (a monotone with plenty of change and no weariness) has been made into a drama where successive phases of passion in one person take the place of successive persons." At the end of "Maud," he declared, "I've always said that 'Maud' and 'Guinevere' were the finest things I've written."

To Dr. Van Dyke, who in the first edition of "The Poetry of Tennyson" had called "Maud" a "splendid failure," he said: "I want to read this to you because I want you to feel what the poem means. It is dramatic; it is the story of a man who has a morbid nature, with a touch of inherited insanity, and very selfish. The poem is to show what love does for him. The war is only an episode. You must remember that it is not I myself speaking. It is this man with the strain of madness in his blood, and the memory of a great trouble and wrong that has put him out with the world."

I felt, when I heard the poet read "Maud," that it was the best possible commentary on the poem. I had not misunderstood it, as Dr. Van Dyke did at first, but the reading made me see heights and depths in it of which I had had no conception before. Especially was I amazed, as my friend was, at "the intensity with which the poet had felt, and the tenacity with which he had pursued, the moral meaning of the poem. It was love, but not love in itself alone, as an emotion, an inward experience, a selfish possession, that he was revealing. It was love as a vital force, love as a part of life, love as an influence,—nay, *the* influence which rescues the soul from the prison, or the madhouse, of self, and leads it into the larger, saner existence. This was the theme of 'Maud.' And the poet's voice brought it out and rang the changes on it, so that it was unmistakable and unforgettable,— the history of a man saved from selfish despair by a pure love." For his last reading of the poem, see the "Memoir," vol. i. page 395.

The motto of "Maud" might well have been the lines from "Locksley Hall" which the poet was fond of copying when friends asked for his autograph:—

Love took up the harp of Life, and smote on all the chords with might;
Smote the chord of Self, that, trembling, past in music out of sight.
From W. J. Rolfe's Cambridge Edition

PART I

· I ·

I

I hate the dreadful hollow behind the little wood;
Its lips in the field above are dabbled with blood-red heath,
The red-ribb'd ledges drip with a silent horror of blood,
And Echo there, whatever is ask'd her, answers "Death."

II

For there in the ghastly pit long since a body was found,
His who had given me life—O father! O God! was it well?—
Mangled, and flatten'd, and crush'd, and dinted into the ground;
There yet lies the rock that fell with him when he fell.

III

Did he fling himself down? who knows? for a vast speculation had fail'd,
And ever he mutter'd and madden'd, and ever wann'd with despair,   10
And out he walk'd when the wind like a broken worldling wail'd,
And the flying gold of the ruin'd woodlands drove thro' the air.

IV

I remember the time, for the roots of my hair were stirr'd
By a shuffled step, by a dead weight trail'd, by a whisper'd fright,

And my pulses closed their gates with a shock on my heart as
    I heard
The shrill-edged shriek of a mother divide the shuddering night.

V

Villainy somewhere! whose? One says, we are villains all.
Not he; his honest fame should at least by me be maintained;
But that old man, now lord of the broad estate and the Hall,
Dropt off gorged from a scheme that had left us flaccid and
    drain'd.   20

VI

Why do they prate of the blessings of peace? we have made
    them a curse,
Pickpockets, each hand lusting for all that is not its own;
And lust of gain, in the spirit of Cain, is it better or worse
Than the heart of the citizen hissing in war on his own hearth-
    stone?

VII

But these are the days of advance, the works of the men of mind,
When who but a fool would have faith in a tradesman's ware or
    his word?
Is it peace or war? Civil war, as I think, and that of a kind
The viler, as underhand, not openly bearing the sword.

VIII

Sooner or later I too may passively take the print
Of the golden age—why not? I have neither hope nor trust;   30
May make my heart as a millstone, set my face as a flint,
Cheat and be cheated, and die—who knows? we are ashes and
    dust.

IX

Peace sitting under her olive, and slurring the days gone by,
When the poor are hovell'd and hustled together, each sex, like
    swine,

When only the ledger lives, and when only not all men lie;
Peace in her vineyard—yes!—but a company forges the wine.

X

And the vitriol madness flushes up in the ruffian's head,
Till the filthy by-lane rings to the yell of the trampled wife,
And chalk and alum and plaster are sold to the poor for bread,
And the spirit of murder works in the very means of life,   40

XI

And Sleep must lie down arm'd, for the villainous centre-bits
Grind on the wakeful ear in the hush of the moonless nights,
While another is cheating the sick of a few last gasps, as he sits
To pestle a poison'd poison behind his crimson lights.

XII

When a Mammonite mother kills her babe for a burial fee,
And Timour-Mammon grins on a pile of children's bones,
Is it peace or war? better, war! loud war by land and by sea,
War with a thousand battles, and shaking a hundred thrones!

XIII

For I trust if an enemy's fleet came yonder round by the hill,
And the rushing battle-bolt sang from the three-decker out of
      the foam,   50
That the smooth-faced, snub-nosed rogue would leap from his
      counter and till,
And strike, if he could, were it but with his cheating yardwand,
      home.—

XIV

What! am I raging alone as my father raged in his mood?
Must *I* too creep to the hollow and dash myself down and die
Rather than hold by the law that I made, nevermore to brood
On a horror of shatter'd limbs and a wretched swindler's lie?

XV

Would there be sorrow for *me?* there was *love* in the passionate
    shriek,
Love for the silent thing that had made false haste to the grave—
Wrapt in a cloak, as I saw him, and thought he would rise and
    speak
And rave at the lie and the liar, ah God, as he used to rave.   60

XVI

I am sick of the Hall and the hill, I am sick of the moor and
    the main.
Why should I stay? can a sweeter chance ever come to me here?
O, having the nerves of motion as well as the nerves of pain,
Were it not wise if I fled from the place and the pit and the
    fear?

XVII

Workmen up at the Hall!—they are coming back from abroad;
The dark old place will be gilt by the touch of a millionaire.
I have heard, I know not whence, of the singular beauty of Maud;
I play'd with the girl when a child; she promised then to be fair.

XVIII

Maud, with her venturous climbings and tumbles and childish
    escapes,
Maud, the delight of the village, the ringing joy of the Hall,   70
Maud, with her sweet purse-mouth when my father dangled the
    grapes,
Maud, the beloved of my mother, the moon-faced darling of all,—

XIX

What is she now? My dreams are bad. She may bring me a
    curse.
No, there is fatter game on the moor; she will let me alone.

Thanks; for the fiend best knows whether woman or man be the
    worse.
I will bury myself in myself, and the Devil may pipe to his own.

· II ·

Long have I sigh'd for a calm; God grant I may find it at last!
It will never be broken by Maud; she has neither savor nor salt,
But a cold and clear-cut face, as I found when her carriage past,
Perfectly beautiful; let it be granted her; where is the fault?   80
All that I saw—for her eyes were downcast, not to be seen—
Faultily faultless, icily regular, splendidly null,
Dead perfection, no more; nothing more, if it had not been
For a chance of travel, a paleness, an hour's defect of the rose,
Or an underlip, you may call it a little too ripe, too full,
Or the least little delicate aquiline curve in a sensitive nose,
From which I escaped heart-free, with the least little touch of
    spleen.

· III ·

Cold and clear-cut face, why come you so cruelly meek,
Breaking a slumber in which all spleenful folly was drown'd?
Pale with the golden beam of an eyelash dead on the cheek,   90
Passionless, pale, cold face, star-sweet on a gloom profound;
Womanlike, taking revenge too deep for a transient wrong
Done but in thought to your beauty, and ever as pale as before
Growing and fading and growing upon me without a sound,
Luminous, gemlike, ghostlike, deathlike, half the night long
Growing and fading and growing, till I could bear it no more,
But arose, and all by myself in my own dark garden ground,
Listening now to the tide in its broad-flung shipwrecking roar,
Now to the scream of a madden'd beach dragg'd down by the
    wave,
Walk'd in a wintry wind by a ghastly glimmer, and found   100
The shining daffodil dead, and Orion low in his grave.

· IV ·

I

A million emeralds break from the ruby-budded lime
In the little grove where I sit—ah, wherefore cannot I be
Like things of the season gay, like the bountiful season bland,
When the far-off sail is blown by the breeze of a softer clime,
Half-lost in the liquid azure bloom of a crescent of sea,
The silent sapphire-spangled marriage ring of the land?

II

Below me, there, is the village, and looks how quiet and small!
And yet bubbles o'er like a city, with gossip, scandal, and spite;
And Jack on his ale-house bench has as many lies as a Czar;
And here on the landward side, by a red rock, glimmers the
    Hall;   111
And up in the high Hall-garden I see her pass like a light;
But sorrow seize me if ever that light be my leading star!

III

When have I bow'd to her father, the wrinkled head of the race?
I met her to-day with her brother, but not to her brother I bow'd;
I bow'd to his lady-sister as she rode by on the moor,
But the fire of a foolish pride flash'd over her beautiful face.
O child, you wrong your beauty, believe it, in being so proud;
Your father has wealth well-gotten, and I am nameless and poor.

IV

I keep but a man and a maid, ever ready to slander and steal;
I know it, and smile a hard-set smile, like a stoic, or like   121
A wiser epicurean, and let the world have its way.
For nature is one with rapine, a harm no preacher can heal;
The Mayfly is torn by the swallow, the sparrow spear'd by the
    shrike,
And the whole little wood where I sit is a world of plunder and
    prey.

V

We are puppets, Man in his pride, and Beauty fair in her flower;
Do we move ourselves, or are moved by an unseen hand at a
    game
That pushes us off from the board, and others ever succeed?
Ah yet, we cannot be kind to each other here for an hour;
We whisper, and hint, and chuckle, and grin at a brother's
    shame;
However we brave it out, we men are a little breed.

VI

A monstrous eft was of old the lord and master of earth,
For him did his high sun flame, and his river billowing ran,
And he felt himself in his force to be Nature's crowning race.
As nine months go to the shaping an infant ripe for his birth,
So many a million of ages have gone to the making of man:
He now is first, but is he the last? is he not too base?

VII

The man of science himself is fonder of glory, and vain,
An eye well-practised in nature, a spirit bounded and poor;
The passionate heart of the poet is whirl'd into folly and vice.   140
I would not marvel at either, but keep a temperate brain;
For not to desire or admire, if a man could learn it, were more
Than to walk all day like the sultan of old in a garden of spice.

VIII

For the drift of the Maker is dark, an Isis hid by the veil.
Who knows the ways of the world, how God will bring them
    about?
Our planet is one, the suns are many, the world is wide.
Shall I weep if a Poland fall? shall I shriek if a Hungary fail?
Or an infant civilization be ruled with rod or with knout?
I have not made the world, and He that made it will guide.

IX

Be mine a philosopher's life in the quiet woodland ways,   150
Where if I cannot be gay let a passionless peace be my lot,
Far-off from the clamor of liars belied in the hubbub of lies;
From the long-neck'd geese of the world that are ever hissing
    dispraise
Because their natures are little, and, whether he heed it or not,
Where each man walks with his head in a cloud of poisonous
    flies.

X

And most of all would I flee from the cruel madness of love
The honey of poison-flowers and all the measureless ill.
Ah, Maud, you milk-white fawn, you are all unmeet for a wife.
Your mother is mute in her grave as her image in marble above;
Your father is ever in London, you wander about at your will; 160
You have but fed on the roses and lain in the lilies of life.

· V ·

I

A voice by the cedar tree
In the meadow under the Hall!
She is singing an air that is known to me,
A passionate ballad gallant and gay,
A martial song like a trumpet's call!
Singing alone in the morning of life,
In the happy morning of life of May,
Singing of men that in battle array,
Ready in heart and ready in hand,   170
March with banner and bugle and fife
To the death, for their native land.

II

Maud with her exquisite face,
And wild voice pealing up to the sunny sky,

And feet like sunny gems on an English green,
Maud in the light of her youth and her grace,
Singing of Death, and of Honor that cannot die,
Till I well could weep for a time so sordid and mean,
And myself so languid and base.

III

Silence, beautiful voice!   180
Be still, for you only trouble the mind
With a joy in which I cannot rejoice,
A glory I shall not find.
Still! I will hear you no more,
For your sweetness hardly leaves me a choice
But to move to the meadow and fall before
Her feet on the meadow grass, and adore,
Not her, who is neither courtly nor kind,
Not her, not her, but a voice.

· VI ·

I

Morning arises stormy and pale,   190
No sun, but a wannish glare
In fold upon fold of hueless cloud;
And the budded peaks of the wood, are bow'd,
Caught, and cuff'd by the gale:
I had fancied it would be fair.

II

Whom but Maud should I meet
Last night, when the sunset burn'd
On the blossom'd gable-ends
At the head of the village street,
Whom but Maud should I meet?   200
And she touch'd my hand with a smile so sweet,
She made me divine amends
For a courtesy not return'd.

III

And thus a delicate spark
Of glowing and growing light
Thro' the livelong hours of the dark
Kept itself warm in the heart of my dreams,
Ready to burst in a color'd flame;
Till at last, when the morning came
In a cloud, it faded, and seems   210
But an ashen-gray delight.

IV

What if with her sunny hair,
And smile as sunny as cold,
She meant to weave me a snare
Of some coquettish deceit,
Cleopatra-like as of old
To entangle me when we met,
To have her lion roll in a silken net
And fawn at a victor's feet.

V

Ah, what shall I be at fifty   220
Should Nature keep me alive,
If I find the world so bitter
When I am but twenty-five?
Yet, if she were not a cheat,
If Maud were all that she seem'd,
And her smile were all that I dream'd,
Then the world were not so bitter
But a smile could make it sweet.

VI

What if, tho' her eye seem'd full
Of a kind intent to me,   230
What if that dandy-despot, he,
That jewell'd mass of millinery,

That oil'd and curl'd Assyrian bull
Smelling of musk and of insolence,
Her brother, from whom I keep aloof,
Who wants the finer politic sense
To mask, tho' but in his own behoof,
With a glassy smile his brutal scorn—
What if he had told her yestermorn
How prettily for his own sweet sake   240
A face of tenderness might be feign'd,
And a moist mirage in desert eyes,
That so, when the rotten hustings shake
In another month to his brazen lies,
A wretched vote may be gain'd?

VII

For a raven ever croaks, at my side,
Keep watch and ward, keep watch and ward,
Or thou wilt prove their tool.
Yea, too, myself from myself I guard,
For often a man's own angry pride   250
Is cap and bells for a fool.

VIII

Perhaps the smile and tender tone
Came out of her pitying womanhood,
For am I not, am I not, here alone
So many a summer since she died,
My mother, who was so gentle and good?
Living alone in an empty house,
Here half-hid in the gleaming wood,
Where I hear the dead at midday moan,
And the shrieking rush of the wainscot mouse,   260
And my own sad name in corners cried,
When the shiver of dancing leaves is thrown
About its echoing chambers wide,
Till a morbid hate and horror have grown
Of a world in which I have hardly mixt,

And a morbid eating lichen fixt
On a heart half-turn'd to stone.

IX

O heart of stone, are you flesh, and caught
By that you swore to withstand?
For what was it else within me wrought   270
But, I fear, the new strong wine of love,
That made my tongue so stammer and trip
When I saw the treasured splendor, her hand,
Come sliding out of her sacred glove,
And the sunlight broke from her lip?

X

I have play'd with her when a child;
She remembers it now we meet.
Ah, well, well, well, I *may* be beguiled
By some coquettish deceit.
Yet, if she were not a cheat,   280
If Maud were all that she seem'd,
And her smile had all that I dream'd,
Then the world were not so bitter
But a smile could make it sweet.

· VII ·

I

Did I hear it half in a doze
    Long since, I know not where?
Did I dream it an hour ago,
    When asleep in this arm-chair?

II

Men were drinking together,
    Drinking and talking of me: 290
"Well, if it prove a girl, the boy
    Will have plenty; so let it be."

III

Is it an echo of something
    Read with a boy's delight,
Viziers nodding together
    In some Arabian night?

IV

Strange, that I hear two men,
    Somewhere, talking of me:
"Well, if it prove a girl, my boy
    Will have plenty; so let it be."   300

· VIII ·

She came to the village church,
And sat by a pillar alone;
An angel watching an urn
Wept over her, carved in stone;
And once, but once, she lifted her eyes,
And suddenly, sweetly, strangely blush'd
To find they were met by my own;
And suddenly, sweetly, my heart beat stronger
And thicker, until I heard no longer
The snowy-banded, dilettante,   310
Delicate-handed priest intone;
And thought, is it pride? and mused and sigh'd,
"No surely, now it cannot be pride."

· IX ·

I was walking a mile,
More than a mile from the shore,
The sun look'd out with a smile
Betwixt the cloud and the moor;
And riding at set of day
Over the dark moor land,

Rapidly riding far away,   320
She waved to me with her hand.
There were two at her side,
Something flash'd in the sun,
Down by the hill I saw them ride,
In a moment they were gone;
Like a sudden spark
Struck vainly in the night,
Then returns the dark
With no more hope of light.

· X ·

I

Sick, am I sick of a jealous dread?   330
Was not one of the two at her side
This new-made lord, whose splendor plucks
The slavish hat from the villager's head?
Whose old grandfather has lately died,
Gone to a blacker pit, for whom
Grimy nakedness dragging his trucks
And laying his trams in a poison'd gloom
Wrought, till he crept from a gutted mine
Master of half a servile shire,
And left his coal all turn'd into gold   340
To a grandson, first of his noble line,
Rich in the grace all women desire,
Strong in the power that all men adore,
And simper and set their voices lower,
And soften as if to a girl, and hold
Awe-stricken breaths at a work divine,
Seeing his gewgaw castle shine,
New as his title, built last year,
There amid perky larches and pine,
And over the sullen-purple moor—   350
Look at it—pricking a cockney ear.

II

What, has he found my jewel out?
For one of the two that rode at her side
Bound for the Hall, I am sure was he;
Bound for the Hall, and I think for a bride.
Blithe would her brother's acceptance be
Maud could be gracious too, no doubt,
To a lord, a captain, a padded shape,
A bought commission, a waxen face,
A rabbit mouth that is ever agape—   360
Bought? what is it he cannot buy?
And therefore splenetic, personal, base,
A wounded thing with a rancorous cry,
At war with myself and a wretched race,
Sick, sick to the heart of life, am I.

III

Last week came one to the county town,
To preach our poor little army down,
And play the game of the despot kings,
Tho' the state has done it and thrice as well.
This broad-brimm'd hawker of holy things,   370
Whose ear is cramm'd with his cotton, and rings
Even in dreams to the chink of his pence,
This huckster put down war! can he tell
Whether war be a cause or a consequence?
Put down the passions that make earth hell!
Down with ambition, avarice, pride,
Jealousy, down! cut off from the mind
The bitter springs of anger and fear!
Down too, down at your own fireside,
With the evil tongue and the evil ear,   380
For each is at war with mankind!

IV

I wish I could hear again
The chivalrous battle-song
That she warbled alone in her joy!
I might persuade myself then
She would not do herself this great wrong,
To take a wanton dissolute boy
For a man and leader of men.

V

Ah God, for a man with heart, head, hand,
Like some of the simple great ones gone   390
For ever and ever by,
One still strong man in a blatant land,
Whatever they call him—what care I?—
Aristocrat, democrat, autocrat—one
Who can rule and dare not lie!

VI

And ah for a man to arise in me,
That the man I am may cease to be!

· XI ·

I

O, let the solid ground
    Not fail beneath my feet
Before my life has found   400
    What some have found so sweet!
Then let come what come may,
What matter if I go mad,
I shall have had my day.

II

Let the sweet heavens endure,
   Not close and darken above me
Before I am quite quite sure
   That there is one to love me!
Then let come what come may
To a life that has been so sad,   410
I shall have had my day.

· XII ·

I

Birds in the high Hall-garden
   When twilight was falling,
Maud, Maud, Maud, Maud,
   They were crying and calling.

II

Where was Maud? in our wood;
   And I—who else?—was with her,
Gathering woodland lilies,
   Myriads blow together.

III

Birds in our wood sang   420
   Ringing thro' the valleys,
Maud is here, here, here
   In among the lilies.

IV

I kiss'd her slender hand,
   She took the kiss sedately;
Maud is not seventeen,
   But she is tall and stately.

V

I to cry out on pride
    Who have won her favor!
O, Maud were sure of heaven   430
    If lowliness could save her!

VI

I know the way she went
    Home with her maiden posy,
For her feet have touch'd the meadows
    And left the daisies rosy.

VII

Birds in the high Hall-garden
    Were crying and calling to her,
Where is Maud, Maud, Maud?
    One is come to woo her.

VIII

Look, a horse at the door,   440
    And little King Charley snarling!
Go back, my lord, across the moor,
    You are not her darling.

· XIII ·

I

Scorn'd, to be scorn'd by one that I scorn,
Is that a matter to make me fret?
That a calamity hard to be borne?
Well, he may live to hate me yet.
Fool that I am to be vext with his pride!
I past him, I was crossing his lands;
He stood on the path a little aside;   450
His face, as I grant, in spite of spite,

Has a broad-blown comeliness, red and white,
And six feet two, as I think, he stands;
But his essences turn'd the live air sick,
And barbarous opulence jewel-thick
Sunn'd itself on his breast and his hands.

II

Who shall call me ungentle, unfair?
I long'd so heartily then and there
To give him the grasp of fellowship;
But while I past he was humming an air,   460
Stopt, and then with a riding-whip
Leisurely tapping a glossy boot,
And curving a contumelious lip,
Gorgonized me from head to foot
With a stony British stare.

III

Why sits he here in his father's chair?
That old man never comes to his place;
Shall I believe him ashamed to be seen?
For only once, in the village street,
Last year, I caught a glimpse of his face,   470
A gray old wolf and a lean.
Scarcely, now, would I call him a cheat;
For then, perhaps, as a child of deceit,
She might by a true descent be untrue;
And Maud is as true as Maud is sweet,
Tho' I fancy her sweetness only due
To the sweeter blood by the other side;
Her mother has been a thing complete,
However she came to be so allied.
And fair without, faithful within,   480
Maud to him is nothing akin.
Some peculiar mystic grace
Made her only the child of her mother,
And heap'd the whole inherited sin

On that huge scapegoat of the race,
All, all upon the brother.

IV

Peace, angry spirit, and let him be!
Has not his sister smiled on me?

· XIV ·

I

Maud has a garden of roses
And lilies fair on a lawn;   490
There she walks in her state
And tends upon bed and bower,
And thither I climb'd at dawn
And stood by her garden-gate.
A lion ramps at the top,
He is claspt by a passion-flower.

II

Maud's own little oak-room—
Which Maud, like a precious stone
Set in the heart of the carven gloom,
Lights with herself, when alone   500
She sits by her music and books
And her brother lingers late
With a roystering company—looks
Upon Maud's own garden-gate;
And I thought as I stood, if a hand, as white
As ocean-foam in the moon, were laid
On the hasp of the window, and my Delight
Had a sudden desire, like a glorious ghost, to glide,
Like a beam of the seventh heaven, down to my side,
There were but a step to be made.   510

III

The fancy flatter'd my mind,
And again seem'd overbold;
Now I thought that she cared for me,
Now I thought she was kind
Only because she was cold.

IV

I heard no sound where I stood
But the rivulet on from the lawn
Running down to my own dark wood,
Or the voice of the long sea-wave as it swell'd
Now and then in the dim-gray dawn;   520
But I look'd, and round, all round the house I beheld
The death-white curtain drawn,
Felt a horror over me creep,
Prickle my skin and catch my breath,
Knew that the death-white curtain meant but sleep,
Yet I shudder'd and thought like a fool of the sleep of death.

· XV ·

So dark a mind within me dwells,
    And I make myself such evil cheer,
That if *I* be dear to some one else,
    Then some one else may have much to fear;   530
But if *I* be dear to some one else,
    Then I should be to myself more dear.
Shall I not take care of all that I think,
Yea, even of wretched meat and drink,
If I be dear,
If I be dear to some one else?

· XVI ·

I

This lump of earth has left his estate
The lighter by the loss of his weight;
And so that he find what he went to seek,
And fulsome pleasure clog him, and drown   540
His heart in the gross mud-honey of town,
He may stay for a year who has gone for a week.
But this is the day when I must speak,
And I see my Oread coming down,
O, this is the day!
O beautiful creature, what am I
That I dare to look her way?
Think I may hold dominion sweet,
Lord of the pulse that is lord of her breast,
And dream of her beauty with tender dread,   550
From the delicate Arab arch of her feet
To the grace that, bright and light as the crest
Of a peacock, sits on her shining head,
And she knows it not—O, if she knew it,
To know her beauty might half undo it!
I know it the one bright thing to save
My yet young life in the wilds of Time,
Perhaps from madness, perhaps from crime,
Perhaps from a selfish grave.

II

What, if she be fasten'd to this fool lord,   560
Dare I bid her abide by her word?
Should I love her so well if she
Had given her word to a thing so low?
Shall I love her as well if she
Can break her word were it even for me?
I trust that it is not so.

III

Catch not my breath, O clamorous heart,
Let not my tongue be a thrall to my eye,
For I must tell her before we part,
I must tell her, or die.   570

· XVII ·

Go not, happy day,
   From the shining fields,
Go not, happy day,
   Till the maiden yields.
Rosy is the West,
   Rosy is the South,
Roses are her cheeks,
   And a rose her mouth.
When the happy Yes
   Falters from her lips,   580
Pass and blush the news
   Over glowing ships;
Over blowing seas,
   Over seas at rest,
Pass the happy news,
   Blush it thro' the West;
Till the red man dance
   By his red cedar-tree,
And the red man's babe
   Leap, beyond the sea.   590
Blush from West to East,
   Blush from East to West,
Till the West is East,
   Blush it thro' the West.
Rosy is the West,
   Rosy is the South,
Roses are her cheeks,
   And a rose her mouth.

· XVIII ·

I

I have led her home, my love, my only friend.
There is none like her, none.   600
And never yet so warmly ran my blood
And sweetly, on and on
Calming itself to the long-wish'd-for end,
Full to the banks, close on the promised good.

II

None like her, none.
Just now the dry-tongued laurels' pattering talk
Seem'd her light foot along the garden walk,
And shook my heart to think she comes once more.
But even then I heard her close the door;
The gates of heaven are closed, and she is gone.   610

III

There is none like her, none,
Nor will be when our summers have deceased.
O, art thou sighing for Lebanon
In the long breeze that streams to thy delicious East,
Sighing for Lebanon,
Dark cedar, tho' thy limbs have here increased,
Upon a pastoral slope as fair,
And looking to the South and fed
With honey'd rain and delicate air,
And haunted by the starry head   620
Of her whose gentle will has changed my fate,
And made my life a perfumed altar-flame;
And over whom thy darkness must have spread
With such delight as theirs of old, thy great
Forefathers of the thornless garden, there
Shadowing the snow-limb'd Eve from whom she came?

IV

Here will I lie, while these long branches sway,
And you fair stars that crown a happy day
Go in and out as if at merry play,
Who am no more so all forlorn   630
As when it seem'd far better to be born
To labor and the mattock-harden'd hand
Than nursed at ease and brought to understand
A sad astrology, the boundless plan
That makes you tyrants in your iron skies,
Innumerable, pitiless, passionless eyes,
Cold fires, yet with power to burn and brand
His nothingness into man.

V

But now shine on, and what care I,
Who in this stormy gulf have found a pearl   640
The countercharm of space and hollow sky,
And do accept my madness, and would die
To save from some slight shame one simple girl?—

VI

Would die, for sullen-seeming Death may give
More life to Love than is or ever was
In our low world, where yet 't is sweet to live.
Let no one ask me how it came to pass;
It seems that I am happy, that to me
A livelier emerald twinkles in the grass,
A purer sapphire melts into the sea.   650

VII

Not die, but live a life of truest breath,
And teach true life to fight with mortal wrongs.
O, why should Love, like men in drinking-songs,
Spice his fair banquet with the dust of death?
Make answer, Maud my bliss,

Maud made my Maud by that long loving kiss,
Life of my life, wilt thou not answer this?
"The dusky strand of Death inwoven here
With dear Love's tie, makes Love himself more dear."

VIII

Is that enchanted moan only the swell   660
Of the long waves that roll in yonder bay?
And hark the clock within, the silver knell
Of twelve sweet hours that past in bridal white,
And died to live, long as my pulses play;
But now by this my love has closed her sight
And given false death her hand, and stolen away
To dreamful wastes where footless fancies dwell
Among the fragments of the golden day.
May nothing there her maiden grace affright!
Dear heart, I feel with thee the drowsy spell.   670
My bride to be, my evermore delight,
My own heart's heart, my ownest own, farewell;
It is but for a little space I go.
And ye meanwhile far over moor and fell
Beat to the noiseless music of the night!
Has our whole earth gone nearer to the glow
Of your soft splendors that you look so bright?
I have climb'd nearer out of lonely hell.
Beat, happy stars, timing with things below,
Beat with my heart more blest than heart can tell,   680
Blest, but for some dark undercurrent woe
That seems to draw—but it shall not be so;
Let all be well, be well.

· XIX ·

I

Her brother is coming back to-night,
Breaking up my dream of delight.

II

My dream? do I dream of bliss?
I have walk'd awake with Truth.
O, when did a morning shine
So rich in atonement as this
For my dark-dawning youth,   690
Darken'd watching a mother decline
And that dead man at her heart and mine;
For who was left to watch her but I?
Yet so did I let my freshness die.

III

I trust that I did not talk
To gentle Maud in our walk—
For often in lonely wanderings
I have cursed him even to lifeless things—
But I trust that I did not talk,
Not touch on her father's sin.   700
I am sure I did but speak
Of my mother's faded cheek
When it slowly grew so thin
That I felt she was slowly dying
Vext with lawyers and harass'd with debt;
For how often I caught her with eyes all wet,
Shaking her head at her son and sighing
A world of trouble within!

IV

And Maud too, Maud was moved
To speak of the mother she loved   710
As one scarce less forlorn,
Dying abroad and it seems apart
From him who had ceased to share her heart,
And ever mourning over the feud,
The household Fury sprinkled with blood
By which our houses are torn.

How strange was what she said,
When only Maud and the brother
Hung over her dying bed—
That Maud's dark father and mine   720
Had bound us one to the other,
Betrothed us over their wine,
On the day when Maud was born;
Seal'd her mine from her first sweet breath!
Mine, mine by a right, from birth till death!
Mine, mine—our fathers have sworn!

V

But the true blood spilt had in it a heat
To dissolve the precious seal on a bond,
That, if left uncancell'd, had been so sweet;
And none of us thought of a something beyond,   730
A desire that awoke in the heart of the child,
As it were a duty done to the tomb,
To be friends for her sake, to be reconciled;
And I was cursing them and my doom,
And letting a dangerous thought run wild
While often abroad in the fragrant gloom
Of foreign churches—I see her there,
Bright English lily, breathing a prayer
To be friends, to be reconciled!

VI

But then what a flint is he!   740
Abroad, at Florence, at Rome,
I find whenever she touch'd on me
This brother had laugh'd her down,
And at last, when each came home,
He had darken'd into a frown,
Chid her, and forbid her to speak
To me, her friend of the years before;
And this was what had redden'd her cheek
When I bow'd to her on the moor.

VII

Yet Maud, altho' not blind   750
To the faults of his heart and mind,
I see she cannot but love him,
And says he is rough but kind,
And wishes me to approve him,
And tells me, when she lay
Sick once, with a fear of worse,
That he left his wine and horses and play,
Sat with her, read to her, night and day,
And tended her like a nurse.

VIII

Kind? but the death-bed desire   760
Spurn'd by this heir of the liar—
Rough but kind? yet I know
He has plotted against me in this,
That he plots against me still.
Kind to Maud? that were not amiss.
Well, rough but kind; why, let it be so,
For shall not Maud have her will?

IX

For, Maud, so tender and true,
As long as my life endures
I feel I shall owe you a debt   770
That I never can hope to pay;
And if ever I should forget
That I owe this debt to you
And for your sweet sake to yours,
O, then, what then shall I say?—
If ever I *should* forget,
May God make me more wretched
Than ever I have been yet!

X

So now I have sworn to bury
All this dead body of hate,   780
I feel so free and so clear
By the loss of that dead weight,
That I should grow light-headed, I fear,
Fantastically merry,
But that her brother comes, like a blight
On my fresh hope, to the Hall to-night.

· XX ·

I

Strange, that I felt so gay,
Strange, that I tried to-day
To beguile her melancholy;
The Sultan, as we name him—   790
She did not wish to blame him—
But he vext her and perplext her
With his worldly talk and folly.
Was it gentle to reprove her
For stealing out of view
From a little lazy lover
Who but claims her as his due?
Or for chilling his caresses
By the coldness of her manners,
Nay, the plainness of her dresses?   800
Now I know her but in two,
Nor can pronounce upon it
If one should ask me whether
The habit, hat, and feather,
Or the frock and gipsy bonnet
Be the neater and completer;
For nothing can be sweeter
Than maiden Maud in either.

II

But to-morrow, if we live,
Our ponderous squire will give   810
A grand political dinner
To half the squirelings near;
And Maud will wear her jewels,
And the bird of prey will hover,
And the titmouse hope to win her
With his chirrup at her ear.

III

A grand political dinner
To the men of many acres,
A gathering of the Tory,
A dinner and then a dance   820
For the maids and marriage-makers,
And every eye but mine will glance
At Maud in all her glory.

IV

For I am not invited,
But, with the Sultan's pardon,
I am all as well delighted,
For I know her own rose-garden,
And mean to linger in it
Till the dancing will be over;
And then, O, then, come out to me   830
For a minute, but for a minute,
Come out to your own true lover,
That your true lover may see
Your glory also, and render
All homage to his own darling,
Queen Maud in all her splendor.

· XXI ·

Rivulet crossing my ground,
And bringing me down from the Hall
This garden-rose that I found,
Forgetful of Maud and me, 840
And lost in trouble and moving round
Here at the head of a tinkling fall,
And trying to pass to the sea;
O rivulet, born at the Hall,
My Maud has sent it by thee—
If I read her sweet will right—
On a blushing mission to me,
Saying in odor and color, "Ah, be
Among the roses to-night."

· XXII ·

I

Come into the garden, Maud, 850
For the black bat, night, has flown,
Come into the garden, Maud,
I am here at the gate alone;
And the woodbine spices are wafted abroad,
And the musk of the rose is blown.

II

For a breeze of morning moves,
And the planet of Love is on high,
Beginning to faint in the light that she loves
On a bed of daffodil sky,
To faint in the light of the sun she loves, 860
To faint in his light, and to die.

III

All night have the roses heard
    The flute, violin, bassoon;
All night has the casement jessamine stirr'd
    To the dancers dancing in tune;
Till a silence fell with the waking bird,
    And a hush with the setting moon.

IV

I said to the lily, "There is but one,
    With whom she has heart to be gay.
When will the dancers leave her alone?   870
    She is weary of dance and play."
Now half to the setting moon are gone,
    And half to the rising day;
Low on the sand and loud on the stone
    The last wheel echoes away.

V

I said to the rose, "The brief night goes
    In babble and revel and wine.
O young lord-lover, what sighs are those,
    For one that will never be thine?
But mine, but mine," so I sware to the rose,   880
    "For ever and ever, mine."

VI

And the soul of the rose went into my blood,
    As the music clash'd in the hall;
And long by the garden lake I stood,
    For I heard your rivulet fall
From the lake to the meadow and on to the wood,
    Our wood, that is dearer than all;

VII

From the meadow your walks have left so sweet
    That whenever a March-wind sighs

He sets the jewel-print of your feet   890
  In violets blue as your eyes,
To the woody hollows in which we meet
  And the valleys of Paradise.

VIII

The slender acacia would not shake
  One long milk-bloom on the tree;
The white lake-blossom fell into the lake
  As the pimpernel dozed on the lea;
But the rose was awake all night for your sake,
  Knowing your promise to me;
The lilies and roses were all awake,   900
  They sigh'd for the dawn and thee.

IX

Queen rose of the rosebud garden of girls,
  Come hither, the dances are done,
In gloss of satin and glimmer of pearls,
  Queen lily and rose in one;
Shine out, little head, sunning over with curls,
  To the flowers, and be their sun.

X

There has fallen a splendid tear
  From the passion-flower at the gate.
She is coming, my dove, my dear;   910
  She is coming, my life, my fate.
The red rose cries, "She is near, she is near;"
  And the white rose weeps, "She is late;"
The larkspur listens, "I hear, I hear;"
  And the lily whispers, "I wait."

XI

She is coming, my own, my sweet;
  Were it ever so airy a tread,

My heart would hear her and beat,
    Were it earth in an earthy bed;
My dust would hear her and beat,   920
    Had I lain for a century dead,
Would start and tremble under her feet,
    And blossom in purple and red.

PART II

· I ·

I

"The fault was mine, the fault was mine"—
Why am I sitting here so stunn'd and still,
Plucking the harmless wild-flower on the hill?—
It is this guilty hand!—
And there rises ever a passionate cry
From underneath in the darkening land—
What is it, that has been done?
O dawn of Eden bright over earth and sky,
The fires of hell brake out of thy rising sun,
The fires of hell and of hate;   10
For she, sweet soul, had hardly spoken a word,
When her brother ran in his rage to the gate,
He came with the babe-faced lord,
Heap'd on her terms of disgrace;
And while she wept, and I strove to be cool,
He fiercely gave me the lie,
Till I with as fierce an anger spoke,
And he struck me, madman, over the face,
Struck me before the languid fool,
Who was gaping and grinning by;   20
Struck for himself an evil stroke,
Wrought for his house an irredeemable woe.
For front to front in an hour we stood,

And a million horrible bellowing echoes broke
From the red-ribb'd hollow behind the wood,
And thunder'd up into heaven the Christless code
That must have life for a blow.
Ever and ever afresh they seem'd to grow.
Was it he lay there with a fading eye?
"The fault was mine," he whisper'd, "fly!"　　　　30
Then glided out of the joyous wood
The ghastly Wraith of one that I know,
And there rang on a sudden a passionate cry,
A cry for a brother's blood;
It will ring in my heart and my ears, till I die, till I die.

II

Is it gone? my pulses beat—
What was it? a lying trick of the brain?
Yet I thought I saw her stand,
A shadow there at my feet,
High over the shadowy land.　　　　40
It is gone; and the heavens fall in a gentle rain,
When they should burst and drown with deluging storms
The feeble vassals of wine and anger and lust,
The little hearts that know not how to forgive.
Arise, my God, and strike, for we hold Thee just,
Strike dead the whole weak race of venomous worms,
That sting each other here in the dust;
We are not worthy to live.

· II ·

I

　　See what a lovely shell,
　　Small and pure as a pearl,　　　　50
　　Lying close to my foot,
　　Frail, but a work divine,
　　Made so fairily well

With delicate spire and whorl,
How exquisitely minute,
A miracle of design!

II

What is it? a learned man
Could give it a clumsy name.
Let him name it who can,
The beauty would be the same.   60

III

The tiny cell is forlorn,
Void of the little living will
That made it stir on the shore.
Did he stand at the diamond door
Of his house in a rainbow frill?
Did he push, when he was uncurl'd,
A golden foot or a fairy horn
Thro' his dim water-world?

IV

Slight, to be crush'd with a tap
Of my finger-nail on the sand,   70
Small, but a work divine,
Frail, but of force to withstand,
Year upon year, the shock
Of cataract seas that snap
The three-decker's oaken spine
Athwart the ledges of rock,
Here on the Breton strand!

V

Breton, not Briton; here
Like a shipwreck'd man on a coast
Of ancient fable and fear—   80
Plagued with a flitting to and fro,
A disease, a hard mechanic ghost

That never came from on high
Nor ever arose from below,
But only moves with the moving eye,
Flying along the land and the main—
Why should it look like Maud?
Am I to be overawed
By what I cannot but know
Is a juggle born of the brain?   90

VI

Back from the Breton coast,
Sick of a nameless fear,
Back to the dark sea-line
Looking, thinking of all I have lost;
An old song vexes my ear,
But that of Lamech is mine.

VII

For years, a measureless ill,
For years, for ever, to part—
But she, she would love me still;
And as long, O God, as she   100
Have a grain of love for me,
So long, no doubt, no doubt,
Shall I nurse in my dark heart,
However weary, a spark of will
Not to be trampled out.

VIII

Strange, that the mind, when fraught
With a passion so intense
One would think that it well
Might drown all life in the eye,—
That it should, by being so overwrought,   110
Suddenly strike on a sharper sense
For a shell, or a flower, little things

Which else would have been past by!
And now I remember, I,
When he lay dying there,
I noticed one of his many rings—
For he had many, poor worm—and thought,
It is his mother's hair.

IX

Who knows if he be dead?
Whether I need have fled?   120
Am I guilty of blood?
However this may be,
Comfort her, comfort her, all things good,
While I am over the sea!
Let me and my passionate love go by,
But speak to her all things holy and high,
Whatever happen to me!
Me and my harmful love go by;
But come to her waking, find her asleep,
Powers of the height, Powers of the deep,   130
And comfort her tho' I die!

· III ·

Courage, poor heart of stone!
I will not ask thee why
Thou canst not understand
That thou art left for ever alone;
Courage, poor stupid heart of stone!—
Or if I ask thee why,
Care not thou to reply:
She is but dead, and the time is at hand
When thou shalt more than die.   140

· IV ·

I

O that 't were possible
After long grief and pain
To find the arms of my true love
Round me once again!

II

When I was wont to meet her
In the silent woody places
By the home that gave me birth,
We stood tranced in long embraces
Mixt with kisses sweeter, sweeter
Than anything on earth.   150

III

A shadow flits before me,
Not thou, but like to thee.
Ah, Christ, that it were possible
For one short hour to see
The souls we loved, that they might tell us
What and where they be!

IV

It leads me forth at evening,
It lightly winds and steals
In a cold white robe before me,
When all my spirit reels   160
At the shouts, the leagues of lights,
And the roaring of the wheels.

V

Half the night I waste in sighs,
Half in dreams I sorrow after

The delight of early skies;
In a wakeful doze I sorrow
For the hand, the lips, the eyes,
For the meeting of the morrow,
The delight of happy laughter,
The delight of low replies.   170

VI

'T is a morning pure and sweet,
And a dewy splendor falls
On the little flower that clings
To the turrets and the walls;
'T is a morning pure and sweet,
And the light and shadow fleet.
She is walking in the meadow,
And the woodland echo rings;
In a moment we shall meet.
She is singing in the meadow,   180
And the rivulet at her feet
Ripples on in light and shadow
To the ballad that she sings.

VII

Do I hear her sing as of old,
My bird with the shining head,
My own dove with the tender eye?
But there rings on a sudden a passionate cry,
There is some one dying or dead,
And a sullen thunder is roll'd;
For a tumult shakes the city,   190
And I wake, my dream is fled.
In the shuddering dawn, behold,
Without knowledge, without pity,
By the curtains of my bed
That abiding phantom cold!

VIII

Get thee hence, nor come again,
Mix not memory with doubt,
Pass, thou deathlike type of pain,
Pass and cease to move about!
'T is the blot upon the brain   200
That *will* show itself without.

IX

Then I rise, the eave-drops fall,
And the yellow vapors choke
The great city sounding wide;
The day comes, a dull red ball
Wrapt in drifts of lurid smoke
On the misty river-tide.

X

Thro' the hubbub of the market
I steal, a wasted frame;
It crosses here, it crosses there,   210
Thro' all that crowd confused and loud,
The shadow still the same;
And on my heavy eyelids
My anguish hangs like shame.

XI

Alas for her that met me,
That heard me softly call,
Came glimmering thro' the laurels
At the quiet evenfall,
In the garden by the turrets
Of the old manorial hall!   220

XII

Would the happy spirit descend
From the realms of light and song,

In the chamber or the street,
As she looks among the blest,
Should I fear to greet my friend
Or to say "Forgive the wrong,"
Or to ask her, "Take me, sweet,
To the regions of thy rest"?

XIII

But the broad light glares and beats,
And the shadow flits and fleets   230
And will not let me be;
And I loathe the squares and streets,
And the faces that one meets,
Hearts with no love for me.
Always I long to creep
Into some still cavern deep,
There to weep, and weep, and weep
My whole soul out to thee.

· V ·

I

Dead, long dead,
Long dead!   240
And my heart is a handful of dust,
And the wheels go over my head,
And my bones are shaken with pain,
For into a shallow grave they are thrust,
Only a yard beneath the street,
And the hoofs of the horses beat, beat,
The hoofs of the horses beat,
Beat into my scalp and my brain,
With never an end to the stream of passing feet,
Driving, hurrying, marrying, burying,   250
Clamor and rumble, and ringing and clatter;
And here beneath it is all as bad,

For I thought the dead had peace, but it is not so.
To have no peace in the grave, is that not sad?
But up and down and to and fro,
Ever about me the dead men go;
And then to hear a dead man chatter
Is enough to drive one mad.

II

Wretchedest age, since Time began,
They cannot even bury a man;   260
And tho' we paid our tithes in the days that are gone,
Not a bell was rung, not a prayer was read.
It is that which makes us loud in the world of the dead;
There is none that does his work, not one.
A touch of their office might have sufficed,
But the churchmen fain would kill their church,
As the churches have kill'd their Christ.

III

See, there is one of us sobbing,
No limit to his distress;
And another, a lord of all things, praying   270
To his own great self, as I guess;
And another, a statesman there, betraying
His party-secret, fool, to the press;
And yonder a vile physician, blabbing
The case of his patient—all for what?
To tickle the maggot born in an empty head,
And wheedle a world that loves him not,
For it is but a world of the dead.

IV

Nothing but idiot gabble!
For the prophecy given of old   280
And then not understood,
Has come to pass as foretold;
Not let any man think for the public good,

But babble, merely for babble.
For I never whisper'd a private affair
Within the hearing of cat or mouse,
No, not to myself in the closet alone,
But I heard it shouted at once from the top of the house;
Everything came to be known.
Who told *him* we were there? 290

V

Not that gray old wolf, for he came not back
From the wilderness, full of wolves, where he used to lie;
He has gather'd the bones for his o'ergrown whelp to crack—
Crack them now for yourself, and howl, and die.

VI

Prophet, curse me the blabbing lip,
And curse me the British vermin, the rat;
I know not whether he came in the Hanover ship,
But I know that he lies and listens mute
In an ancient mansion's crannies and holes.
Arsenic, arsenic, sure, would do it, 300
Except that now we poison our babes, poor souls!
It is all used up for that.

VII

Tell him now: she is standing here at my head;
Not beautiful now, not even kind;
He may take her now; for she never speaks her mind,
But is ever the one thing silent here.
She is not *of* us, as I divine;
She comes from another stiller world of the dead,
Stiller, not fairer than mine.

VIII

But I know where a garden grows, 310
Fairer than aught in the world beside,
All made up of the lily and rose

That blow by night, when the season is good,
To the sound of dancing music and flutes:
It is only flowers, they had no fruits,
And I almost fear they are not roses, but blood;
For the keeper was one, so full of pride,
He linkt a dead man there to a spectral bride;
For he, if he had not been a Sultan of brutes,
Would he have that hole in his side?   320

IX

But what will the old man say?
He laid a cruel snare in a pit
To catch a friend of mine one stormy day;
Yet now I could even weep to think of it;
For what will the old man say
When he comes to the second corpse in the pit?

X

Friend, to be struck by the public foe,
Then to strike him and lay him low,
That were a public merit, far,
Whatever the Quaker holds, from sin;   330
But the red life spilt for a private blow—
I swear to you, lawful and lawless war
Are scarcely even akin.

XI

O me, why have they not buried me deep enough?
Is it kind to have made me a grave so rough,
Me, that was never a quiet sleeper?
Maybe still I am but half-dead;
Then I cannot be wholly dumb.
I will cry to the steps above my head
And somebody, surely, some kind heart will come   340
To bury me, bury me
Deeper, ever so little deeper.

PART III

I

My life has crept so long on a broken wing
Thro' cells of madness, haunts of horror and fear,
That I come to be grateful at last for a little thing.
My mood is changed, for it fell at a time of year
When the face of night is fair on the dewy downs,
And the shining daffodil dies, and the Charioteer
And starry Gemini hang like glorious crowns
Over Orion's grave low down in the west,
That like a silent lightning under the stars
She seem'd to divide in a dream from a band of the blest,   10
And spoke of a hope for the world in the coming wars—
"And in that hope, dear soul, let trouble have rest,
Knowing I tarry for thee," and pointed to Mars
As he glow'd like a ruddy shield on the Lion's breast.

II

And it was but a dream, yet it yielded a dear delight
To have look'd, tho' but in a dream, upon eyes so fair,
That had been in a weary world my one thing bright;
And it was but a dream, yet it lighten'd my despair
When I thought that a war would arise in defence of the right,
That an iron tyranny now should bend or cease,   20
The glory of manhood stand on his ancient height,
Nor Britain's one sole God be the millionaire.
No more shall commerce be all in all, and Peace
Pipe on her pastoral hillock a languid note,
And watch her harvest ripen, her herd increase,
Nor the cannon-bullet rust on a slothful shore,
And the cobweb woven across the cannon's throat
Shall shake its threaded tears in the wind no more.

III

And as months ran on and rumor of battle grew,
"It is time, it is time, O passionate heart," said I,—   30
For I cleaved to a cause that I felt to be pure and true,—
"It is time, O passionate heart and morbid eye,
That old hysterical mock-disease should die."
And I stood on a giant deck and mixt my breath
With a loyal people shouting a battle cry,
Till I saw the dreary phantom arise and fly
Far into the North, and battle, and seas of death.

IV

Let it go or stay, so I wake to the higher aims
Of a land that has lost for a little her lust of gold,
And love of a peace that was full of wrongs and shames,   40
Horrible, hateful, monstrous, not to be told;
And hail once more to the banner of battle unroll'd!
Tho' many a light shall darken, and many shall weep
For those that are crush'd in the clash of jarring claims,
Yet God's just wrath shall be wreak'd on a giant liar,
And many a darkness into the light shall leap,
And shine in the sudden making of splendid names,
And noble thought be freer under the sun,
And the heart of a people beat with one desire;
For the peace, that I deem'd no peace, is over and done,   50
And now by the side of the Black and the Baltic deep,
And deathful-grinning mouths of the fortress, flames
The blood-red blossom of war with a heart of fire.

V

Let it flame or fade, and the war roll down like a wind,
We have proved we have hearts in a cause, we are noble still,
And myself have awaked, as it seems, to the better mind.
It is better to fight for the good than to rail at the ill;
I have felt with my native land, I am one with my kind,
I embrace the purpose of God, and the doom assign'd.

I come from haunts of coot and hern,
 I make a sudden sally,
And sparkle out among the fern,
 To bicker down a valley.

By thirty hills I hurry down,
 Or slip between the ridges,
By twenty thorps, a little town,
 And half a hundred bridges.

Till last by Philip's farm I flow
 To join the brimming river,   10
For men may come and men may go,
 But I go on for ever.

  . . . .

I chatter over stony ways,
 In little sharps and trebles,
I bubble into eddying bays,
 I babble on the pebbles.

With many a curve my banks I fret
 By many a field and fallow,
And many a fairy foreland set
 With willow-weed and mallow.   20

I chatter, chatter, as I flow
 To join the brimming river,
For men may come and men may go,
 But I go on for ever.

  . . . .

I wind about, and in and out,
   With here a blossom sailing,
And here and there a lusty trout,
   And here and there a grayling,

And here and there a foamy flake
   Upon me, as I travel   30
With many a silvery water-break
   Above the golden gravel,

And draw them all along, and flow
   To join the brimming river,
For men may come and men may go,
   But I go on for ever.

.   .   .   .   .   .

I steal by lawns and grassy plots,
   I slide by hazel covers;
I move the sweet forget me nots
   That grow for happy lovers.   40

I slip, I slide, I gloom, I glance,
   Among my skimming swallows;
I make the netted sunbeam dance
   Against my sandy shallows.

I murmur under moon and stars
   In brambly wildernesses;
I linger by my shingly bars,
   I loiter round my cresses;

And out again I curve and flow
   To join the brimming river,   50
For men may come and men may go,
   But I go on for ever.

THE DAISY

WRITTEN AT EDINBURGH

O love, what hours were thine and mine,
In lands of palm and southern pine;
    In lands of palm, or orange-blossom,
Of olive, aloe, and maize and vine!

What Roman strength Turbìa show'd
In ruin, by the mountain road;
    How like a gem, beneath, the city
Of little Monaco, basking, glow'd!

How richly down the rocky dell
The torrent vineyard streaming fell   10
    To meet the sun and sunny waters,
That only heaved with a summer swell!

What slender campanili grew
By bays, the peacock's neck in hue;
    Where, here and there, on sandy beaches
A milky-bell'd amaryllis blew!

How young Columbus seem'd to rove,
Yet present in his natal grove,
    Now watching high on mountain cornice,
And steering, now, from a purple cove,   20

Now pacing mute by ocean's rim;
Till, in a narrow street and dim,
    I stay'd the wheels at Cogoletto,
And drank, and loyally drank to him!

Nor knew we well what pleased us most;
Not the clipt palm of which they boast,

But distant color, happy hamlet,
A moulder'd citadel on the coast,

Or tower, or high hill-convent, seen
A light amid its olives green;
  Or olive-hoary cape in ocean;
Or rosy blossom in hot ravine,

30

Where oleanders flush'd the bed
Of silent torrents, gravel-spread;
  And, crossing, oft we saw the glisten
Of ice, far up on a mountain head.

We loved that hall, tho' white and cold,
Those niched shapes of noble mould,
  A princely people's awful princes,
The grave, severe Genovese of old.

40

At Florence too what golden hours,
In those long galleries, were ours;
  What drives about the fresh Cascinè,
Or walks in Boboli's ducal bowers!

In bright vignettes, and each complete,
Of tower or duomo, sunny-sweet,
  Or palace, how the city glitter'd,
Thro' cypress avenues, at our feet!

But when we crost the Lombard plain
Remember what a plague of rain;
  Of rain at Reggio, rain at Parma,
At Lodi rain, Piacenza rain.

50

And stern and sad—so rare the smiles
Of sunlight—look'd the Lombard piles;
  Porch-pillars on the lion resting,
And sombre, old, colonnaded aisles.

O Milan, O the chanting quires,
The giant windows' blazon'd fires,
   The height, the space, the gloom, the glory!
A mount of marble, a hundred spires!   60

I climb'd the roofs at break of day;
Sun-smitten Alps before me lay.
   I stood among the silent statues,
And statued pinnacles, mute as they.

How faintly-flush'd, how phantom-fair,
Was Monte Rosa, hanging there
   A thousand shadowy-pencill'd valleys
And snowy dells in a golden air!

Remember how we came at last
To Como; shower and storm and blast   70
   Had blown the lake beyond his limit,
And all was flooded; and how we past

From Como, when the light was gray,
And in my head, for half the day,
   The rich Virgilian rustic measure
Of "Lari Maxume," all the way,

Like ballad-burthen music, kept,
As on the Lariano crept
   To that fair port below the castle
Of Queen Theodolind, where we slept;   80

Or hardly slept, but watch'd awake
A cypress in the moonlight shake,
   The moonlight touching o'er a terrace
One tall agavè above the lake.

What more? we took our last adieu,
And up the snowy Splügen drew;

But ere we reach'd the highest summit
I pluck'd a daisy, I gave it you.

It told of England then to me,
And now it tells of Italy. 90
   O love, we two shall go no longer
To lands of summer across the sea,

So dear a life your arms enfold
Whose crying is a cry for gold;
   Yet here to-night in this dark city,
When ill and weary, alone and cold,

I found, tho' crush'd to hard and dry,
This nursling of another sky
   Still in the little book you lent me,
And where you tenderly laid it by; 100

And I forgot the clouded Forth,
The gloom that saddens heaven and earth,
   The bitter east, the misty summer
And gray metropolis of the North.

Perchance to lull the throbs of pain,
Perchance to charm a vacant brain,
   Perchance to dream you still beside me,
My fancy fled to the South again.

ODE ON THE DEATH OF THE DUKE OF WELLINGTON

I

Bury the Great Duke
   With an empire's lamentation;
Let us bury the Great Duke
   To the noise of the mourning of a mighty nation;

Mourning when their leaders fall,
Warriors carry the warrior's pall,
And sorrow darkens hamlet and hall.

II

Where shall we lay the man whom we deplore?
Here, in streaming London's central roar.
Let the sound of those he wrought for,   10
And the feet of those he fought for,
Echo round his bones for evermore.

III

Lead out the pageant: sad and slow,
As fits an universal woe,
Let the long, long procession go,
And let the sorrowing crowd about it grow,
And let the mournful martial music blow;
The last great Englishman is low.

IV

Mourn, for to us he seems the last,
Remembering all his greatness in the past.   20
No more in soldier fashion will he greet
With lifted hand the gazer in the street.
O friends, our chief state-oracle is mute!
Mourn for the man of long-enduring blood,
The statesman-warrior, moderate, resolute,
Whole in himself, a common good.
Mourn for the man of amplest influence,
Yet clearest of ambitious crime,
Our greatest yet with least pretence,
Great in council and great in war,   30
Foremost captain of his time,
Rich in saving common-sense,
And, as the greatest only are,
In his simplicity sublime.
O good gray head which all men knew,

O voice from which their omens all men drew,
O iron nerve to true occasion true,
O fallen at length that tower of strength
Which stood four-square to all the winds that blew!
Such was he whom we deplore.   40
The long self-sacrifice of life is o'er.
The great World-victor's victor will be seen no more.

V

All is over and done.
Render thanks to the Giver,
England, for thy son.
Let the bell be toll'd.
Render thanks to the Giver,
And render him to the mould.
Under the cross of gold
That shines over city and river,   50
There he shall rest for ever
Among the wise and the bold.
Let the bell be toll'd,
And a reverent people behold
The towering car, the sable steeds.
Bright let it be with its blazon'd deeds,
Dark in its funeral fold.
Let the bell be toll'd,
And a deeper knell in the heart be knoll'd;
And the sound of the sorrowing anthem roll'd   60
Thro' the dome of the golden cross;
And the volleying cannon thunder his loss;
He knew their voices of old.
For many a time in many a clime
His captain's-ear has heard them boom
Bellowing victory, bellowing doom.
When he with those deep voices wrought,
Guarding realms and kings from shame,
With those deep voices our dead captain taught
The tyrant, and asserts his claim   70

In that dread sound to the great name
Which he has worn so pure of blame,
In praise and in dispraise the same,
A man of well-attemper'd frame.
O civic muse, to such a name,
To such a name for ages long,
To such a name,
Preserve a broad approach of fame,
And ever-echoing avenues of song!

VI

"Who is he that cometh, like an honor'd guest,   80
With banner and with music, with soldier and with priest,
With a nation weeping, and breaking on my rest?"—
Mighty Seaman, this is he
Was great by land as thou by sea.
Thine island loves thee well, thou famous man,
The greatest sailor since our world began.
Now, to the roll of muffled drums,
To thee the greatest soldier comes;
For this is he
Was great by land as thou by sea.   90
His foes were thine; he kept us free;
O, give him welcome, this is he
Worthy of our gorgeous rites,
And worthy to be laid by thee;
For this is England's greatest son,
He that gain'd a hundred fights,
Nor ever lost an English gun;
This is he that far away
Against the myriads of Assaye
Clash'd with his fiery few and won;   100
And underneath another sun,
Warring on a later day,
Round affrighted Lisbon drew
The treble works, the vast designs
Of his labor'd rampart-lines,

Where he greatly stood at bay,
Whence he issued forth anew,
And ever great and greater grew,
Beating from the wasted vines
Back to France her banded swarms,   110
Back to France with countless blows,
Till o'er the hills her eagles flew
Beyond the Pyrenean pines,
Follow'd up in valley and glen
With blare of bugle, clamor of men,
Roll of cannon and clash of arms,
And England pouring on her foes.
Such a war had such a close.
Again their ravening eagle rose
In anger, wheel'd on Europe-shadowing wings,   120
And barking for the thrones of kings;
Till one that sought but Duty's iron crown
On that loud Sabbath shook the spoiler down;
A day of onsets of despair!
Dash'd on every rocky square,
Their surging charges foam'd themselves away;
Last, the Prussian trumpet blew;
Thro' the long-tormented air
Heaven flash'd a sudden jubilant ray,
And down we swept and charged and overthrew.   130
So great a soldier taught us there
What long-enduring hearts could do
In that world-earthquake, Waterloo!
Mighty Seaman, tender and true,
And pure as he from taint of craven guile,
O saviour of the silver-coasted isle,
O shaker of the Baltic and the Nile,
If aught of things that here befall
Touch a spirit among things divine,
If love of country move thee there at all,   140
Be glad, because his bones are laid by thine
And thro' the centuries let a people's voice

In full acclaim,
A people's voice,
The proof and echo of all human fame,
A people's voice, when they rejoice
At civic revel and pomp and game,
Attest their great commander's claim
With honor, honor, honor, honor to him,
Eternal honor to his name.   150

VII

A people's voice! we are a people yet.
Tho' all men else their nobler dreams forget,
Confused by brainless mobs and lawless Powers,
Thank Him who isled us here, and roughly set
His Briton in blown seas and storming showers,
We have a voice with which to pay the debt
Of boundless love and reverence and regret
To those great men who fought, and kept it ours.
And keep it ours, O God, from brute control!
O Statesmen, guard us, guard the eye, the soul   160
Of Europe, keep our noble England whole,
And save the one true seed of freedom sown
Betwixt a people and their ancient throne,
That sober freedom out of which there springs
Our loyal passion for our temperate kings!
For, saving that, ye help to save mankind
Till public wrong be crumpled into dust,
And drill the raw world for the march of mind,
Till crowds at length be sane and crowns be just.
But wink no more in slothful overtrust.   170
Remember him who led your hosts;
He bade you guard the sacred coasts.
Your cannons moulder on the seaward wall;
His voice is silent in your council-hall
For ever; and whatever tempests lour
For ever silent; even if they broke
In thunder, silent; yet remember all

He spoke among you, and the Man who spoke;
Who never sold the truth to serve the hour,
Nor palter'd with Eternal God for power;   180
Who let the turbid streams of rumor flow
Thro' either babbling world of high and low;
Whose life was work, whose language rife
With rugged maxims hewn from life;
Who never spoke against a foe;
Whose eighty winters freeze with one rebuke
All great self-seekers trampling on the right.
Truth-teller was our England's Alfred named;
Truth-lover was our English Duke;
Whatever record leap to light   190
He never shall be shamed.

VIII

Lo! the leader in these glorious wars
Now to glorious burial slowly borne,
Follow'd by the brave of other lands,
He, on whom from both her open hands
Lavish Honor shower'd all her stars,
And affluent Fortune emptied all her horn.
Yea, let all good things await
Him who cares not to be great
But as he saves or serves the state.   200
Not once or twice in our rough island-story
The path of duty was the way to glory.
He that walks it, only thirsting
For the right, and learns to deaden
Love of self, before his journey closes,
He shall find the stubborn thistle bursting
Into glossy purples, which outredden
All voluptuous garden-roses.
Not once or twice in our fair island-story
The path of duty was the way to glory.   210
He, that ever following her commands,
On with toil of heart and knees and hands,

Thro' the long gorge to the far light has won
His path upward, and prevail'd,
Shall find the toppling crags of Duty scaled
Are close upon the shining table-lands
To which our God Himself is moon and sun.
Such was he: his work is done.
But while the races of mankind endure
Let his great example stand   220
Colossal, seen of every land,
And keep the soldier firm, the statesman pure;
Till in all lands and thro' all human story
The path of duty be the way to glory.
And let the land whose hearths he saved from shame
For many and many an age proclaim
At civic revel and pomp and game,
And when the long-illumined cities flame,
Their ever-loyal iron leader's fame,
With honor, honor, honor, honor to him,   230
Eternal honor to his name.

IX

Peace, his triumph will be sung
By some yet unmoulded tongue
Far on in summers that we shall not see.
Peace, it is a day of pain
For one about whose patriarchal knee
Late the little children clung.
O peace, it is a day of pain
For one upon whose hand and heart and brain
Once the weight and fate of Europe hung.   240
Ours the pain, be his the gain!
More than is of man's degree
Must be with us, watching here
At this, our great solemnity.
Whom we see not we revere;
We revere, and we refrain

From talk of battles loud and vain,
And brawling memories all too free
For such a wise humility
As befits a solemn fane: 250
We revere, and while we hear
The tides of Music's golden sea
Setting toward eternity,
Uplifted high in heart and hope are we,
Until we doubt not that for one so true
There must be other nobler work to do
Than when he fought at Waterloo,
And Victor he must ever be.
For tho' the Giant Ages heave the hill
And break the shore, and evermore   260
Make and break, and work their will,
Tho' world on world in myriad myriads roll
Round us, each with different powers,
And other forms of life than ours,
What know we greater than the soul?
On God and Godlike men we build our trust.
Hush, the Dead March wails in the people's ears;
The dark crowd moves, and there are sobs and tears;
The black earth yawns; the mortal disappears;
Ashes to ashes, dust to dust;   270
He is gone who seem'd so great.—
Gone, but nothing can bereave him
Of the force he made his own
Being here, and we believe him
Something far advanced in State,
And that he wears a truer crown
Than any wreath that man can weave him.
Speak no more of his renown,
Lay your earthly fancies down,
And in the vast cathedral leave him,   280
God accept him, Christ receive him!

1852.

THE CHARGE OF THE LIGHT BRIGADE

I

Half a league, half a league,
Half a league onward,
All in the valley of Death
  Rode the six hundred.
"Forward the Light Brigade!
Charge for the guns!" he said.
Into the valley of Death
  Rode the six hundred.

II

"Forward, the Light Brigade!"
Was there a man dismay'd? 10
Not tho' the soldier knew
  Some one had blunder'd.
Theirs not to make reply,
Theirs not to reason why,
Theirs but to do and die.
Into the valley of Death
  Rode the six hundred.

III

Cannon to right of them,
Cannon to left of them,
Cannon in front of them 20
  Volley'd and thunder'd;
Storm'd at with shot and shell,
Boldly they rode and well,
Into the jaws of Death,
Into the mouth of hell
  Rode the six hundred.

IV

Flash'd all their sabres bare,
Flash'd as they turn'd in air
Sabring the gunners there,
Charging an army, while   30
   All the world wonder'd.
Plunged in the battery-smoke
Right thro' the line they broke;
Cossack and Russian
Reel'd from the sabre-stroke
   Shatter'd and sunder'd.
Then they rode back, but not,
   Not the six hundred.

V

Cannon to right of them,
Cannon to left of them,   40
Cannon behind them
   Volley'd and thunder'd;
Storm'd at with shot and shell,
While horse and hero fell,
They that had fought so well
Came thro' the jaws of Death,
Back from the mouth of hell,
All that was left of them,
   Left of six hundred.

VI

When can their glory fade?   50
O the wild charge they made!
   All the world wonder'd.
Honor the charge they made!
Honor the Light Brigade,
   Noble six hundred!

FROM IDYLLS OF THE KING

IN TWELVE BOOKS

"Flos Regum Arthurus."—JOSEPH OF EXETER

The poet became interested in the Arthurian story long before the first series of the "Idylls" was published. "The Lady of Shalott," which appeared in 1832, is founded upon the legend which was later made the subject of "Lancelot and Elaine." "The Palace of Art" in the same volume contained an allusion to "that deep-wounded child of Pendragon," or "mythic Uther's deeply wounded son," as it now reads. "Sir Galahad" and "Sir Lancelot and Queen Guinevere" were printed in 1842, when the "Morte d'Arthur" was also given to the world. This latter poem, afterwards incorporated in "The Passing of Arthur," must have been written as early as 1835, when Fitzgerald heard it read from manuscript ("Memoir," vol. i. p. 194). Landor also writes under date of December 9, 1837: "Yesterday a Mr. Moreton, a young man of rare judgment, read to me a manuscript by Mr. Tennyson, very different in style from his printed poems. The subject is the death of Arthur. It is more Homeric than any poem of our time, and rivals some of the noblest parts of the Odyssea" (Forster's "Life of Landor," ii. 323).

The first instalment of the "Idylls" as finally published in July, 1859, included "Enid," "Vivien," "Elaine," and "Guinevere," as they were then entitled. Ten thousand copies were sold in about six weeks, and the critics were almost unanimous in their praise of the book. Among its warmest admirers was Prince Albert, who sent his copy to the poet, asking him to write his name in it. The note continued:—

"You would thus add a peculiar interest to the book containing those beautiful songs, from the perusal of which I derived the greatest enjoyment. They quite rekindle the feeling with which the legends of King Arthur must have inspired the chivalry of old, whilst the graceful form in which they are presented blends those feelings with the softer tone of our present age."

In 1862, a new edition of the "Idylls" appeared, with the dedication to the memory of the Prince, who died in December, 1861.

In 1869, four more Idylls were brought out,—"The Coming of Arthur," "The Holy Grail," "Pelleas and Ettarre," and "The Passing of Arthur," in which, as already mentioned, the "Morte d'Arthur" of 1842 is incorporated.

In 1872, "The Last Tournament" (contributed to the "Contemporary Review" for December, 1871) and "Gareth and Lynette" appeared; and in 1885 "Balin and Balan," the last of the series, was included in "Tiresias and Other Poems."

In 1884, "Enid," already entitled "Geraint and Enid," was divided into two parts (numbered I. and II.), and in 1888 these parts received their present titles. The poems were now described as "twelve books," and arranged in the order in which the author intended they should be read.

THE COMING OF ARTHUR

Leodogran, the king of Cameliard,
Had one fair daughter, and none other child;
And she was fairest of all flesh on earth,
Guinevere, and in her his one delight.

For many a petty king ere Arthur came
Ruled in this isle and, ever waging war
Each upon other, wasted all the land;
And still from time to time the heathen host
Swarm'd over-seas, and harried what was left.
And so there grew great tracts of wilderness,   10
Wherein the beast was ever more and more,
But man was less and less, till Arthur came.
For first Aurelius lived and fought and died,
And after him King Uther fought and died,
But either fail'd to make the kingdom one.
And after these King Arthur for a space,
And thro' the puissance of his Table Round,
Drew all their petty princedoms under him,
Their king and head, and made a realm and reign'd.

And thus the land of Cameliard was waste,   20
Thick with wet woods, and many a beast therein,
And none or few to scare or chase the beast;

So that wild dog and wolf and boar and bear
Came night and day, and rooted in the fields,
And wallow'd in the gardens of the King.
And ever and anon the wolf would steal
The children and devour, but now and then,
Her own brood lost or dead, lent her fierce teat
To human sucklings; and the children, housed
In her foul den, there at their meat would growl,   30
And mock their foster-mother on four feet,
Till, straighten'd, they grew up to wolf-like men,
Worse than the wolves. And King Leodogran
Groan'd for the Roman legions here again
And Cæsar's eagle. Then his brother king,
Urien, assail'd him; last a heathen horde,
Reddening the sun with smoke and earth with blood,
And on the spike that split the mother's heart
Spitting the child, brake on him, till, amazed,
He knew not whither he should turn for aid.   40

But—for he heard of Arthur newly crown'd,
Tho' not without an uproar made by those
Who cried, "He is not Uther's son"—the King
Sent to him, saying, "Arise, and help us thou!
For here between the man and beast we die."

And Arthur yet had done no deed of arms,
But heard the call and came; and Guinevere
Stood by the castle walls to watch him pass;
But since he neither wore on helm or shield
The golden symbol of his kinglihood,   50
But rode a simple knight among his knights,
And many of these in richer arms than he,
She saw him not, or mark'd not, if she saw,
One among many, tho' his face was bare.
But Arthur, looking downward as he past,
Felt the light of her eyes into his life
Smite on the sudden, yet rode on, and pitch'd

His tents beside the forest. Then he drave
The heathen; after, slew the beast, and fell'd
The forest, letting in the sun, and made   60
Broad pathways for the hunter and the knight,
And so return'd.

    For while he linger'd there,
A doubt that ever smoulder'd in the hearts
Of those great lords and barons of his realm
Flash'd forth and into war; for most of these,
Colleaguing with a score of petty kings,
Made head against him, crying: "Who is he
That he should rule us? who hath proven him
King Uther's son? for lo! we look at him,
And find nor face nor bearing, limbs nor voice,   70
Are like to those of Uther whom we knew.
This is the son of Gorloïs, not the King;
This is the son of Anton, not the King."

 And Arthur, passing thence to battle, felt
Travail, and throes and agonies of the life,
Desiring to be join'd with Guinevere,
And thinking as he rode: "Her father said
That there between the man and beast they die.
Shall I not lift her from this land of beasts
Up to my throne and side by side with me?   80
What happiness to reign a lonely king,
Vext—O ye stars that shudder over me,
O earth that soundest hollow under me,
Vext with waste dreams? for saving I be join'd
To her that is the fairest under heaven,
I seem as nothing in the mighty world,
And cannot will my will nor work my work
Wholly, nor make myself in mine own realm
Victor and lord. But were I join'd with her,
Then might we live together as one life,   90
And reigning with one will in everything

Have power on this dark land to lighten it,
And power on this dead world to make it live."

   Thereafter—as he speaks who tells the tale—
When Arthur reach'd a field of battle bright
With pitch'd pavilions of his foe, the world
Was all so clear about him that he saw
The smallest rock far on the faintest hill,
And even in high day the morning star.
So when the King had set his banner broad,   100
At once from either side, with trumpet-blast,
And shouts, and clarions shrilling unto blood,
The long-lanced battle let their horses run.
And now the barons and the kings prevail'd,
And now the King, as here and there that war
Went swaying; but the Powers who walk the world
Made lightnings and great thunders over him,
And dazed all eyes, till Arthur by main might,
And mightier of his hands with every blow,
And leading all his knighthood threw the kings,   110
Carádos, Urien, Cradlemont of Wales,
Claudius, and Clariance of Northumberland,
The King Brandagoras of Latangor,
With Anguisant of Erin, Morganore,
And Lot of Orkney. Then, before a voice
As dreadful as the shout of one who sees
To one who sins, and deems himself alone
And all the world asleep, they swerved and brake
Flying, and Arthur call'd to stay the brands
That hack'd among the flyers, "Ho! they yield!"   120
So like a painted battle the war stood
Silenced, the living quiet as the dead,
And in the heart of Arthur joy was lord.
He laugh'd upon his warrior whom he loved
And honor'd most. "Thou dost not doubt me King,
So well thine arm hath wrought for me to-day."
"Sir and my liege," he cried, "the fire of God

Descends upon thee in the battle-field.
I know thee for my King!" Whereat the two,
For each had warded either in the fight,   130
Sware on the field of death a deathless love.
And Arthur said, "Man's word is God in man;
Let chance what will, I trust thee to the death."

Then quickly from the foughten field he sent
Ulfius, and Brastias, and Bedivere,
His new-made knights, to King Leodogran,
Saying, "If I in aught have served thee well,
Give me thy daughter Guinevere to wife."

Whom when he heard, Leodogran in heart
Debating—"How should I that am a king,   140
However much he holp me at my need,
Give my one daughter saving to a king,
And a king's son?"—lifted his voice, and call'd
A hoary man, his chamberlain, to whom
He trusted all things, and of him required
His counsel: "Knowest thou aught of Arthur's birth?"

Then spake the hoary chamberlain and said:
"Sir King, there be but two old men that know;
And each is twice as old as I; and one
Is Merlin, the wise man that ever served   150
King Uther thro' his magic art, and one
Is Merlin's master—so they call him—Bleys,
Who taught him magic; but the scholar ran
Before the master, and so far that Bleys
Laid magic by, and sat him down, and wrote
All things and whatsoever Merlin did
In one great annal-book, where after-years
Will learn the secret of our Arthur's birth."

To whom the King Leodogran replied:
"O friend, had I been holpen half as well   160

By this King Arthur as by thee to-day,
Then beast and man had had their share of me;
But summon here before us yet once more
Ulfius, and Brastias, and Bedivere."

Then, when they came before him, the king said:
"I have seen the cuckoo chased by lesser fowl,
And reason in the chase; but wherefore now
Do these your lords stir up the heat of war,
Some calling Arthur born of Gorloïs,
Others of Anton? Tell me, ye yourselves,   170
Hold ye this Arthur for King Uther's son?"

And Ulfius and Brastias answer'd, "Ay."
Then Bedivere, the first of all his knights
Knighted by Arthur at his crowning, spake—
For bold in heart and act and word was he,
Whenever slander breathed against the King—

"Sir, there be many rumors on this head;
For there be those who hate him in their hearts,
Call him baseborn, and since his ways are sweet,
And theirs are bestial, hold him less than man;   180
And there be those who deem him more than man,
And dream he dropt from heaven. But my belief
In all this matter—so ye care to learn—
Sir, for ye know that in King Uther's time
The prince and warrior Gorloïs, he that held
Tintagil castle by the Cornish sea,
Was wedded with a winsome wife, Ygerne.
And daughters had she borne him,—one whereof,
Lot's wife, the Queen of Orkney, Bellicent,
Hath ever like a loyal sister cleaved   190
To Arthur,—but a son she had not borne.
And Uther cast upon her eyes of love;
But she, a stainless wife to Gorloïs,
So loathed the bright dishonor of his love

That Gorloïs and King Uther went to war,
And overthrown was Gorloïs and slain.
Then Uther in his wrath and heat besieged
Ygerne within Tintagil, where her men,
Seeing the mighty swarm about their walls,
Left her and fled, and Uther enter'd in,   200
And there was none to call to but himself.
So, compass'd by the power of the king,
Enforced she was to wed him in her tears,
And with a shameful swiftness; afterward,
Not many moons, King Uther died himself,
Moaning and wailing for an heir to rule
After him, lest the realm should go to wrack.
And that same night, the night of the new year,
By reason of the bitterness and grief
That vext his mother, all before his time   210
Was Arthur born, and all as soon as born
Deliver'd at a secret postern-gate
To Merlin, to be holden far apart
Until his hour should come, because the lords
Of that fierce day were as the lords of this,
Wild beasts, and surely would have torn the child
Piecemeal among them, had they known; for each
But sought to rule for his own self and hand,
And many hated Uther for the sake
Of Gorloïs. Wherefore Merlin took the child,   220
And gave him to Sir Anton, an old knight
And ancient friend of Uther; and his wife
Nursed the young prince, and rear'd him with her own;
And no man knew. And ever since the lords
Have foughten like wild beasts among themselves,
So that the realm has gone to wrack; but now,
This year, when Merlin—for his hour had come—
Brought Arthur forth, and set him in the hall,
Proclaiming, 'Here is Uther's heir, your king,'
A hundred voices cried: 'Away with him!   230
No king of ours! a son of Gorloïs he,

Or else the child of Anton, and no king,
Or else baseborn.' Yet Merlin thro' his craft,
And while the people clamor'd for a king,
Had Arthur crown'd; but after, the great lords
Banded, and so brake out in open war."

Then while the king debated with himself
If Arthur were the child of shamefulness,
Or born the son of Gorloïs after death,
Or Uther's son and born before his time.   240
Or whether there were truth in anything
Said by these three, there came to Cameliard,
With Gawain and young Modred, her two sons,
Lot's wife, the Queen of Orkney, Bellicent;
Whom as he could, not as he would, the king
Made feast for, saying, as they sat at meat:
"A doubtful throne is ice on summer seas.
Ye come from Arthur's court. Victor his men
Report him! Yea, but ye—think ye this king—
So many those that hate him, and so strong,   250
So few his knights, however brave they be—
Hath body enow to hold his foemen down?"

"O King," she cried, "and I will tell thee: few,
Few, but all brave, all of one mind with him;
For I was near him when the savage yells
Of Uther's peerage died, and Arthur sat
Crowned on the daïs, and his warriors cried,
'Be thou the king, and we will work thy will
Who love thee.' Then the King in low deep tones,
And simple words of great authority,   260
Bound them by so strait vows to his own self
That when they rose, knighted from kneeling, some
Were pale as at the passing of a ghost,
Some flush'd, and others dazed, as one who wakes
Half-blinded at the coming of a light.

"But when he spake, and cheer'd his Table Round
With large, divine, and comfortable words,
Beyond my tongue to tell thee—I beheld
From eye to eye thro' all their Order flash
A momentary likeness of the King; 270
And ere it left their faces, thro' the cross
And those around it and the Crucified,
Down from the casement over Arthur, smote
Flame-color, vert, and azure, in three rays,
One falling upon each of three fair queens
Who stood in silence near his throne, the friends
Of Arthur, gazing on him, tall, with bright
Sweet faces, who will help him at his need.

"And there I saw mage Merlin, whose vast wit
And hundred winters are but as the hands 280
Of loyal vassals toiling for their liege.

"And near him stood the Lady of the Lake,
Who knows a subtler magic than his own—
Clothed in white samite, mystic, wonderful.
She gave the King his huge cross-hilted sword,
Whereby to drive the heathen out. A mist
Of incense curl'd about her, and her face
Wellnigh was hidden in the minster gloom;
But there was heard among the holy hymns
A voice as of the waters, for she dwells 290
Down in a deep—calm, whatsoever storms
May shake the world—and when the surface rolls,
Hath power to walk the waters like our Lord.

"There likewise I beheld Excalibur
Before him at his crowning borne, the sword
That rose from out the bosom of the lake,
And Arthur row'd across and took it—rich
With jewels, elfin Urim, on the hilt,

Bewildering heart and eye—the blade so bright
That men are blinded by it—on one side,   300
Graven in the oldest tongue of all this world,
'Take me,' but turn the blade and ye shall see,
And written in the speech ye speak yourself,
'Cast me away!' And sad was Arthur's face
Taking it, but old Merlin counsell'd him,
'Take thou and strike! the time to cast away
Is yet far-off.' So this great brand the king
Took, and by this will beat his foemen down."

Thereat Leodogran rejoiced, but thought
To sift his doubtings to the last, and ask'd,   310
Fixing full eyes of question on her face,
"The swallow and the swift are near akin,
But thou art closer to this noble prince,
Being his own dear sister;" and she said,
"Daughter of Gorloïs and Ygerne am I;"
"And therefore Arthur's sister?" ask'd the king.
She answer'd, "These be secret things," and sign'd
To those two sons to pass, and let them be.
And Gawain went, and breaking into song
Sprang out, and follow'd by his flying hair   320
Ran like a colt, and leapt at all he saw;
But Modred laid his ear beside the doors,
And there half-heard—the same that afterward
Struck for the throne, and striking found his doom.

And then the Queen made answer: "What know I?
For dark my mother was in eyes and hair,
And dark in hair and eyes am I; and dark
Was Gorloïs; yea, and dark was Uther too,
Wellnigh to blackness; but this king is fair
Beyond the race of Britons and of men.   330
Moreover, always in my mind I hear
A cry from out the dawning of my life,
A mother weeping, and I hear her say,

'O that ye had some brother, pretty one,
To guard thee on the rough ways of the world.' "

"Ay," said the king, "and hear ye such a cry?
But when did Arthur chance upon thee first?"

"O King!" she cried, "and I will tell thee true.
He found me first when yet a little maid.
Beaten I had been for a little fault   340
Whereof I was not guilty; and out I ran
And flung myself down on a bank of heath,
And hated this fair world and all therein,
And wept, and wish'd that I were dead; and he—
I know not whether of himself he came,
Or brought by Merlin, who, they say, can walk
Unseen at pleasure—he was at my side,
And spake sweet words, and comforted my heart,
And dried my tears, being a child with me.
And many a time he came, and evermore   350
As I grew greater grew with me; and sad
At times he seem'd, and sad with him was I,
Stern too at times, and then I loved him not,
But sweet again, and then I loved him well.
And now of late I see him less and less,
But those first days had golden hours for me,
For then I surely thought he would be king.

"But let me tell thee now another tale:
For Bleys, our Merlin's master, as they say,
Died but of late, and sent his cry to me,   360
To hear him speak before he left his life.
Shrunk like a fairy changeling lay the mage;
And when I enter'd told me that himself
And Merlin ever served about the king,
Uther, before he died; and on the night
When Uther in Tintagil past away
Moaning and wailing for an heir, the two

Left the still king, and passing forth to breathe,
Then from the castle gateway by the chasm
Descending thro' the dismal night—a night   370
In which the bounds of heaven and earth were lost—
Beheld, so high upon the dreary deeps
It seem'd in heaven, a ship, the shape thereof
A dragon wing'd, and all from stem to stern
Bright with a shining people on the decks,
And gone as soon as seen. And then the two
Dropt to the cove, and watch'd the great sea fall,
Wave after wave, each mightier than the last,
Till last, a ninth one, gathering half the deep
And full of voices, slowly rose and plunged   380
Roaring, and all the wave was in a flame;
And down the wave and in the flame was borne
A naked babe, and rode to Merlin's feet,
Who stoopt and caught the babe, and cried, 'The King!
Here is an heir for Uther!' And the fringe
Of that great breaker, sweeping up the strand,
Lash'd at the wizard as he spake the word,
And all at once all round him rose in fire,
So that the child and he were clothed in fire.
And presently thereafter follow'd calm,   390
Free sky and stars. 'And this same child,' he said,
'Is he who reigns; nor could I part in peace
Till this were told.' And saying this the seer
Went thro' the strait and dreadful pass of death,
Not ever to be question'd any more
Save on the further side; but when I met
Merlin, and ask'd him if these things were truth—
The shining dragon and the naked child
Descending in the glory of the seas—
He laugh'd as is his wont, and answer'd me   400
In riddling triplets of old time, and said:—

    " 'Rain, rain, and sun! a rainbow in the sky!
    A young man will be wiser by and by;
    An old man's wit may wander ere he die.

" 'Rain, rain, and sun! a rainbow on the lea!
And truth is this to me, and that to thee;
And truth or clothed or naked let it be.

" 'Rain, sun, and rain! and the free blossom blows;
Sun, rain, and sun! and where is he who knows?
From the great deep to the great deep he goes.' 410

"So Merlin riddling anger'd me; but thou
Fear not to give this King thine only child,
Guinevere; so great bards of him will sing
Hereafter, and dark sayings from of old
Ranging and ringing thro' the minds of men,
And echo'd by old folk beside their fires
For comfort after their wage-work is done,
Speak of the King; and Merlin in our time
Hath spoken also, not in jest, and sworn
Tho' men may wound him that he will not die, 420
But pass, again to come, and then or now
Utterly smite the heathen underfoot,
Till these and all men hail him for their king."

She spake and King Leodogran rejoiced,
But musing "Shall I answer yea or nay?"
Doubted, and drowsed, nodded and slept, and saw,
Dreaming, a slope of land that ever grew,
Field after field, up to a height, the peak
Haze-hidden, and thereon a phantom king,
Now looming, and now lost; and on the slope 430
The sword rose, the hind fell, the herd was driven,
Fire glimpsed; and all the land from roof and rick,
In drifts of smoke before a rolling wind,
Stream'd to the peak, and mingled with the haze
And made it thicker; while the phantom king
Sent out at times a voice; and here or there
Stood one who pointed toward the voice, the rest
Slew on and burnt, crying, "No king of ours,

No son of Uther, and no king of ours;"
Till with a wink his dream was changed, the haze   440
Descended, and the solid earth became
As nothing, but the King stood out in heaven,
Crown'd. And Leodogran awoke, and sent
Ulfius, and Brastias, and Bedivere,
Back to the court of Arthur answering yea.

    Then Arthur charged his warrior whom he loved
And honor'd most, Sir Lancelot, to ride forth
And bring the Queen, and watch'd him from the gates;
And Lancelot past away among the flowers—
For then was latter April—and return'd   450
Among the flowers, in May, with Guinevere.
To whom arrived, by Dubric the high saint,
Chief of the church in Britain, and before
The stateliest of her altar-shrines, the King
That morn was married, while in stainless white,
The fair beginners of a nobler time,
And glorying in their vows and him, his knights
Stood round him, and rejoicing in his joy.
Far shone the fields of May thro' open door,
The sacred altar blossom'd white with May,   460
The sun of May descended on their King,
They gazed on all earth's beauty in their Queen,
Roll'd incense, and there past along the hymns
A voice as of the waters, while the two
Sware at the shrine of Christ a deathless love.
And Arthur said, "Behold, thy doom is mine.
Let chance what will, I love thee to the death!"
To whom the Queen replied with drooping eyes,
"King and my lord, I love thee to the death!"
And holy Dubric spread his hands and spake: 470
"Reign ye, and live and love, and make the world
Other, and may thy Queen be one with thee,
And all this Order of thy Table Round
Fulfil the boundless purpose of their King!"

So Dubric said; but when they left the shrine
Great lords from Rome before the portal stood,
In scornful stillness gazing as they past;
Then while they paced a city all on fire
With sun and cloth of gold, the trumpets blew,
And Arthur's knighthood sang before the King:—   480

"Blow trumpet, for the world is white with May!
Blow trumpet, the long night hath roll'd away!
Blow thro' the living world—'Let the King reign!'

"Shall Rome or Heathen rule in Arthur's realm?
Flash brand and lance, fall battle-axe upon helm,
Fall battle-axe, and flash brand! Let the King reign!

"Strike for the King and live! his knights have heard
That God hath told the King a secret word.
Fall battle-axe, and flash brand! Let the King reign!

"Blow trumpet! he will lift us from the dust.   490
Blow trumpet! live the strength, and die the lust!
Clang battle-axe, and clash brand! Let the King reign!

"Strike for the King and die! and if thou diest,
The King is king, and ever wills the highest.
Clang battle-axe, and clash brand! Let the King reign!

"Blow, for our Sun is mighty in his May!
Blow, for our Sun is mightier day by day!
Clang battle-axe, and clash brand! Let the King reign!

"The King will follow Christ, and we the King,
In whom high God hath breathed a secret thing.   500
Fall battle-axe, and clash brand! Let the King reign!"

So sang the knighthood, moving to their hall.
There at the banquet those great lords from Rome,

The slowly-fading mistress of the world,
Strode in and claim'd their tribute as of yore.
But Arthur spake: 'Behold, for these have sworn
To wage my wars, and worship me their King;
The old order changeth, yielding place to new,
And we that fight for our fair father Christ,
Seeing that ye be grown too weak and old   510
To drive the heathen from your Roman wall,
No tribute will we pay.' So those great lords
Drew back in wrath, and Arthur strove with Rome.

And Arthur and his knighthood for a space
Were all one will, and thro' that strength the King
Drew in the petty princedoms under him,
Fought, and in twelve great battles overcame
The heathen hordes, and made a realm and reign'd.

THE LAST TOURNAMENT

Dagonet, the fool, whom Gawain in his mood
Had made mock-knight of Arthur's Table Round,
At Camelot, high above the yellowing woods,
Danced like a wither'd leaf before the hall.
And toward him from the hall, with harp in hand,
And from the crown thereof a carcanet
Of ruby swaying to and fro, the prize
Of Tristram in the jousts of yesterday,
Came Tristram, saying, "Why skip ye so, Sir Fool?"

For Arthur and Sir Lancelot riding once   10
Far down beneath a winding wall of rock
Heard a child wail. A stump of oak half-dead,
From roots like some black coil of carven snakes,
Clutch'd at the crag, and started thro' mid air
Bearing an eagle's nest; and thro' the tree

Rush'd ever a rainy wind, and thro' the wind
Pierced ever a child's cry; and crag and tree
Scaling, Sir Lancelot from the perilous nest,
This ruby necklace thrice around her neck,
And all unscarr'd from beak or talon, brought   20
A maiden babe, which Arthur pitying took,
Then gave it to his Queen to rear. The Queen,
But coldly acquiescing, in her white arms
Received, and after loved it tenderly,
And named it Nestling; so forgot herself
A moment, and her cares; till that young life
Being smitten in mid heaven with mortal cold
Past from her, and in time the carcanet
Vext her with plaintive memories of the child.
So she, delivering it to Arthur, said,   30
"Take thou the jewels of this dead innocence,
And make them, an thou wilt, a tourney-prize."

  To whom the King: "Peace to thine eagle-borne
Dead nestling, and this honor after death,
Following thy will! but, O my Queen, I muse
Why ye not wear on arm, or neck, or zone
Those diamonds that I rescued from the tarn,
And Lancelot won, methought, for thee to wear."

  "Would rather you had let them fall," she cried,
"Plunge and be lost—ill-fated as they were,   40
A bitterness to me!—ye look amazed,
Not knowing they were lost as soon as given—
Slid from my hands when I was leaning out
Above the river—that unhappy child
Past in her barge; but rosier luck will go
With these rich jewels, seeing that they came
Not from the skeleton of a brother-slayer,
But the sweet body of a maiden babe.
Perchance—who knows?—the purest of thy knights
May win them for the purest of my maids."   50

She ended, and the cry of a great jousts
With trumpet-blowings ran on all the ways
From Camelot in among the faded fields
To furthest towers; and everywhere the knights
Arm'd for a day of glory before the King.

But on the hither side of that loud morn
Into the hall stagger'd, his visage ribb'd
From ear to ear with dogwhip-weals, his nose
Bridge-broken, one eye out, and one hand off,
And one with shatter'd fingers dangling lame,   60
A churl, to whom indignantly the King:

"My churl, for whom Christ died, what evil beast
Hath drawn his claws athwart thy face? or fiend?
Man was it who marr'd heaven's image in thee thus?"

Then, sputtering thro' the hedge of splinter'd teeth,
Yet strangers to the tongue, and with blunt stump
Pitch-blacken'd sawing the air, said the maim'd churl:

"He took them and he drave them to his tower—
Some hold he was a table-knight of thine—
A hundred goodly ones—the Red Knight, he—   70
Lord, I was tending swine, and the Red Knight
Brake in upon me and drave them to his tower;
And when I call'd upon thy name as one
That doest right by gentle and by churl,
Maim'd me and maul'd, and would outright have slain,
Save that he sware me to a message, saying:
'Tell thou the King and all his liars that I
Have founded my Round Table in the North,
And whatsoever his own knights have sworn
My knights have sworn the counter to it—and say   80
My tower is full of harlots, like his court,
But mine are worthier, seeing they profess
To be none other than themselves—and say

My knights are all adulterers like his own,
But mine are truer, seeing they profess
To be none other; and say his hour is come,
The heathen are upon him, his long lance
Broken, and his Excalibur a straw.'"

    Then Arthur turn'd to Kay the seneschal:
"Take thou my churl, and tend him curiously   90
Like a king's heir, till all his hurts be whole.
The heathen—but that ever-climbing wave,
Hurl'd back again so often in empty foam,
Hath lain for years at rest—and renegades,
Thieves, bandits, leavings of confusion, whom
The wholesome realm is purged of otherwhere,
Friends, thro' your manhood and your fealty,—now
Make their last head like Satan in the North.
My younger knights, new-made, in whom your flower
Waits to be solid fruit of golden deeds,   100
Move with me toward their quelling, which achieved,
The loneliest ways are safe from shore to shore.
But thou, Sir Lancelot, sitting in my place
Enchair'd to-morrow, arbitrate the field;
For wherefore shouldst thou care to mingle with it,
Only to yield my Queen her own again?
Speak, Lancelot, thou are silent; is it well?"

    Thereto Sir Lancelot answer'd: "It is well;
Yet better if the King abide, and leave
The leading of his younger knights to me.   110
Else, for the King has will'd it, it is well."

    Then Arthur rose and Lancelot follow'd him,
And while they stood without the doors, the King
Turn'd to him saying: "Is it then so well?
Or mine the blame that oft I seem as he
Of whom was written, 'A sound is in his ears'?
The foot that loiters, bidden go,—the glance

That only seems half-loyal to command,—
A manner somewhat fallen from reverence—
Or have I dream'd the bearing of our knights   120
Tells of a manhood ever less and lower?
Or whence the fear lest this my realm, uprear'd,
By noble deeds at one with noble vows,
From flat confusion and brute violences,
Reel back into the beast, and be no more?"

    He spoke, and taking all his younger knights,
Down the slope city rode, and sharply turn'd
North by the gate. In her high bower the Queen,
Working a tapestry, lifted up her head,
Watch'd her lord pass, and knew not that she sigh'd.   130
Then ran across her memory the strange rhyme
Of bygone Merlin, "Where is he who knows?
From the great deep to the great deep he goes."

    But when the morning of a tournament,
By these in earnest those in mockery call'd
The Tournament of the Dead Innocence,
Brake with a wet wind blowing, Lancelot,
Round whose sick head all night, like birds of prey,
The words of Arthur flying shriek'd, arose,
And down a streetway hung with folds of pure   140
White samite, and by fountains running wine,
Where children sat in white with cups of gold,
Moved to the lists, and there, with slow sad steps
Ascending, fill'd his double-dragon'd chair.

    He glanced and saw the stately galleries,
Dame, damsel, each thro' worship of their Queen
White-robed in honor of the stainless child,
And some with scatter'd jewels, like a bank
Of maiden snow mingled with sparks of fire.
He look'd but once, and vail'd his eyes again.   150

The sudden trumpet sounded as in a dream
To ears but half-awaked, then one low roll
Of autumn thunder, and the jousts began;
And ever the wind blew, and yellowing leaf,
And gloom and gleam, and shower and shorn plume
Went down it. Sighing weariedly, as one
Who sits and gazes on a faded fire,
When all the goodlier guests are past away,
Sat their great umpire looking o'er the lists.
He saw the laws that ruled the tournament   160
Broken, but spake not; once, a knight cast down
Before his throne of arbitration cursed
The dead babe and the follies of the King;
And once the laces of a helmet crack'd,
And show'd him, like a vermin in its hole,
Modred, a narrow face. Anon he heard
The voice that billow'd round the barriers roar
An ocean-sounding welcome to one knight,
But newly-enter'd, taller than the rest,
And armor'd all in forest green, whereon   170
There tript a hundred tiny silver deer,
And wearing but a holly-spray for crest,
With ever scattering berries, and on shield
A spear, a harp, a bugle—Tristram—late
From over-seas in Brittany return'd,
And marriage with a princess of that realm,
Isolt the White—Sir Tristram of the Woods—
Whom Lancelot knew, had held sometime with pain
His own against him, and now yearn'd to shake
The burthen off his heart in one full shock   180
With Tristram even to death. His strong hands gript
And dinted the gilt dragons right and left,
Until he groan'd for wrath—so many of those
That ware their ladies' colors on the casque
Drew from before Sir Tristram to the bounds,
And there with gibes and flickering mockeries
Stood, while he mutter'd, "Craven crests! O shame!

What faith have these in whom they sware to love?
The glory of our Round Table is no more."

So Tristram won, and Lancelot gave, the gems,   190
Not speaking other word than, "Hast thou won?
Art thou the purest, brother? See, the hand
Wherewith thou takest this is red!" to whom
Tristram, half plagued by Lancelot's languorous mood,
Made answer: "Ay, but wherefore toss me this
Like a dry bone cast to some hungry hound?
Let be thy fair Queen's fantasy. Strength of heart
And might of limb, but mainly use and skill,
Are winners in this pastime of our King.
My hand—belike the lance hath dript upon it—   200
No blood of mine, I trow; but O chief knight,
Right arm of Arthur in the battle-field,
Great brother, thou nor I have made the world;
Be happy in thy fair Queen as I in mine."

And Tristram round the gallery made his horse
Caracole; then bow'd his homage, bluntly saying,
"Fair damsels, each to him who worships each
Sole Queen of Beauty and of love, behold
This day my Queen of Beauty is not here."
And most of these were mute, some anger'd, one   210
Murmuring, "All courtesy is dead," and one,
"The glory of our Round Table is no more."

Then fell thick rain, plume droopt and mantle clung,
And pettish cries awoke, and the wan day
Went glooming down in wet and weariness;
But under her black brows a swarthy one
Laugh'd shrilly, crying: "Praise the patient saints,
Our one white day of Innocence hath past,
Tho' somewhat draggled at the skirt. So be it.
The snowdrop only, flowering thro' the year,   220
Would make the world as blank as winter-tide.

Come—let us gladden their sad eyes, our Queen's
And Lancelot's, at this night's solemnity
With all the kindlier colors of the field."

So dame and damsel glitter'd at the feast
Variously gay; for he that tells the tale
Liken'd them, saying, as when an hour of cold
Falls on the mountain in midsummer snows,
And all the purple slopes of mountain flowers
Pass under white, till the warm hour returns   230
With veer of wind and all are flowers again,
So dame and damsel cast the simple white,
And glowing in all colors, the live grass,
Rose-campion, bluebell, kingcup, poppy, glanced
About the revels, and with mirth so loud
Beyond all use, that, half-amazed, the Queen,
And wroth at Tristram and the lawless jousts,
Brake up their sports, then slowly to her bower
Parted, and in her bosom pain was lord.

And little Dagonet on the morrow morn,   240
High over all the yellowing autumn-tide,
Danced like a wither'd leaf before the hall.
Then Tristram saying, "Why skip ye so, Sir Fool?"
Wheel'd round on either heel, Dagonet replied,
"Belike for lack of wiser company;
Or being fool, and seeing too much wit
Makes the world rotten, why, belike I skip
To know myself the wisest knight of all."
"Ay, fool," said Tristram, "but 't is eating dry
To dance without a catch, a roundelay   250
To dance to." Then he twangled on his harp,
And while he twangled little Dagonet stood
Quiet as any water-sodden log
Stay'd in the wandering warble of a brook,
But when the twangling ended, skipt again;
And being ask'd, "Why skipt ye not, Sir Fool?"

Made answer, "I had liefer twenty years
Skip to the broken music of my brains
Than any broken music thou canst make."
Then Tristram, waiting for the quip to come,   260
"Good now, what music have I broken, fool?"
And little Dagonet, skipping, "Arthur, the King's;
For when thou playest that air with Queen Isolt,
Thou makest broken music with thy bride,
Her daintier namesake down in Brittany—
And so thou breakest Arthur's music too."
"Save for that broken music in thy brains,
Sir Fool," said Tristram, "I would break thy head.
Fool, I came late, the heathen wars were o'er,
The life had flown, we sware but by the shell—   270
I am but a fool to reason with a fool—
Come, thou art crabb'd and sour; but lean me down,
Sir Dagonet, one of thy long asses' ears,
And harken if my music be not true.

        " 'Free love—free field—we love but while we may.
The woods are hush'd, their music is no more;
The leaf is dead, the yearning past away.
New leaf, new life—the days of frost are o'er;
New life, new love, to suit the newer day;
New loves are sweet as those that went before.   280
Free love—free field—we love but while we may.'

     "Ye might have moved slow-measure to my tune,
Not stood stock-still. I made it in the woods,
And heard it ring as true as tested gold."

    But Dagonet with one foot poised in his hand:
"Friend, did ye mark that fountain yesterday,
Made to run wine?—but this had run itself
All out like a long life to a sour end—
And them that round it sat with golden cups

To hand the wine to whosoever came—   290
The twelve small damosels white as Innocence,
In honor of poor Innocence the babe,
Who left the gems which Innocence the Queen
Lent to the King, and Innocence the King
Gave for a prize—and one of those white slips
Handed her cup and piped, the pretty one,
'Drink, drink, Sir Fool,' and thereupon I drank,
Spat—pish—the cup was gold, the draught was mud."

    And Tristram: "Was it muddier than thy gibes?
Is all the laughter gone dead out of thee?—   300
Not marking how the knighthood mock thee, fool—
'Fear God: honor the King—his one true knight—
Sole follower of the vows'—for here be they
Who knew thee swine enow before I came,
Smuttier than blasted grain. But when the King
Had made thee fool, thy vanity so shot up
It frighted all free fool from out thy heart;
Which left thee less than fool, and less than swine,
A naked aught—yet swine I hold thee still,
For I have flung thee pearls and find thee swine."   310

    And little Dagonet mincing with his feet:
"Knight, an ye fling those rubies round my neck
In lieu of hers, I 'll hold thou hast some touch
Of music, since I care not for thy pearls.
Swine? I have wallow'd, I have wash'd—the world
Is flesh and shadow—I have had my day.
The dirty nurse, Experience, in her kind
Hath foul'd me—an I wallow'd, then I wash'd—
I have had my day and my philosophies—
And thank the Lord I am King Arthur's fool.   320
Swine, say ye? swine, goats, asses, rams, and geese
Troop'd round a Paynim harper once, who thrumm'd
On such a wire as musically as thou
Some such fine song—but never a king's fool."

And Tristram, "Then were swine, goats, asses, geese
The wiser fools, seeing thy Paynim bard
Had such a mastery of his mystery
That he could harp his wife up out of hell."

Then Dagonet, turning on the ball of his foot,
"And whither harp'st thou thine? down! and thyself   330
Down! and two more; a helpful harper thou,
That harpest downward! Dost thou know the star
We call the Harp of Arthur up in heaven?"

And Tristram, "Ay, Sir Fool, for when our King
Was victor wellnigh day by day, the knights,
Glorying in each new glory, set his name
High on all hills and in the signs of heaven."

And Dagonet answer'd: "Ay, and when the land
Was freed, and the Queen false, ye set yourself
To babble about him, all to show your wit—   340
And whether he were king by courtesy,
Or king by right—and so went harping down
The black king's highway, got so far and grew
So witty that ye play'd at ducks and drakes
With Arthur's vows on the great lake of fire.
Tuwhoo! do ye see it? do ye see the star?"

"Nay, fool," said Tristram, "not in open day."
And Dagonet: "Nay, nor will; I see it and hear.
It makes a silent music up in heaven,
And I and Arthur and the angels hear,   350
And then we skip." "Lo, fool," he said, "ye talk
Fool's treason; is the King thy brother fool?"
Then little Dagonet clapt his hands and shrill'd:
"Ay, ay, my brother fool, the king of fools!
Conceits himself as God that he can make
Figs out of thistles, silk from bristles, milk

From burning spurge, honey from hornet-combs,
And men from beasts—Long live the king of fools!"

And down the city Dagonet danced away;
But thro' the slowly-mellowing avenues   360
And solitary passes of the wood
Rode Tristram toward Lyonnesse and the west.
Before him fled the face of Queen Isolt
With ruby-circled neck, but evermore
Past, as a rustle or twitter in the wood
Made dull his inner, keen his outer eye
For all that walk'd, or crept, or perch'd, or flew.
Anon the face, as, when a gust hath blown,
Unruffling waters re-collect the shape
Of one that in them sees himself, return'd;   370
But at the slot or fewmets of a deer,
Or even a fallen feather, vanish'd again.

So on for all that day from lawn to lawn
Thro' many a league-long bower he rode. At length
A lodge of intertwisted beechen-boughs,
Furze-cramm'd and bracken-rooft, the which himself
Built for a summer day with Queen Isolt
Against a shower, dark in the golden grove
Appearing, sent his fancy back to where
She lived a moon in that low lodge with him;   380
Till Mark her lord had past, the Cornish King,
With six or seven, when Tristram was away,
And snatch'd her thence, yet, dreading worse than shame
Her warrior Tristram, spake not any word,
But bode his hour, devising wretchedness.

And now that desert lodge to Tristram lookt
So sweet that, halting, in he past and sank
Down on a drift of foliage random-blown;
But could not rest for musing how to smooth
And sleek his marriage over to the queen.   390

Perchance in lone Tintagil far from all
The tonguesters of the court she had not heard.
But then what folly had sent him over-seas
After she left him lonely here? a name?
Was it the name of one in Brittany,
Isolt, the daughter of the king? "Isolt
Of the White Hands" they call'd her: the sweet name
Allured him first, and then the maid herself,
Who served him well with those white hands of hers,
And loved him well, until himself had thought   400
He loved her also, wedded easily,
But left her all as easily, and return'd.
The black-blue Irish hair and Irish eyes
Had drawn him home—what marvel? then he laid
His brows upon the drifted leaf and dream'd.

He seem'd to pace the strand of Brittany
Between Isolt of Britain and his bride,
And show'd them both the ruby-chain, and both
Began to struggle for it, till his queen
Graspt it so hard that all her hand was red.   410
Then cried the Breton, "Look, her hand is red!
These be no rubies, this is frozen blood,
And melts within her hand—her hand is hot
With ill desires, but this I gave thee, look,
Is all as cool and white as any flower."
Follow'd a rush of eagle's wings, and then
A whimpering of the spirit of the child,
Because the twain had spoil'd her carcanet.

He dream'd; but Arthur with a hundred spears
Rode far, till o'er the illimitable reed,   420
And many a glancing plash and sallowy isle,
The wide-wing'd sunset of the misty marsh
Glared on a huge machicolated tower
That stood with open doors, whereout was roll'd
A roar of riot, as from men secure

Amid their marshes, ruffians at their ease
Among their harlot-brides, an evil song.
"Lo there," said one of Arthur's youth, for there,
High on a grim dead tree before the tower,
A goodly brother of the Table Round   430
Swung by the neck; and on the boughs a shield
Showing a shower of blood in a field noir,
And therebeside a horn, inflamed the knights
At that dishonor done the gilded spur,
Till each would clash the shield and blow the horn.
But Arthur waved them back. Alone he rode.
Then at the dry harsh roar of the great horn,
That sent the face of all the marsh aloft
An ever upward-rushing storm and cloud
Of shriek and plume, the Red Knight heard, and all,   440
Even to tipmost lance and topmost helm,
In blood-red armor sallying, howl'd to the King:

   "The teeth of Hell flay bare and gnash thee flat!—
Lo! art thou not that eunuch-hearted king
Who fain had clipt free manhood from the world—
The woman-worshipper? Yea, God's curse, and I!
Slain was the brother of my paramour
By a knight of thine, and I that heard her whine
And snivel, being eunuch-hearted too,
Sware by the scorpion-worm that twists in hell   450
And stings itself to everlasting death,
To hang whatever knight of thine I fought
And tumbled. Art thou king?—Look to thy life!"

   He ended. Arthur knew the voice; the face
Wellnigh was helmet-hidden, and the name
Went wandering somewhere darkling in his mind.
And Arthur deign'd not use of word or sword,
But let the drunkard, as he stretch'd from horse
To strike him, overbalancing his bulk,
Down from the causeway heavily to the swamp   460

Fall, as the crest of some slow-arching wave,
Heard in dead night along that table-shore,
Drops flat, and after the great waters break
Whitening for half a league, and thin themselves,
Far over sands marbled with moon and cloud,
From less and less to nothing; thus he fell
Head-heavy. Then the knights, who watch'd him, roar'd
And shouted and leapt down upon the fallen,
There trampled out his face from being known,
And sank his head in mire, and slimed themselves;   470
Nor heard the King for their own cries, but sprang
Thro' open doors, and swording right and left
Men, women, on their sodden faces, hurl'd
The tables over and the wines, and slew
Till all the rafters rang with woman-yells,
And all the pavement stream'd with massacre.
Then, echoing yell with yell, they fired the tower,
Which half that autumn night, like the live North,
Red-pulsing up thro' Alioth and Alcor,
Made all above it, and a hundred meres   480
About it, as the water Moab saw
Come round by the east, and out beyond them flush'd
The long low dune and lazy-plunging sea.

So all the ways were safe from shore to shore,
But in the heart of Arthur pain was lord.

Then, out of Tristram waking, the red dream
Fled with a shout, and that low lodge return'd,
Mid-forest, and the wind among the boughs.
He whistled his good war-horse left to graze
Among the forest greens, vaulted upon him,   490
And rode beneath an ever-showering leaf,
Till one lone woman, weeping near a cross,
Stay'd him. "Why weep ye?" "Lord," she said, "my man
Hath left me or is dead;" whereon he thought—
"What, if she hate me now? I would not this.

What, if she love me still? I would not that.
I know not what I would"—but said to her,
"Yet weep not thou, lest, if thy mate return,
He find thy favor changed and love thee not"—
Then pressing day by day thro' Lyonnesse   500
Last in a roky hollow, belling, heard
The hounds of Mark, and felt the goodly hounds
Yelp at his heart, but, turning, past and gain'd
Tintagil, half in sea and high on land,
A crown of towers.

              Down in a casement sat,
A low sea-sunset glorying round her hair
And glossy-throated grace, Isolt the queen.
And when she heard the feet of Tristram grind
The spiring stone that scaled about her tower,
Flush'd, started, met him at the doors, and there   510
Belted his body with her white embrace,
Crying aloud: "Not Mark—not Mark, my soul!
The footstep flutter'd me at first—not he!
Catlike thro' his own castle steals my Mark,
But warrior-wise thou stridest thro' his halls
Who hates thee, as I him—even to the death.
My soul, I felt my hatred for my Mark
Quicken within me, and knew that thou wert nigh."
To whom Sir Tristram smiling, "I am here;
Let be thy Mark, seeing he is not thine."   520

   And drawing somewhat backward she replied:
"Can he be wrong'd who is not even his own,
But save for dread of thee had beaten me,
Scratch'd, bitten, blinded, marr'd me somehow—Mark?
What rights are his that dare not strike for them?
Not lift a hand—not, tho' he found me thus!
But harken! have ye met him? hence he went
To-day for three days' hunting—as he said—
And so returns belike within an hour.

Mark's way, my soul!—but eat not thou with Mark,   530
Because he hates thee even more than fears,
Nor drink; and when thou passest any wood
Close vizor, lest an arrow from the bush
Should leave me all alone with Mark and hell.
My God, the measure of my hate for Mark
Is as the measure of my love for thee!"

So, pluck'd one way by hate and one by love,
Drain'd of her force, again she sat, and spake
To Tristram, as he knelt before her, saying:
"O hunter, and O blower of the horn,   540
Harper, and thou hast been a rover too,
For, ere I mated with my shambling king,
Ye twain had fallen out about the bride
Of one—his name is out of me—the prize,
If prize she were—what marvel?—she could see—
Thine, friend; and ever since my craven seeks
To wreck thee villainously—but, O Sir Knight,
What dame or damsel have ye kneel'd to last?"

And Tristram, "Last to my Queen Paramount,
Here now to my queen paramount of love   550
And loveliness—ay, lovelier than when first
Her light feet fell on our rough Lyonnesse,
Sailing from Ireland."

Softly laugh'd Isolt:
"Flatter me not, for hath not our great Queen
My dole of beauty trebled?" and he said:
"Her beauty is her beauty, and thine thine,
And thine is more to me—soft, gracious, kind—
Save when thy Mark is kindled on thy lips
Most gracious; but she, haughty, even to him,
Lancelot; for I have seen him wan enow   560
To make one doubt if ever the great Queen
Have yielded him her love."

To whom Isolt:
"Ah, then, false hunter and false harper, thou
Who brakest thro' the scruple of my bond,
Calling me thy white hind, and saying to me
That Guinevere had sinn'd against the highest,
And I—misyoked with such a want of man—
That I could hardly sin against the lowest."

He answer'd: "O my soul, be comforted!
If this be sweet, to sin in leading-strings,   570
If here be comfort, and if ours be sin,
Crown'd warrant had we for the crowning sin
That made us happy; but how ye greet me—fear
And fault and doubt—no word of that fond tale—
Thy deep heart-yearnings, thy sweet memories
Of Tristram in that year he was away."

And, saddening on the sudden, spake Isolt:
"I had forgotten all in my strong joy
To see thee—yearnings?—ay! for, hour by hour,
Here in the never-ended afternoon,   580
O, sweeter than all memories of thee,
Deeper than any yearnings after thee
Seem'd those far-rolling, westward-smiling seas,
Watch'd from this tower. Isolt of Britain dash'd
Before Isolt of Brittany on the strand,
Would that have chill'd her bride-kiss? Wedded her?
Fought in her father's battles? wounded there?
The King was all fulfill'd with gratefulness,
And she, my namesake of the hands, that heal'd
Thy hurt and heart with unguent and caress—   590
Well—can I wish her any huger wrong
Than having known thee? her too hast thou left
To pine and waste in those sweet memories.
O, were I not my Mark's, by whom all men
Are noble, I should hate thee more than love."

And Tristram, fondling her light hands, replied:
"Grace, queen, for being loved; she loved me well.
Did I love her? the name at least I loved.
Isolt?—I fought his battles, for Isolt!
The night was dark; the true star set. Isolt!   600
The name was ruler of the dark—Isolt?
Care not for her! patient, and prayerful, meek,
Pale-blooded, she will yield herself to God."

And Isolt answer'd: "Yea, and why not I?
Mine is the larger need, who am not meek,
Pale-blooded, prayerful. Let me tell thee now.
Here one black, mute midsummer night I sat,
Lonely, but musing on thee, wondering where,
Murmuring a light song I had heard thee sing,
And once or twice I spake thy name aloud.   610
Then flash'd a levin-brand; and near me stood,
In fuming sulphur blue and green, a fiend—
Mark's way to steal behind one in the dark—
For there was Mark: 'He has wedded her,' he said,
Not said, but hiss'd it; then this crown of towers
So shook to such a roar of all the sky,
That here in utter dark I swoon'd away,
And woke again in utter dark, and cried,
'I will flee hence and give myself to God'—
And thou wert lying in thy new leman's arms."   620

Then Tristram, ever dallying with her hand,
"May God be with thee, sweet, when old and gray,
And past desire!" a saying that anger'd her.
" 'May God be with thee, sweet, when thou art old,
And sweet no more to me!' I need Him now.
For when had Lancelot utter'd aught so gross
Even to the swineherd's malkin in the mast?
The greater man the greater courtesy.
Far other was the Tristram, Arthur's knight!

But thou, thro' ever harrying thy wild beasts—   630
Save that to touch a harp, tilt with a lance
Becomes thee well—art grown wild beast thyself.
How darest thou, if lover, push me even
In fancy from thy side, and set me far
In the gray distance, half a life away.
Her to be loved no more? Unsay it, unswear!
Flatter me rather, seeing me so weak,
Broken with Mark and hate and solitude,
Thy marriage and mine own, that I should suck
Lies like sweet wines. Lie to me; I believe.   640
Will ye not lie? not swear, as there ye kneel,
And solemnly as when ye sware to him,
The man of men, our King—My God, the power
Was once in vows when men believed the King!
They lied not then who sware, and thro' their vows
The King prevailing made his realm—I say,
Swear to me thou wilt love me even when old,
Gray-hair'd, and past desire, and in despair."

    Then Tristram, pacing moodily up and down:
"Vows! did you keep the vow you made to Mark   650
More than I mine? Lied, say ye? Nay, but learnt,
The vow that binds too strictly snaps itself—
My knighthood taught me this—ay, being snapt—
We run more counter to the soul thereof
Than had we never sworn. I swear no more.
I swore to the great King, and am forsworn.
For once—even to the height—I honor'd him.
'Man, is he man at all?' methought, when first
I rode from our rough Lyonnesse, and beheld
That victor of the Pagan throned in hall—   660
His hair, a sun that ray'd from off a brow
Like hill-snow high in heaven, the steel-blue eyes,
The golden beard that clothed his lips with light—
Moreover, that weird legend of his birth,
With Merlin's mystic babble about his end

Amazed me; then, his foot was on a stool
Shaped as a dragon; he seem'd to me no man,
But Michael trampling Satan; so I sware,
Being amazed. But this went by—The vows!
O, ay—the wholesome madness of an hour—   670
They served their use, their time; for every knight
Believed himself a greater than himself,
And every follower eyed him as a God;
Till he, being lifted up beyond himself,
Did mightier deeds than elsewise he had done,
And so the realm was made. But then their vows—
First mainly thro' that sullying of our Queen—
Began to gall the knighthood, asking whence
Had Arthur right to bind them to himself?
Dropt down from heaven? wash'd up from out the deep?   680
They fail'd to trace him thro' the flesh and blood
Of our old kings. Whence then? a doubtful lord
To bind them by inviolable vows,
Which flesh and blood perforce would violate;
For feel this arm of mine—the tide within
Red with free chase and heather-scented air,
Pulsing full man. Can Arthur make me pure
As any maiden child? lock up my tongue
From uttering freely what I freely hear?
Bind me to one? The wide world laughs at it.   690
And worldling of the world am I, and know
The ptarmigan that whitens ere his hour
Woos his own end; we are not angels here
Nor shall be. Vows—I am woodman of the woods,
And hear the garnet-headed yaffingale
Mock them—my soul, we love but while we may;
And therefore is my love so large for thee,
Seeing it is not bounded save by love."

  Here ending, he moved toward her, and she said:
"Good; an I turn'd away my love for thee   700

To some one thrice as courteous as thyself—
For courtesy wins woman all as well
As valor may, but he that closes both
Is perfect, he is Lancelot—taller indeed,
Rosier and comelier, thou—but say I loved
This knightliest of all knights, and cast thee back
Thine own small saw, 'We love but while we may,'
Well then, what answer?"

            He that while she spake,
Mindful of what he brought to adorn her with,
The jewels, had let one finger lightly touch   710
The warm white apple of her throat, replied,
"Press this a little closer, sweet, until—
Come, I am hunger'd and half-anger'd—meat,
Wine, wine—and I will love thee to the death,
And out beyond into the dream to come."

  So then, when both were brought to full accord,
She rose, and set before him all he will'd;
And after these had comforted the blood
With meats and wines, and satiated their hearts—
Now talking of their woodland paradise,   720
The deer, the dews, the fern, the founts, the lawns;
Now mocking at the much ungainliness,
And craven shifts, and long crane legs of Mark—
Then Tristram laughing caught the harp and sang:

  "Ay, ay, O, ay—the winds that bend the brier!
A star in heaven, a star within the mere!
Ay, ay, O, ay—a star was my desire,
And one was far apart and one was near.
Ay, ay, O, ay—the winds that bow the grass!
And one was water and one star was fire,   730
And one will ever shine and one will pass.
Ay, ay, O, ay—the winds that move the mere!"

Then in the light's last glimmer Tristram show'd
And swung the ruby carcanet. She cried,
"The collar of some Order, which our King
Hath newly founded, all for thee, my soul,
For thee, to yield thee grace beyond thy peers."

"Not so, my queen," he said, "but the red fruit
Grown on a magic oak-tree in mid-heaven,
And won by Tristram as a tourney-prize,   740
And hither brought by Tristram for his last
Love-offering and peace-offering unto thee."

He spoke, he turn'd, then, flinging round her neck,
Claspt it, and cried, "Thine Order, O my queen!"
But, while he bow'd to kiss the jewell'd throat,
Out of the dark, just as the lips had touch'd,
Behind him rose a shadow and a shriek—
"Mark's way," said Mark, and clove him thro' the brain.

That night came Arthur home, and while he climb'd,
All in a death-dumb autumn-dripping gloom,   750
The stairway to the hall, and look'd and saw
The great Queen's bower was dark,—about his feet
A voice clung sobbing till he question'd it,
"What art thou?" and the voice about his feet
Sent up an answer, sobbing, "I am thy fool,
And I shall never make thee smile again."

RIZPAH

17—

I

Wailing, wailing, wailing, the wind over land and sea—
And Willy's voice in the wind, "O mother, come out to me!"
Why should he call me to-night, when he knows that I cannot go?
For the downs are as bright as day, and the full moon stares at
    the snow.

II

We should be seen, my dear; they would spy us out of the town.
The loud black nights for us, and the storm rushing over the
    down,
When I cannot see my own hand, but am led by the creak of the
    chain,
And grovel and grope for my son till I find myself drenched
    with the rain.

III

Anything fallen again? nay—what was there left to fall?
I have taken them home, I have number'd the bones, I have
    hidden them all.   10
What am I saying? and what are *you?* do you come as a spy?
Falls? what falls? who knows? As the tree falls so must it lie.

IV

Who let her in? how long has she been? you—what have you
    heard?
Why did you sit so quiet? you never have spoken a word.

O—to pray with me—yes—a lady—none of their spies—
But the night has crept into my heart, and begun to darken my
  eyes.

V

Ah—you, that have lived so soft, what should *you* know of the
  night,
The blast and the burning shame and the bitter frost and the
  fright?
I have done it, while you were asleep—you were only made for
  the day.
I have gather'd my baby together—and now you may go your
  way.   20

VI

Nay—for it 's kind of you, madam, to sit by an old dying wife.
But say nothing hard of my boy, I have only an hour of life.
I kiss'd my boy in the prison, before he went out to die.
"They dared me to do it," he said, and he never has told me a
  lie.
I whipt him for robbing an orchard once when he was but a
  child—
"The farmer dared me to do it," he said; he was always so wild—
And idle—and could n't be idle—my Willy—he never could rest.
The King should have made him a soldier, he would have been
  one of his best.

VII

But he lived with a lot of wild mates, and they never would let
  him be good;
They swore that he dare not rob the mail, and he swore that he
  would;   30
And he took no life, but he took one purse, and when all was
  done
He flung it among his fellows—"I 'll none of it," said my son.

VIII

I came into court to the judge and the lawyers. I told them my
    tale,
God's own truth—but they kill'd him, they kill'd him for rob-
    bing the mail.
They hang'd him in chains for a show—we had always borne a
    good name—
To be hang'd for a thief—and then put away—is n't that enough
    shame?
Dust to dust—low down—let us hide! but they set him so high
That all the ships of the world could stare at him, passing by.
God 'ill pardon the hell-black raven and horrible fowls of the air,
But not the black heart of the lawyer who kill'd him and hang'd
    him there.   40

IX

And the jailer forced me away. I had bid him my last good-bye,
They had fasten'd the door of his cell. "O mother!" I heard him
    cry.
I could n't get back tho' I tried, he had something further to say,
And now I never shall know it. The jailer forced me away.

X

Then since I could n't but hear that cry of my boy that was dead,
They seized me and shut me up: they fasten'd me down on my
    bed.
"Mother, O mother!"—he call'd in the dark to me year after
    year—
They beat me for that, they beat me—you know that I could n't
    but hear;
And then at the last they found I had grown so stupid and still
They let me abroad again—but the creatures had worked their
    will.   50

XI

Flesh of my flesh was gone, but bone of my bone was left—
I stole them all from the lawyers—and you, will you call it a
   theft?—
My baby, the bones that had suck'd me, the bones that had
   laughed and had cried—
Theirs? O, no! they are mine—not theirs—they had moved in
   my side.

XII

Do you think I was scared by the bones? I kiss'd 'em, I buried
   'em all—
I can't dig deep, I am old—in the night by the churchyard wall.
My Willy 'ill rise up whole when the trumpet of judgment 'ill
   sound,
But I charge you never to say that I laid him in holy ground.

XIII

They would scratch him up—they would hang him again on the
   cursed tree.
Sin? O, yes, we are sinners, I know—let all that be,   60
And read me a Bible verse of the Lord's goodwill toward men—
"Full of compassion and mercy, the Lord"—let me hear it again;
"Full of compassion and mercy—long-suffering." Yes, O, yes!
For the lawyer is born but to murder—the Saviour lives but to
   bless.
He 'll never put on the black cap except for the worst of the
   worst,
And the first may be last—I have heard it in church—and the
   last may be first.
Suffering—O, long-suffering—yes, as the Lord must know,
Year after year in the mist and the wind and the shower and
   the snow.

XIV

Heard, have you? what? they have told you he never repented
his sin.
How do they know it? are *they* his mother? are *you* of his kin?
Heard!ᵔ have you ever heard, when the storm on the downs
began,   71
The wind that 'ill wail like a child and the sea that 'ill moan
like a man?

XV

Election, Election, and Reprobation—it 's all very well,
But I go to-night to my boy, and I shall not find him in hell.
For I cared so much for my boy that the Lord has look'd into
my care,
And He means me I 'm sure to be happy with Willy, I know not
where.

XVI

And if *he* be lost—but to save *my* soul, that is all your desire—
Do you think that I care for *my* soul if my boy be gone to the
fire?
I have been with God in the dark—go, go, you may leave me
alone—   79
You never have borne a child—you are just as hard as a stone.

XVII

Madam, I beg your pardon! I think that you mean to be kind,
But I cannot hear what you say for my Willy's voice in the
wind—
The snow and the sky so bright—he used but to call in the dark,
And he calls to me now from the church and not from the gibbet
—for hark!
Nay—you can hear it yourself—it is coming—shaking the walls—
Willy—the moon 's in a cloud——Good-night. I am going. He
calls.

THE REVENGE

A BALLAD OF THE FLEET

First published in "The Nineteenth Century" for March, 1878, with the title, "Sir Richard Grenville, a Ballad of the Fleet;" afterwards included in the "Ballads," 1880, with the present title.

According to Sir Walter Raleigh, who wrote a "Report of the truth of the fight about the Iles of Açores this last Sommer," the engagement began at 3 P.M. on the 31st of August, Old Style, or the 10th of September, New Style, in the year 1591. Gervase Markham, who commemorated the event in a poem entitled "The Most Honorable Tragedie of Sir Richard Grinuile, Knight" (1595), gives the main facts in his "Argument," or introduction, as follows:—

"Sir Richard *Grinuile*, lying at anchor neere vnto *Flores*, one of the westerlie Ilands of the *Azores*, the last of August in the after noone, had intelligence by one Captayne *Midleton* of the aproch of the Spanish *Armada*, beeing in number fiftie three saile of great ships, and fifteene thousand men to man them. Sir *Richard*, staying to recouer his men which were vpon the Iland, and disdayning to flie from his Countries enemy, not beeing able to recouer the winde, was instantlie inuironed with that hudge Nauie, betweene whom began a dreadfull fight, continuing the space of fifteene howers, in which conflict, Sir *Richard* sunck the great *San Phillip* of *Spaine*, the *Ascension* of *Siuel*, the Admirall of the *Hulks*, and two other great *Armados*; about midnight Sir *Richard* receiued a wound through the bodie, and as he was dressing, was shot againe into the head, and his Surgion slaine. Sir *Richard* mayntained the fight, till he had not one corne of powder left, nor one whole pike, nor fortie lyuing men; which seeing, hee would haue sunke his owne ship, but that was gaine-stood by the Maister thereof, who contrarie to his will came to composition with the *Spanyards*, and so saued those which were left aliue. Sir *Richard* dyed aboard the Admyrall of *Spayne*, about the fourth day after the battaile, and was mightlie bewaild of all men."

A Dutch writer, Jan Huygen van Linschoten, whose book was translated into English in 1598, gives the following account of Sir Richard's death:—

"All the rest of the Captaines and Gentlemen went to visite hym.

and to comfort him in his hard fortune, wondring at his courage, and
stout hart, for that he shewed not any signe of faintnes nor changing
of colour. But feeling the hower of death to approch, hee spake
these wordes in Spanish and said: Heere die I, *Richard Greenfield*,
with **a** ioyfull and quiet mind, for that I haue ended my life as a
true soldier ought to do, yat hath fought for his countrey, Queene,
religion, and honor, whereby my soule most ioyfull departeth out of
this bodie, and shall alwaies leaue behinde it an euerlasting fame of
a valiant and true soldier that hath done his dutie, as he was bound
to doe. When he had finished these or such other like words, hee
gaue vp the ghost, with great and stout courage, and no man could
perceiue any true signe of heauinesse in him."

I

At Flores in the Azores Sir Richard Grenville lay,
And a pinnace, like a flutter'd bird, came flying from far away:
"Spanish ships of war at sea! we have sighted fifty-three!"
Then sware Lord Thomas Howard: " 'Fore God I am no coward;
But I cannot meet them here, for my ships are out of gear,
And the half my men are sick. I must fly, but follow quick.
We are six ships of the line; can we fight with fifty-three?"

II

Then spake Sir Richard Grenville: "I know you are no coward;
You fly them for a moment to fight with them again.
But I 've ninety men and more that are lying sick ashore.   10
I should count myself the coward if I left them, my Lord
        Howard,
To these Inquisition dogs and the devildoms of Spain."

III

So Lord Howard past away with five ships of war that day,
Till he melted like a cloud in the silent summer heaven;
But Sir Richard bore in hand all his sick men from the land
Very carefully and slow,
Men of Bideford in Devon,
And we laid them on the ballast down below;

For we brought them all aboard,
And they blest him in their pain, that they were not left to
     Spain,   20
To the thumb-screw and the stake, for the glory of the Lord.

IV

He had only a hundred seamen to work the ship and to fight,
And he sailed away from Flores till the Spaniard came in sight,
With his huge sea-castles heaving upon the weather bow.
"Shall we fight or shall we fly?
Good Sir Richard, tell us now,
For to fight is but to die!
There 'll be little of us left by the time this sun be set."
And Sir Richard said again: "We be all good English men.
Let us bang these dogs of Seville, the children of the devil,   30
For I never turn'd my back upon Don or devil yet."

V

Sir Richard spoke and he laugh'd, and we roar'd a hurrah, and so
The little Revenge ran on sheer into the heart of the foe,
With her hundred fighters on deck, and her ninety sick below;
For half of their fleet to the right and half to the left were seen,
And the little Revenge ran on thro' the long sea-lane between.

VI

Thousands of their soldiers look'd down from their decks and
     laugh'd,
Thousands of their seamen made mock at the mad little craft
Running on and on, till delay'd   39
By their mountain-like San Philip that, of fifteen hundred tons,
And up-shadowing high above us with her yawning tiers of guns,
Took the breath from our sails, and we stay'd.

VII

And while now the great San Philip hung above us like a cloud
Whence the thunderbolt will fall
Long and loud,

Four galleons drew away
From the Spanish fleet that day,
And two upon the larboard and two upon the starboard lay,
And the battle-thunder broke from them all.

VIII

But anon the great San Philip, she bethought herself and went,
Having that within her womb that had left her ill content;   51
And the rest they came aboard us, and they fought us hand to
    hand,
For a dozen times they came with their pikes and musqueteers,
And a dozen times we shook 'em off as a dog that shakes his ears
When he leaps from the water to the land.

IX

And the sun went down, and the stars came out far over the
    summer sea,
But never a moment ceased the fight of the one and the fifty-three.
Ship after ship, the whole night long, their high-built galleons
    came,
Ship after ship, the whole night long, with her battle-thunder
    and flame;
Ship after ship, the whole night long, drew back with her dead
    and her shame.   60
For some were sunk and many were shatter'd, and so could
    fight us no more—
God of battles, was ever a battle like this in the world before?

X

For he said, "Fight on! fight on!"
Tho' his vessel was all but a wreck;
And it chanced that, when half of the short summer night was
    gone,
With a grisly wound to be drest he had left the deck,
But a bullet struck him that was dressing it suddenly dead,
And himself he was wounded again in the side and the head,
And he said, "Fight on! fight on!"

XI

And the night went down, and the sun smiled out far over the
 summer sea,   70
And the Spanish fleet with broken sides lay round us all in a
 ring;
But they dared not touch us again, for they fear'd that we still
 could sting,
So they watch'd what the end would be.
And we had not fought them in vain,
But in perilous plight were we,
Seeing forty of our poor hundred were slain,
And half of the rest of us maim'd for life
In the crash of the cannonades and the desperate strife;
And the sick men down in the hold were most of them stark
 and cold,
And the pikes were all broken or bent, and the powder was all
 of it spent;   80
And the masts and the rigging were lying over the side;
But Sir Richard cried in his English pride:
"We have fought such a fight for a day and a night
As may never be fought again!
We have won great glory, my men!
And a day less or more
At sea or ashore,
We die—does it matter when?
Sink me the ship, Master Gunner—sink her, split her in twain!
Fall into the hands of God, not into the hands of Spain!" 90

XII

And the gunner said, "Ay, ay," but the seamen made reply:
"We have children, we have wives,
And the Lord hath spared our lives.
We will make the Spaniard promise, if we yield, to let us go;
We shall live to fight again and to strike another blow."
And the lion there lay dying, and they yielded to the foe.

XIII

And the stately Spanish men to their flagship bore him then,
Where they laid him by the mast, old Sir Richard caught at last,
And they praised him to his face with their courtly foreign
    grace;
But he rose upon their decks, and he cried: 100
"I have fought for Queen and Faith like a valiant man and true;
I have only done my duty as a man is bound to do.
With a joyful spirit I Sir Richard Grenville die!"
And he fell upon their decks, and he died.

XIV

And they stared at the dead that had been so valiant and true,
And had holden the power and glory of Spain so cheap
That he dared her with one little ship and his English few;
Was he devil or man? He was devil for aught they knew,
But they sank his body with honor down into the deep,
And they mann'd the Revenge with a swarthier alien crew,   110
And away she sail'd with her loss and long'd for her own;
When a wind from the lands they had ruin'd awoke from sleep,
And the water began to heave and the weather to moan,
And or ever that evening ended a great gale blew,
And a wave like the wave that is raised by an earthquake grew,
Till it smote on their hulls and their sails and their masts and
    their flags,
And the whole sea plunged and fell on the shot-shatter'd navy of
    Spain,
And the little Revenge herself went down by the island crags
To be lost evermore in the main.

THE VOYAGE OF MAELDUNE

(FOUNDED ON AN IRISH LEGEND. A. D. 700)

The original story may be found in P. W. Joyce's "Old Celtic
Romances" (London, 1879).

According to the tale, Maildun (*Mail Duin*, chief of the fort) sets forth with sixty chosen men, to seek the murderer of his father. They come, as in the poem, to an island where the man lives, but are driven away by a tempest. After three days they arrive at "the island of the monstrous ants," each "as large as a foal;" but, not liking the "eager and hungry look" of the insects, they do not land. Three days later they reach "the terraced island of birds," of which they take great numbers, and then sail away to a large sandy island, from whose shores they are frightened by a monster "somewhat like a horse in shape," but with legs like a dog and blue claws. On the next island they see a "demon horse-race," and continue their voyage to another, whereon is a magnificent palace. Here they find "abundance of food and ale," but see no inhabitants; so after eating and drinking their fill, they thank God and put to sea again. The "island of the wonderful apple-tree," a single apple from which serves to supply the travellers with food and drink for forty days, and successive islands infested with "blood-thirsty quadrupeds," strange monsters, and "red-hot animals," are visited in turn; also an island where a "little cat," living in a spendid palace, kills one of Maildun's brothers; another island that "dyed white and black" —everything on one side of a wall across is becoming black, and on the other side white; the island "of the burning river," and that "of the miller of hell," who grinds up all the good things that men complain of, and all that they "try to conceal from God;" with the isles of "weeping," of "the four precious walls," of "the crystal bridge," of "speaking birds," of "the aged hermit," and of "the big blacksmiths," who remind one of the Cyclops of old. The voyagers also sail over "the crystal sea," and another transparent sea beneath whose waters they see a country beautiful indeed, but infested with strange and monstrous animals. Later they come to another island, about which the sea rose up, forming, "as it were, a wall all round it;" and to another spanned by a stream of water in the form of a rainbow, "and they hooked down from it many large salmon." A mighty "silver pillar standing in the sea" and an "island standing on one pillar" are other wonders they encounter before arriving at a lovely island, the queen of which detains them long by her magic arts. Escaping at last, they visit "the isle of intoxicating wine-fruits" and that of "the mystic lake," whose waters renewed the youth of the bather, and a third where the people were "all continually laughing." They pass "the isle of the blest" without venturing to land,

and soon see a lonely rock whereon a holy hermit dwelt, who, after telling the wonderful story of his life, said to them: "You shall all reach your own country in safety; and you, Maildun, you shall find in an island on your way the very man that slew your father; but you are neither to kill him nor take revenge on him in any way. As God has delivered you from the many dangers you have passed through, though you were very guilty and well deserved death at His hands, so do you forgive your enemy the crime he committed against you." Sailing away, the voyagers come again to the island where this enemy dwelt. It is evening, and the man is at supper with his friends. Maildun and his companions stand outside the house and listen to the conversation going on within. The people happen to be talking of Maildun, and one asks, "Supposing he came now, what should we do?" "I can easily answer that," said the man of the house; "Maildun has been for a long time suffering great afflictions and hardships; and if he were to come now, though we were enemies once, I should certainly give him a welcome and a kind reception." Maildun at once knocked at the door and made himself known. The wanderers were invited to enter, and "were joyfully welcomed by the whole household; new garments were given to them; and they feasted and rested, till they forgot their weariness and their hardships."

It will be seen that while the old Celtic tale has suggested to Tennyson a few of the main incidents in the poem, the details are almost entirely of his own invention. The date which he assigns to the legend (A. D. 700) is that which Joyce and others, from internal evidence, accept for the events on which it is founded.

I

I was the chief of the race—he had stricken my father dead—
But I gather'd my fellows together, I swore I would strike off
    his head.
Each of them look'd like a king, and was noble in birth as in
    worth,
And each of them boasted he sprang from the oldest race upon
    earth.
Each was as brave in the fight as the bravest hero of song,
And each of them liefer had died than have done one another
    a wrong.

He lived on an isle in the ocean—we sail'd on a Friday morn—
He that had slain my father the day before I was born.

II

And we came to the isle in the ocean, and there on the shore
    was he.   9
But a sudden blast blew us out and away thro' a boundless sea.

III

And we came to the Silent Isle that we never had touch'd at
    before,
Where a silent ocean always broke on a silent shore,
And the brooks glitter'd on in the light without sound, and the
    long waterfalls
Pour'd in a thunderless plunge to the base of the mountain
    walls,
And the poplar and cypress unshaken by storm flourish'd up
    beyond sight,
And the pine shot aloft from the crag to an unbelievable height,
And high in the heaven above it there flicker'd a songless lark,
And the cock could n't crow, and the bull could n't low, and the
    dog could n't bark.
And round it we went, and thro' it, but never a murmur, a
    breath—
It was all of it fair as life, it was all of it quiet as death,   20
And we hated the beautiful isle, for whenever we strove to
    speak
Our voices were thinner and fainter than any flittermouse-shriek;
And the men that were mighty of tongue and could raise such
    a battle-cry
That a hundred who heard it would rush on a thousand lances and
    die—
O, they to be so dumb'd by the charm!—so fluster'd with anger
    were they
They almost fell on each other; but after we sail'd away.

IV

And we came to the Isle of Shouting; we landed, a score of wild
    birds
Cried from the topmost summit with human voices and words.
Once in an hour they cried, and whenever their voices peal'd
The steer fell down at the plow and the harvest died from the
    field,   30
And the men dropt dead in the valleys and half of the cattle
    went lame,
And the roof sank in on the hearth, and the dwelling broke into
    flame;
And the shouting of these wild birds ran into the hearts of my
    crew,
Till they shouted along with the shouting and seized one another
    and slew.
But I drew them the one from the other; I saw that we could
    not stay,
And we left the dead to the birds, and we sail'd with our wounded
    away.

V

And we came to the Isle of Flowers; their breath met us out
    on the seas,
For the Spring and the middle Summer sat each on the lap of
    the breeze;
And the red passion-flower to the cliffs, and the dark-blue clematis,
    clung,
And starr'd with a myriad blossom the long convolvulus hung;   40
And the topmost spire of the mountain was lilies in lieu of snow,
And the lilies like glaciers winded down, running out below
Thro' the fire of the tulip and poppy, the blaze of gorse, and the
    blush
Of millions of roses that sprang without leaf or a thorn from
    the bush;
And the whole isle-side flashing down from the peak without
    ever a tree

Swept like a torrent of gems from the sky to the blue of the
  sea,
And we roll'd upon capes of crocus and vaunted our kith and
  our kin,
And we wallow'd in beds of lilies, and chanted the triumph of
  Finn,
Till each like a golden image was pollen'd from head to feet
And each was as dry as a cricket, with thirst in the middle-day
  heat.   50
Blossom and blossom, and promise of blossom, but never a
  fruit!
And we hated the Flowering Isle, as we hated the isle that was
  mute,
And we tore up the flowers by the million and flung them in
  bight and bay,
And we left but a naked rock, and in anger we sail'd away.

VI

And we came to the Isle of Fruits; all round from the cliffs and
  the capes,
Purple or amber, dangled a hundred fathom of grapes,
And the warm melon lay like a little sun on the tawny sand,
And the fig ran up from the beach and rioted over the land,
And the mountain arose like a jewell'd throne thro' the fragrant
  air,
Glowing with all-color'd plums and with golden masses of pear, 60
And the crimson and scarlet of berries that flamed upon bine
  and vine,
But in every berry and fruit was the poisonous pleasure of wine;
And the peak of the mountain was apples, and the hugest that
  ever were seen,
And they prest, as they grew, on each other, with hardly a
  leaflet between,
And all of them redder than rosiest health or than utterest shame,
And setting, when Even descended, the very sunset aflame.

And we stay'd three days, and we gorged and we madden'd, till
    every one drew
His sword on his fellow to slay him, and ever they struck and
    they slew;
And myself, I had eaten but sparely, and fought till I sunder'd
    the fray,
Then I bade them remember my father's death, and we sail'd
    away.   70

VII

And we came to the Isle of Fire; we were lured by the light
    from afar,
For the peak sent up one league of fire to the Northern Star;
Lured by the glare and the blare, but scarcely could stand upright,
For the whole isle shudder'd and shook like a man in a mortal
    affright.
We were giddy besides with the fruits we had gorged, and so
    crazed that at last
There were some leap'd into the fire; and away we sail'd, and
    we past
Over that undersea isle, where the water is clearer than air.
Down we look'd—what a garden! O bliss, what a Paradise there!
Towers of a happier time, low down in a rainbow deep
Silent palaces, quiet fields of eternal sleep!   80
And three of the gentlest and best of my people, whate'er I
    could say,
Plunged head-down in the sea, and the Paradise trembled away.

VIII

And we came to the Bounteous Isle, where the heavens lean low
    on the land,
And ever at dawn from the cloud glitter'd o'er us a sun-bright
    hand,
Then it open'd and dropt at the side of each man, as he rose
    from his rest,

Bread enough for his need till the laborless day dipt under the
  west;
And we wander'd about it and thro' it. O, never was time so
  good!
And we sang of the triumphs of Finn, and the boast of our
  ancient blood,
And we gazed at the wandering wave as we sat by the gurgle
  of springs,
And we chanted the songs of the Bards and the glories of fairy
  kings.   90
But at length we began to be weary, to sigh, and to stretch and
  yawn,
Till we hated the Bounteous Isle and the sun-bright hand of the
  dawn,
For there was not an enemy near, but the whole green isle was
  our own,
And we took to playing at ball, and we took to throwing the
  stone,
And we took to playing at battle, but that was a perilous play,
For the passion of battle was in us, we slew and we sail'd away.

                                IX

And we came to the Isle of Witches and heard their musical
  cry—
"Come to us, O, come, come!" in the stormy red of a sky
Dashing the fires and the shadows of dawn on the beautiful
  shapes,
For a wild witch naked as heaven stood on each of the loftiest
  capes,   100
And a hundred ranged on the rock like white sea-birds in a row,
And a hundred gamboll'd and pranced on the wrecks in the
  sand below,
And a hundred splash'd from the ledges, and bosom'd the burst
  of the spray;
But I knew we should fall on each other, and hastily sail'd
  away.

X

And we came in an evil time to the Isle of the Double Towers,
One was of smooth-cut stone, one carved all over with flowers,
But an earthquake always moved in the hollows under the dells,
And they shock'd on each other and butted each other with
    clashing of bells,
And the daws flew out of the towers and jangled and wrangled
    in vain,
And the clash and boom of the bells rang into the heart and the
    brain, 110
Till the passion of battle was on us, and all took sides with the
    towers,
There were some for the clean-cut stone, there were more for
    the carven flowers,
And the wrathful thunder of God peal'd over us all the day,
For the one half slew the other, and after we sail'd away.

XI

And we came to the Isle of a Saint who had sail'd with Saint
    Brendan of yore,
He had lived ever since on the isle and his winters were fifteen
    score,
And his voice was low as from other worlds, and his eyes were
    sweet,
And his white hair sank to his heels, and his white beard fell to
    his feet,
And he spake to me: "O Maeldune, let be this purpose of thine!
Remember the words of the Lord when he told us, 'Vengeance
    is mine!' 120
His fathers have slain thy fathers in war or in single strife,
Thy fathers have slain his fathers, each taken a life for a life,
Thy father had slain his father, how long shall the murder last?
Go back to the Isle of Finn and suffer the Past to be Past."
And we kiss'd the fringe of his beard, and we pray'd as we
    heard him pray,
And the holy man he assoil'd us, and sadly we sail'd away.

XII

And we came to the isle we were blown from, and there on the
    shore was he,
The man that had slain my father. I saw him and let him be.
O, weary was I of the travel, the trouble, the strife, and the sin,
When I landed again with a tithe of my men, on the Isle of
    Finn!   130

TO E. FITZGERALD

This introduction to the poem that follows was apparently written on
or about March 31, 1883, when Fitzgerald was seventy-five years
of age. He was rather more than a year older than Tennyson, who
was born August 6, 1809. He died June 14, 1883, before the volume
containing the poem was published.

Old Fitz, who from your suburb grange,
    Where once I tarried for a while,
Glance at the wheeling orb of change,
    And greet it with a kindly smile;
Whom yet I see as there you sit
    Beneath your sheltering garden-tree,
And watch your doves about you flit,
    And plant on shoulder, hand, and knee,
Or on your head their rosy feet,
    As if they knew your diet spares   10
Whatever moved in that full sheet
    Let down to Peter at his prayers;
Who live on milk and meal and grass;
    And once for ten long weeks I tried
Your table of Pythagoras,
    And seem'd at first "a thing enskied,"
As Shakespeare has it, airy-light
    To float above the ways of men,
Then fell from that half-spiritual height

Chill'd, till I tasted flesh again   20
One night when earth was winter-black,
   And all the heavens flash'd in frost;
And on me, half-asleep, came back
   That wholesome heat the blood had lost,
And set me climbing icy capes
   And glaciers, over which there roll'd
To meet me long-arm'd vines with grapes
   Of Eshcol hugeness; for the cold
Without, and warmth within me, wrought
   To mould the dream; but none can say   30
That Lenten fare makes Lenten thought
   Who reads your golden Eastern lay,
Than which I know no version done
   In English more divinely well;
A planet equal to the sun
   Which cast it, that large infidel
Your Omar; and your Omar drew
   Full-handed plaudits from our best
In modern letters, and from two,
   Old friends outvaluing all the rest,   40
Two voices heard on earth no more;
   But we old friends are still alive,
And I am nearing seventy-four,
   While you have touch'd at seventy-five,
And so I send a birthday line
   Of greeting; and my son, who dipt
In some forgotten book of mine
   With sallow scraps of manuscript,
And dating many a year ago,
   Has hit on this, which you will take,   50
My Fitz, and welcome, as I know,
   Less for its own than for the sake
Of one recalling gracious times,
   When, in our younger London days,
You found some merit in my rhymes,
   And I more pleasure in your praise.

TIRESIAS

Tiresias and Other Poems was published in 1885, with the following dedication:

TO MY GOOD FRIEND

ROBERT BROWNING

WHOSE GENIUS AND GENIALITY
WILL BEST APPRECIATE WHAT MAY BE BEST
AND MAKE MOST ALLOWANCE FOR WHAT MAY BE WORST
THIS VOLUME
IS
AFFECTIONATELY DEDICATED

Mr. Arthur Waugh ("Alfred Lord Tennyson," 2d ed., London, 1893), remarks: "It is characteristic of a certain shyness in Tennyson that he never told Browning of the dedication, and it was not until the book was in the hands of the public that the latter learned the circumstance from a friend."

I wish I were as in the years of old,
While yet the blessed daylight made itself
Ruddy thro' both the roofs of sight, and woke
These eyes, now dull, but then so keen to seek
The meanings ambush'd under all they saw,
The flight of birds, the flame of sacrifice,
What omens may foreshadow fate to man
And woman, and the secret of the Gods.
  My son, the Gods, despite of human prayer,
Are slower to forgive than human kings.   10
The great God Arês burns in anger still
Against the guiltless heirs of him from Tyre,
Our Cadmus, out of whom thou art, who found
Beside the springs of Dircê, smote, and still'd
Thro' all its folds the multitudinous beast,
The dragon, which our trembling fathers call'd
The God's own son.
                A tale, that told to me,

When but thine age, by age as winter-white
As mine is now, amazed, but made me yearn
For larger glimpses of that more than man   20
Which rolls the heavens, and lifts and lays the deep,
Yet loves and hates with mortal hates and loves,
And moves unseen among the ways of men.
    Then, in my wanderings all the lands that lie
Subjected to the Heliconian ridge
Have heard this footstep fall, altho' my wont
Was more to scale the highest of the heights
With some strange hope to see the nearer God.
    One naked peak—the sister of the Sun
Would climb from out the dark, and linger there   30
To silver all the valleys with her shafts—
There once, but long ago, five-fold thy term
Of years, I lay; the winds were dead for heat;
The noonday crag made the hand burn; and sick
For shadow—not one bush was near—I rose,
Following a torrent till its myriad falls
Found silence in the hollows underneath.
    There is a secret olive glade I saw
Pallas Athene climbing from the bath
In anger; yet one glittering foot disturb'd   40
The lucid well; one snowy knee was prest
Against the margin flowers; a dreadful light
Came from her golden hair, her golden helm
And all her golden armor on the grass,
And from her virgin breast, and virgin eyes
Remaining fixt on mine, till mine grew dark
For ever, and I heard a voice that said,
"Henceforth be blind, for thou hast seen too much,
And speak the truth that no man may believe."
    Son, in the hidden world of sight that lives   50
Behind this darkness, I behold her still,
Beyond all work of those who carve the stone,
Beyond all dreams of Godlike womanhood,
Ineffable beauty, out of whom, at a glance,

And as it were, perforce, upon me flash'd
The power of prophesying—but to me
No power—so chain'd and coupled with the curse
Of blindness and their unbelief who heard
And heard not, when I spake of famine, plague,
Shrine-shattering earthquake, fire, flood, thunderbolt,   60
And angers of the Gods for evil done
And expiation lack'd—no power on Fate
Theirs, or mine own! for when the crowd would roar
For blood, for war, whose issue was their doom,
To cast wise words among the multitude
Was flinging fruit to lions; nor, in hours
Of civil outbreak, when I knew the twain
Would each waste each, and bring on both the yoke
Of stronger states, was mine the voice to curb
The madness of our cities and their kings.   70

    Who ever turn'd upon his heel to hear
My warning that the tyranny of one
Was prelude to the tyranny of all?
My counsel that the tyranny of all
Led backward to the tyranny of one?

    This power hath work'd no good to aught that lives,
And these blind hands were useless in their wars.
O, therefore, that the unfulfill'd desire,
The grief for ever born from griefs to be,
The boundless yearning of the prophet's heart—   80
Could *that* stand forth, and like a statue, rear'd
To some great citizen, win all praise from all
Who past it, saying, "That was he!"

                            In vain!
Virtue must shape itself in deed, and those
Whom weakness or necessity have cramp'd
Within themselves, immerging, each, his urn
In his own well, draws solace as he may.

    Menœceus, thou hast eyes, and I can hear
Too plainly what full tides of onset sap

Our seven high gates, and what a weight of war   90
Rides on those ringing axles! jingle of bits,
Shouts, arrows, tramp of the horn-footed horse
That grind the glebe to powder! Stony showers
Of that ear-stunning hail of Arês crash
Along the sounding walls. Above, below,
Shock after shock the song-built towers and gates
Reel, bruised and butted with the shuddering
War-thunder of iron rams; and from within
The city comes a murmur void of joy,
Lest she be taken captive—maidens, wives,   100
And mothers with their babblers of the dawn,
And oldest age in shadow from the night,
Falling about their shrines before their Gods,
And wailing, "Save us."
                            And they wail to thee!
These eyeless eyes, that cannot see thine own,
See this, that only in thy virtue lies
The saving of our Thebes; for, yesternight,
To me, the great God Arês, whose one blow
In war and human sacrifice—himself
Blood-red from battle, spear and helmet tipt   110
With stormy light as on a mast at sea,
Stood out before a darkness, crying, "Thebes,
Thy Thebes shall fall and perish, for I loathe
The seed of Cadmus—yet if one of these
By his own hand—if one of these—"
                                  My son,
No sound is breathed so potent to coerce,
And to conciliate, as their names who dare
For that sweet mother land which gave them birth
Nobly to do, nobly to die. Their names,
Graven on memorial columns, are a song   120
Heard in the future; few, but more than wall
And rampart, their examples reach a hand
Far thro' all years, and everywhere they meet

And kindle generous purpose, and the strength
To mould it into action pure as theirs.
   Fairer thy fate than mine, if life's best end
Be to end well! and thou refusing this,
Unvenerable will thy memory be
While men shall move the lips; but if thou dare—
Thou, one of these, the race of Cadmus—then   130
No stone is fitted in yon marble girth
Whose echo shall not tongue thy glorious doom,
Nor in this pavement but shall ring thy name
To every hoof that clangs it, and the springs
Of Dircê laving yonder battle-plain,
Heard from the roofs by night, will murmur thee
To thine own Thebes, while Thebes thro' thee shall stand
Firm-based with all her Gods.
                       The Dragon's cave
Half hid, they tell me, now in flowing vines—
Where once he dwelt and whence he roll'd himself   140
At dead of night—thou knowest, and that smooth rock
Before it, altar-fashion'd, where of late
The woman-breasted Sphinx, with wings drawn back,
Folded her lion paws, and look'd to Thebes.
There blanch the bones of whom she slew, and these
Mixt with her own, because the fierce beast found
A wiser than herself, and dash'd herself
Dead in her rage; but thou art wise enough,
Tho' young, to love thy wiser, blunt the curse
Of Pallas, hear, and tho' I speak the truth   150
Believe I speak it, let thine own hand strike
Thy youthful pulses into rest and quench
The red God's anger, fearing not to plunge
Thy torch of life in darkness, rather—thou
Rejoicing that the sun, the moon, the stars
Send no such light upon the ways of men
As one great deed.
               Thither, my son, and there
Thou, that hast never known the embrace of love,

Offer thy maiden life.
             This useless hand!
I felt one warm tear fall upon it. Gone!   160
He will achieve his greatness.
                  But for me,
I would that I were gather'd to my rest,
And mingled with the famous kings of old,
On whom about their ocean-islets flash
The faces of the Gods—the wise man's word,
Here trampled by the populace underfoot,
There crown'd with worship—and these eyes will find
The men I knew, and watch the chariot whirl
About the goal again, and hunters race
The shadowy lion, and the warrior-kings,   170
In height and prowess more than human, strive
Again for glory, while the golden lyre
Is ever sounding in heroic ears
Heroic hymns, and every way the vales
Wind, clouded with the grateful incense-fume
Of those who mix all odor to the Gods
On one far height in one far-shining fire.

     "One height and one far-shining fire!"
        And while I fancied that my friend
     For this brief idyll would require   180
        A less diffuse and opulent end,
     And would defend his judgment well,
        If I should deem it over nice—
     The tolling of his funeral bell
        Broke on my Pagan Paradise,
     And mixt the dream of classic times,
        And all the phantoms of the dream,
     With present grief, and made the rhymes,
        That miss'd his living welcome, seem
     Like would-be guests an hour too late,   190

Who down the highway moving on
With easy laughter find the gate
   Is bolted, and the master gone.
Gone into darkness, that full light
   Of friendship! past, in sleep, away
By night, into the deeper night!
   The deeper night? A clearer day
Than our poor twilight dawn on earth—
   If night, what barren toil to be!
What life, so maim'd by night, were worth   200
   Our living out? Not mine to me
Remembering all the golden hours
   Now silent, and so many dead,
And him the last; and laying flowers,
   This wreath, above his honor'd head,
And praying that, when I from hence
   Shall fade with him into the unknown,
My close of earth's experience
   May prove as peaceful as his own.

POETS AND THEIR BIBLIOGRAPHIES

Old poets foster'd under friendlier skies,
   Old Virgil who would write ten lines, they say,
   At dawn, and lavish all the golden day
To make them wealthier in his readers' eyes;
And you, old popular Horace, you the wise
   Adviser of the nine-years-ponder'd lay,
   And you, that wear a wreath of sweeter bay,
Catullus, whose dead songster never dies;
If, glancing downward on the kindly sphere
   That once had roll'd you round and round the sun.
You see your Art still shrined in human shelves,
You should be jubilant that you flourish'd here
   Before the Love of Letters, overdone,
Had swampt the sacred poets with themselves.

LOCKSLEY HALL SIXTY YEARS AFTER

Late, my grandson! half the morning have I paced these sandy
    tracts,
Watch'd again the hollow ridges roaring into cataracts,

Wander'd back to living boyhood while I heard the curlews call,
I myself so close on death, and death itself in Locksley Hall.

So—your happy suit was blasted—she the faultless, the divine;
And you liken—boyish babble—this boy-love of yours with mine.

I myself have often babbled doubtless of a foolish past;
Babble, babble; our old England may go down in babble at last.

"Curse him!" curse your fellow-victim? call him dotard in your
    rage?
Eyes that lured a doting boyhood well might fool a dotard's
    age   10

Jilted for a wealthier! wealthier? yet perhaps she was not wiser
I remember how you kiss'd the miniature with those sweet eyes.

In the hall there hangs a painting—Amy's arms about my neck—
Happy children in a sunbeam sitting on the ribs of wreck.

In my life there was a picture, she that clasp'd my neck had
    flown;
I was left within the shadow sitting on the wreck alone.

Yours has been a slighter ailment, will you sicken for her sake?
You, not you! your modern amorist is of easier, earthlier make.

Amy loved me, Amy fail'd me, Amy was a timid child;
But your Judith—but your worldling—*she* had never driven me
    wild.   20

She that holds the diamond necklace dearer than the golden
ring,
She that finds a winter sunset fairer than a morn of spring.

She that in her heart is brooding on his briefer lease of life,
While she vows "till death shall part us," she the would-be-
widow wife.

She the worldling born of worldlings—father, mother—be content,
Even the homely farm can teach us there is something in descent.

Yonder in that chapel, slowly sinking now into the ground,
Lies the warrior, my forefather, with his feet upon the hound.

Cross'd! for once he sail'd the sea to crush the Moslem in his
pride;
Dead the warrior, dead his glory, dead the cause in which he
died.   30

Yet how often I and Amy in the mouldering aisle have stood,
Gazing for one pensive moment on that founder of our blood.

There again I stood to-day, and where of old we knelt in prayer,
Close beneath the casement crimson with the shield of Locksley
—there,

All in white Italian marble, looking still as if she smiled,
Lies my Amy dead in childbirth, dead the mother, dead the child.

Dead—and sixty years ago, and dead her aged husband now—
I, this old white-headed dreamer, stoopt and kiss'd her marble
brow.

Gone the fires of youth, the follies, furies, curses, passionate
tears,
Gone like fires and floods and earthquakes of the planet's dawning
years.   40

Fires that shook me once, but now to silent ashes fallen away.
Cold upon the dead volcano sleeps the gleam of dying day.

Gone the tyrant of my youth, and mute below the chancel stones,
All his virtues—I forgive them—black in white above his bones.

Gone the comrades of my bivouac, some in fight against the foe,
Some thro' age and slow diseases, gone as all on earth will go.

Gone with whom for forty years my life in golden sequence ran,
She with all the charm of woman, she with all the breadth of man,

Strong in will and rich in wisdom, Edith, yet so lowly-sweet,
Woman to her inmost heart, and woman to her tender feet,   50

Very woman of very woman, nurse of ailing body and mind,
She that link'd again the broken chain that bound me to my kind.

Here to-day was Amy with me, while I wander'd down the coast,
Near us Edith's holy shadow, smiling at the slighter ghost.

Gone our sailor son thy father, Leonard early lost at sea;
Thou alone, my boy, of Amy's kin and mine art left to me.

Gone thy tender-natured mother, wearying to be left alone,
Pining for the stronger heart that once had beat beside her own.

Truth, for truth is truth, he worshipt, being true as he was brave;
Good, for good is good, he follow'd, yet he look'd beyond the
        grave.   60

Wiser there than you, that crowning barren Death as lord of all,
Deem this over-tragic drama's closing curtain is the pall!

Beautiful was death in him, who saw the death, but kept the
   deck,
Saving women and their babes, and sinking with the sinking
   wreck,

Gone for ever! Ever? no—for since our dying race began,
Ever, ever, and for ever was the leading light of man.

Those that in barbarian burials kill'd the slave, and slew the wife
Felt within themselves the sacred passion of the second life.

Indian warriors dream of ampler hunting grounds beyond the
   night;   69
Even the black Australian dying hopes he shall return, a white.

Truth for truth, and good for good! The good, the true, the
   pure, the just—
Take the charm "For ever" from them, and they crumble into
   dust.

Gone the cry of "Forward, Forward," lost within a growing
   gloom;
Lost, or only heard in silence from the silence of a tomb.

Half the marvels of my morning, triumphs over time and space,
Staled by frequence, shrunk by usage into commonest commonplace!

"Forward" rang the voices then, and of the many mine was one.
Let us hush this cry of "Forward" till ten thousand years have
   gone.

Far among the vanish'd races, old Assyrian kings would flay
Captives whom they caught in battle—iron-hearted victors they.

Ages after, while in Asia, he that led the wild Moguls,   81
Timur built his ghastly tower of eighty thousand human skulls;

Then, and here in Edward's time, an age of noblest English
    names,
Christian conquerors took and flung the conquer'd Christian into
    flames.

Love your enemy, bless your haters, said the Greatest of the great;
Christian love among the Churches look'd the twin of heathen hate.

From the golden alms of Blessing man had coin'd himself a curse:
Rome of Cæsar, Rome of Peter, which was crueller? which was
    worse?

France had shown a light to all men, preach'd a Gospel, all men's
    good;
Celtic Demos rose a Demon, shriek'd and slaked the light with
    blood.   90

Hope was ever on her mountain, watching till the day begun—
Crown'd with sunlight—over darkness—from the still unrisen sun.

Have we grown at last beyond the passions of the primal clan?
"Kill your enemy, for you hate him," still, "your enemy" was a
    man.

Have we sunk below them? peasants maim the helpless horse, and
    drive
Innocent cattle under thatch, and burn the kindlier brutes alive.

Brutes, the brutes are not your wrongers—burnt at midnight,
    found at morn,
Twisted hard in mortal agony with their offspring, born-unborn,

Clinging to the silent mother! Are we devils? are we men?
Sweet Saint Francis of Assisi, would that he were here again,   100

He that in his Catholic wholeness used to call the very flowers
Sisters, brothers—and the beasts—whose pains are hardly less
    than ours!

Chaos, Cosmos! Cosmos, Chaos! who can tell how all will end?
Read the wide world's annals, you, and take their wisdom for your
     friend.

Hope the best, but hold the Present fatal daughter of the Past,
Shape your heart to front the hour, but dream not that the hour
     will last.

Ay, if dynamite and revolver leave you courage to be wise—
When was age so cramm'd with menace? madness? written,
     spoken lies?

Envy wears the mask of Love, and, laughing sober fact to scorn,
Cries to weakest as to strongest, "Ye are equals, equal-born." 110

Equal-born? O, yes, if yonder hill be level with the flat.
Charm us, orator, till the lion look no larger than the cat,

Till the cat thro' that mirage of overheated language loom
Larger than the lion,—Demos end in working its own doom.

Russia bursts our Indian barrier, shall we fight her? shall we
     yield?
Pause! before you sound the trumpet, hear the voices from the
     field.

Those three hundred millions under one Imperial sceptre now,
Shall we hold them? shall we loose them? take the suffrage of the
     plow.

Nay, but these would feel and follow Truth if only you and you,
Rivals of realm-ruining party, when you speak were wholly true.

Plowmen, shepherds, have I found, and more than once, and still
     could find,   121
Sons of God, and kings of men in utter nobleness of mind,

Truthful, trustful, looking upward to the practised hustings-liar;
So the higher wields the lower, while the lower is the higher.

Here and there a cotter's babe is royal-born by right divine;
Here and there my lord is lower than his oxen or his swine.

Chaos, Cosmos! Cosmos, Chaos! once again the sickening game;
Freedom, free to slay herself, and dying while they shout her
    name.

Step by step we gain'd a freedom known to Europe, known to all;
Step by step we rose to greatness,—thro' the tonguesters we may
    fall.   130

You that woo the Voices—tell them "old experience is a fool,"
Teach your flatter'd kings that only those who cannot read can
    rule.

Pluck the mighty from their seat, but set no meek ones in their
    place;
Pillory Wisdom in your markets, pelt your offal at her face.

Tumble Nature heel o'er head, and, yelling with the yelling street,
Set the feet above the brain and swear the brain is in the feet.

Bring the old dark ages back without the faith, without the hope,
Break the State, the Church, the Throne, and roll their ruins down
    the slope.

Authors—essayist, atheist, novelist, realist, rhymester, play your
    part,
Paint the mortal shame of nature with the living hues of art.   140

Rip your brothers' vices open, strip your own foul passions bare;
Down with Reticence, down with Reverence—forward—naked—
    let them stare.

Feed the budding rose of boyhood with the drainage of your
  sewer;
Send the drain into the fountain, lest the stream should issue pure.

Set the maiden fancies wallowing in the troughs of Zolaism,—
Forward, forward, ay, and backward, downward too into the
  abysm!

Do your best to charm the worst, to lower the rising race of men;
Have we risen from out the beast, then back into the beast again?

Only "dust to dust" for me that sicken at your lawless din,
Dust in wholesome old-world dust before the newer world begin.

Heated am I? you—you wonder—well, it scarce becomes mine
  age—   151
Patience! let the dying actor mouth his last upon the stage.

Cries of unprogressive dotage ere the dotard fall asleep?
Noises of a current narrowing, not the music of a deep?

Ay, for doubtless I am old, and think gray thoughts, for I am gray;
After all the stormy changes shall we find a changeless May?

After madness, after massacre, Jacobinism and Jacquerie,
Some diviner force to guide us thro' the days I shall not see?

When the schemes and all the systems, kingdoms and republics
  fall,   159
Something kindlier, higher, holier—all for each and each for all?

All the full-brain, half-brain races, led by Justice, Love, and Truth;
All the millions one at length with all the visions of my youth?

All diseases quench'd by Science, no man halt, or deaf, or blind;
Stronger ever born of weaker, lustier body, larger mind?

Earth at last a warless world, a single race, a single tongue—
I have seen her far away—for is not Earth as yet so young?—

Every tiger madness muzzled, every serpent passion kill'd,
Every grim ravine a garden, every blazing desert till'd,

Robed in universal harvest up to either pole she smiles,
Universal ocean softly washing all her warless isles.   170

Warless? when her tens are thousands, and her thousands millions, then—
All her harvest all too narrow—who can fancy warless men?

Warless? war will die out late then. Will it ever? late or soon?
Can it, till this outworn earth be dead as yon dead world the moon?

Dead the new astronomy calls her.—On this day and at this hour,
In this gap between the sandhills, whence you see the Locksley tower,

Here we met, our latest meeting—Amy—sixty years ago—
She and I—the moon was falling greenish thro' a rosy glow,

Just above the gateway tower, and even where you see her now—
Here we stood and claspt each other, swore the seeming-deathless vow.—   180

Dead, but how her living glory lights the hall, the dune, the grass!
Yet the moonlight is the sunlight, and the sun himself will pass.

Venus near her! smiling downward at this earthlier earth of ours,
Closer on the sun, perhaps a world of never fading flowers.

Hesper, whom the poet call'd the Bringer home of all good things—
All good things may move in Hesper, perfect peoples, perfect kings.

Hesper—Venus—were we native to that splendor or in Mars,
We should see the globe we groan in, fairest of their evening stars.

Could we dream of wars and carnage, craft and madness, lust and
      spite,   189
Roaring London, raving Paris, in that point of peaceful light?

Might we not in glancing heavenward on a star so silver-fair,
Yearn, and clasp the hands and murmur, "Would to God that we
      were there"?

Forward, backward, backward, forward, in the immeasurable sea,
Sway'd by vaster ebbs and flows than can be known to you or me.

All the suns—are these but symbols of innumerable man,
Man or Mind that sees a shadow of the planner or the plan?

Is there evil but on earth? or pain in every peopled sphere?
Well, be grateful for the sounding watchword "Evolution" here,

Evolution ever climbing after some ideal good,
And Reversion ever dragging Evolution in the mud.   200

What are men that He should heed us? cried the king of sacred
      song;
Insects of an hour, that hourly work their brother insect wrong,

While the silent heavens roll, and suns along their fiery way,
All their planets whirling round them, flash a million miles a day.

Many an æon moulded earth before her highest, man, was born,
Many an æon too may pass when earth is manless and forlorn,

Earth so huge, and yet so bounded—pools of salt, and plots of
      land—
Shallow skin of green and azure—chains of mountain, grains of
      sand!

Only That which made us meant us to be mightier by and by,   209
Set the sphere of all the boundless heavens within the human eye.

Sent the shadow of Himself, the boundless, thro' the human soul;
Boundless inward in the atom, boundless outward in the Whole.

.   .   .   .

Here is Locksley Hall, my grandson, here the lion-guarded gate.
Not to-night in Locksley Hall—to-morrow—you, you come so late.

Wreck'd—your train—or all but wreck'd? a shatter'd wheel? a
    vicious boy!
Good, this forward, you that preach it, is it well to wish you joy?

Is it well that while we range with Science, glorying in the Time,
City children soak and blacken soul and sense in city slime?

There among the glooming alleys Progress halts on palsied feet,
Crime and hunger cast our maidens by the thousand on the street.

There the master scrimps his haggard sempstress of her daily
    bread,   221
There a single sordid attic holds the living and the dead.

There the smouldering fire of fever creeps across the rotted floor,
And the crowded couch of incest in the warrens of the poor.

Nay, your pardon, cry your "Forward," yours are hope and youth,
    but I—
Eighty winters leave the dog too lame to follow with the cry,

Lame and old, and past his time, and passing now into the night;
Yet I would the rising race were half as eager for the light.

Light the fading gleam of even? light the glimmer of the dawn?
Aged eyes may take the growing glimmer for the gleam withdrawn.

Far away beyond her myriad coming changes earth will be　　231
Something other than the wildest modern guess of you and me.

Earth may reach her earthly-worst, or if she gain her earthly-best,
Would she find her human offspring this ideal man at rest?

Forward then, but still remember how the course of Time will
　　swerve,
Crook and turn upon itself in many a backward streaming curve.

Not the Hall to-night, my grandson! Death and Silence hold their
　　own.
Leave the master in the first dark hour of his last sleep alone.

Worthier soul was he than I am, sound and honest, rustic Squire,
Kindly landlord, boon companion—youthful jealousy is a liar.　240

Cast the poison from your bosom, oust the madness from your
　　brain.
Let the trampled serpent show you that you have not lived in vain.

Youthful! youth and age are scholars yet but in the lower school,
Nor is he the wisest man who never proved himself a fool.

Yonder lies our young sea-village—Art and Grace are less and
　　less:
Science grows and Beauty dwindles—roofs of slated hideousness!

There is one old hostel left us where they swing the Locksley
　　shield,
Till the peasant cow shall butt the "lion passant" from his field.

Poor old Heraldry, poor old History, poor old Poetry, passing
　　hence,
In the common deluge drowning old political common-sense!　250

Ere she gain her heavenly-best, a God must mingle with the game.
Nay, there may be those about us whom we neither see nor name,

Felt within us as ourselves, the Powers of Good, the Powers of Ill,
Strowing balm, or shedding poison in the fountains of the will.

Follow you the star that lights a desert pathway, yours or mine.
Forward, till you see the Highest Human Nature is divine.

Follow Light, and do the Right—for man can half-control his
    doom—
Till you find the deathless Angel seated in the vacant tomb.

Forward, let the stormy moment fly and mingle with the past.
I that loathed have come to love him. Love will conquer at the
    last.   280

one at eighty, mine own age, and I and you will bear the pall;
hen I leave thee lord and master, latest lord of Locksley Hall.

TO VIRGIL

WRITTEN AT THE REQUEST OF THE MANTUANS FOR THE
NINETEENTH CENTENARY OF VIRGIL'S DEATH

First printed in "The Nineteenth
Century" for November, 1882.

I

Roman Virgil, thou that singest
    Ilion's lofty temples robed in fire,
Ilion falling, Rome arising,
    wars, and filial faith, and Dido's pyre;

II

Landscape-lover, lord of language
    more than he that sang the "Works and Days,"

Poor old voice of eighty crying after voices that have fled!
All I loved are vanish'd voices, all my steps are on the dead.

All the world is ghost to me, and as the phantom disappears,
Forward far and far from here is all the hope of eighty years.

.   .   .   .

In this hostel—I remember—I repent it o'er his grave—
Like a clown—by chance he met me—I refused the hand he gave.

From that casement where the trailer mantles all the mouldering
    bricks—
I was then in early boyhood, Edith but a child of six—

While I shelter'd in this archway from a day of driving showers—
Peept the winsome face of Edith like a flower among the flowers.

Here to-night! the Hall to-morrow, when they toll the chapel
    bell!   261
Shall I hear in one dark room a wailing, "I have loved thee well"?

Then a peal that shakes the portal—one has come to claim his
    bride,
Her that shrank, and put me from her, shriek'd, and started from
    my side—

Silent echoes! You, my Leonard, use and not abuse your day,
Move among your people, know them, follow him who led the way,

Strove for sixty widow'd years to help his homelier brother men,
Served the poor, and built the cottage, raised the school, and
    drain'd the fen.

Hears he now the voice that wrong'd him? who shall swear it
    cannot be?   269
Earth would never touch her worst, were one in fifty such as he.

All the chosen coin of fancy
    flashing out from many a golden phrase;

III

Thou that singest wheat and woodland,
    tilth and vineyard, hive and horse and herd;
All the charm of all the Muses
    often flowering in a lonely word;

IV

Poet of the happy Tityrus
    piping underneath his beechen bowers;
Poet of the poet-satyr
    whom the laughing shepherd bound with flowers;

V

Chanter of the Pollio, glorying
    in the blissful years again to be,
Summers of the snakeless meadow,
    unlaborious earth and oarless sea;

VI

Thou that seest Universal
    Nature moved by Universal Mind;
Thou majestic in thy sadness
    at the doubtful doom of human kind;

VII

Light among the vanish'd ages;
    star that gildest yet this phantom shore;
Golden branch amid the shadows,
    kings and realms that pass to rise no more;

VIII

Now thy Forum roars no longer,
    fallen every purple Cæsar's dome—

Tho' thine ocean-roll of rhythm
    sound forever of Imperial Rome—

IX

Now the Rome of slaves hath perish'd,
    and the Rome of freemen holds her place,
I, from out the Northern Island
    sunder'd once from all the human race,

X

I salute thee, Mantovano,
    I that loved thee since my day began,
Wielder of the stateliest measure
    ever moulded by the lips of man.

"FRATER AVE ATQUE VALE"

First printed in "The Nineteenth
Century" for March, 1883.

Desenzano is a town at the southern end of Lake Garda, in Italy.
The narrow peninsula of Sermione (the Latin Sirmio), where Catullus
had his country house, is about three miles and a half to the east of
Desenzano. There are some slight remains of an ancient building
on the edge of the lake, said to belong to the poet's villa; and on a
hill near by are fragments of Roman baths.

Row us out from Desenzano, to your Sirmione row!
So they row'd, and there we landed—"O venusta Sirmio!"
There to me thro' all the groves of olive in the summer glow,
There beneath the Roman ruin where the purple flowers grow,
Came that "Ave atque Vale" of the Poet's hopeless woe,
Tenderest of Roman poets nineteen hundred years ago,
"Frater Ave atque Vale"—as we wander'd to and fro
Gazing at the Lydian laughter of the Garda Lake below
Sweet Catullus's all-but-island, olive-silvery Sirmio!

MERLIN AND THE GLEAM

Compare "The Voyage;" and see also "Freedom" (1884):

> "*O follower of the Vision, still*
> *In motion to the distant gleam,*" etc.

Stopford Brooke says of this poem: "It is as lovely in form and rhythm and imagination, as it is noble in thought and emotion. It speaks to all poetic hearts in England; it tells them of his coming death. It then recalls his past, his youth, his manhood; his early poems, his critics, his central labor on Arthur's tale; and we see through its verse clear into the inmost chamber of his heart. What sits there upon the throne, what has always sat thereon? It is the undying longing and search after the ideal light, the mother-passion of all the supreme artists of the world. 'I am Merlin, who follow the Gleam.' I know of no poem of Tennyson's which more takes my heart with magic and beauty."

I

O young Mariner,
You from the haven
Under the sea-cliff,
You that are watching
The gray Magician
With eyes of wonder,
I am Merlin,
And *I* am dying,
I am Merlin
Who follow the Gleam.   10

II

Mighty the Wizard
Who found me at sunrise
Sleeping, and woke me
And learn'd me Magic!

Great the Master,
And sweet the Magic,
When over the valley,
In early summers,
Over the mountain,
On human faces,   20
And all around me,
Moving to melody,
Floated the Gleam.

III

Once at the croak of a Raven
          who crost it
A barbarous people,
Blind to the magic
And deaf to the melody,
Snarl'd at and cursed me.
A demon vext me,
The light retreated,   30
The landskip darken'd,
The melody deaden'd,
The Master whisper'd,
"Follow the Gleam."

IV

Then to the melody,
Over a wilderness
Gliding, and glancing at
Elf of the woodland,
Gnome of the cavern,
Griffin and Giant,   40
And dancing of Fairies
In desolate hollows,
And wraiths of the mountain,
And rolling of dragons
By warble of water.
Or cataract music

Of falling torrents,
Flitted the Gleam.

V

Down from the mountain
And over the level,   50
And streaming and shining on
Silent river,
Silvery willow,
Pasture and plowland,
Innocent maidens,
Garrulous children,
Homestead and harvest,
Reaper and gleaner,
And rough-ruddy faces
Of lowly labor,   60
Slided the Gleam—

VI

Then, with a melody
Stronger and statelier,
Led me at length
To the city and palace
Of Arthur the King;
Touch'd at the golden
Cross of the churches,
Flash'd on the tournament,
Flicker'd and bicker'd   70
From helmet to helmet,
And last on the forehead
Of Arthur the blameless
Rested the Gleam.

VII

Clouds and darkness
Closed upon Camelot;
Arthur had vanish'd

I knew not whither,
The king who loved me,
And cannot die;   80
For out of the darkness
Silent and slowly
The Gleam, that had waned to
      a wintry glimmer
On icy fallow
And faded forest,
Drew to the valley
Named of the shadow,
And slowly brightening
Out of the glimmer,
And slowly moving again to a
      melody   90
Yearningly tender,
Fell on the shadow,
No longer a shadow,
But clothed with the Gleam.

VIII

And broader and brighter
The Gleam flying onward,
Wed to the melody,
Sang thro' the world;
And slower and fainter,
Old and weary,   100
But eager to follow,
I saw, whenever
In passing it glanced upon
Hamlet or city,
That under the Crosses
The dead man's garden,
The mortal hillock,
Would break into blossom;
And so to the land's
Last limit I came—   110

And can no longer,
But die rejoicing,
For thro' the Magic
Of Him the Mighty,
Who taught me in childhood,
There on the border
Of boundless Ocean,
And all but in Heaven
Hovers the Gleam.

IX

Not of the sunlight,   120
Not of the moonlight,
Not of the starlight!
O young Mariner,
Down to the haven,
Call your companions,
Launch your vessel
And crowd your canvas,
And, ere it vanishes
Over the margin,
After it, follow it,   130
Follow the Gleam.

CROSSING THE BAR

This poem first appeared in the "Demeter" volume of 1889, but is placed here in accordance with Lord Tennyson's request that it might be put at the end of all editions of his poems.

Sunset and evening star,
   And one clear call for me!
And may there be no moaning of the bar,
   When I put out to sea,

But such a tide as moving seems asleep,
   Too full for sound and foam,
When that which drew from out the boundless deep
   Turns again home.

Twilight and evening bell,
   And after that the dark!
And may there be no sadness of farewell,
   When I embark;

For tho' from out our bourne of Time and Place
   The flood may bear me far,
I hope to see my Pilot face to face
   When I have crost the bar.

APPENDIX

APPENDIX

from

"ON SOME CHARACTERISTICS OF MODERN POETRY,
AND ON THE LYRICAL POEMS OF ALFRED TENNYSON"

By ARTHUR H. HALLAM

(This review of Tennyson's *Poems, Chiefly Lyrical* [1830] appeared
unsigned in *Moxon's Englishman's Magazine*, August, 1831, pp.
616–628.)

. . . When Mr. Wordsworth, in his celebrated Preface to the
Lyrical Ballads, asserted that immediate or rapid popularity was
not the test of poetry, great was the consternation and clamour
among those farmers of public favour, the established critics.
Never had so audacious an attack been made upon their un-
doubted privileges and hereditary charter of oppression.

"What! *The Edinburgh Review* not infallible!" shrieked the
amiable petulance of Mr. Jeffrey.

"*The Gentleman's Magazine* incapable of decision!" faltered
the feeble garrulity of Silvanus Urban.

And straightway the whole sciolist herd, men of rank, men of
letters, men of wealth, men of business, all the "mob of gentlemen
who think with ease," and a terrible number of old ladies and
boarding-school misses began to scream in chorus, and prolonged
the notes of execration with which they overwhelmed the new
doctrine, until their wits and their voices fairly gave in from
exhaustion. Much, no doubt, they did, for much persons will do
when they fight for their dear selves: but there was one thing
they could not do, and unfortunately it was the only one of any
importance. They could not put down Mr. Wordsworth by clamour,
or prevent his doctrine, once uttered and enforced by his example,
from awakening the minds of men, and giving a fresh impulse
to art. It was the truth, and it prevailed; not only against the
exasperation of that hydra, the Reading Public, whose vanity was

hurt, and the blustering of its keepers, whose delusion was exposed, but even against the false glosses and narrow apprehensions of the Wordsworthians themselves. It is the madness of all who loosen some great principle, long buried under a snow-heap of custom and superstition, to imagine that they can restrain its operation, or circumscribe it by their purposes. But the right of private judgment was stronger than the will of Luther; and even the genius of Wordsworth cannot expand itself to the full periphery of poetic art.

It is not true, as his exclusive admirers would have it, that the highest species of poetry is the reflective; it is a gross fallacy, that because certain opinions are acute or profound, the expression of them by the imagination must be eminently beautiful. Whenever the mind of the artist suffers itself to be occupied, during its periods of creation, by any other predominant motive than the desire of beauty, the result is false in art.

Now there is undoubtedly no reason why he may not find beauty in those moods of emotion, which arise from the combinations of reflective thought; and it is possible that he may delineate these with fidelity, and not be led astray by any suggestions of an unpoetical mood. But though possible, it is hardly probable; for a man whose reveries take a reasoning turn, and who is accustomed to measure his ideas by their logical relations rather than the congruity of the sentiments to which they refer, will be apt to mistake the pleasure he has in knowing a thing to be true, for the pleasure he would have in knowing it to be beautiful, and so will pile his thoughts in a rhetorical battery, that they may convince, instead of letting them flow in a natural course of contemplation, that they may enrapture.

It would not be difficult to shew, by reference to the most admired poems of Wordsworth, that he is frequently chargeable with this error; and that much has been said by him which is good as philosophy, powerful as rhetoric, but false as poetry. Perhaps this very distortion of the truth did more in the peculiar juncture of our literary affairs to enlarge and liberalize the genius of our age, than could have been effected by a less sectarian temper.

However this may be, a new school of reformers soon began to attract attention, who, professing the same independence of immediate favour, took their stand on a different region of Parnassus from that occupied by the Lakers, and one, in our opinion, much less liable to perturbing currents of air from ungenial climates. We shall not hesitate to express our conviction, that the cockney school (as it was termed in derision from a cursory view of its accidental circumstances) contained more genuine inspiration, and adhered more steadily to that portion of truth which it embraced, than any form of art that has existed in this country since the days of Milton. Their *caposetta* was Mr. Leigh Hunt, who did little more than point the way, and was diverted from his aim by a thousand personal predilections and political habits of thought.

But he was followed by two men of very superior make; men who were born poets, lived poets, and went poets to their untimely graves. Shelley and Keats were indeed of opposite genius; that of the one was vast, impetuous, and sublime, the other seemed to be "fed with honeydew," and to have "drunk the milk of Paradise." Even the softness of Shelley comes out in bold, rapid, comprehensive strokes; he has no patience for minute beauties, unless they can be massed into a general effect of grandeur. On the other hand, the tenderness of Keats cannot sustain a lofty flight; he does not generalize or allegorize Nature; his imagination works with few symbols, and reposes willingly on what is given freely.

Yet in this formal opposition of character there is, it seems to us, a groundwork of similarity sufficient for the purposes of classification, and constituting a remarkable point in the progress of literature. They are both poets of sensation rather than reflection. Susceptible of the slightest impulse from external nature, their fine organs trembled into emotion at colors, and sounds, and movements, unperceived or unregarded by duller temperaments. Rich and clear were their perceptions of visible forms; full and deep their feelings of music. So vivid was the delight attending the simple exertions of eye and ear, that it became mingled more and more with their trains of active thought, and tended to absorb their whole being into the energy of sense. Other poets seek for images to illustrate their conceptions; these men had no need to seek; they lived in a world of images; for the most important and extensive portion of their life consisted in those emotions which are immediately conversant with the sensation. Like the hero of Goethe's novel, they would hardly have been affected by what is called the pathetic parts of a book; but the *merely beautiful* passages, "those from which the spirit of the author looks clearly and mildly forth," would have melted them to tears. Hence they are not descriptive, they are picturesque. They are not smooth and *negatively* harmonious; they are full of deep and varied melodies.

This powerful tendency of imagination to a life of immediate sympathy with the external universe, is not nearly so liable to false views of art as the opposite disposition of purely intellectual contemplation. For where beauty is constantly passing before "that inward eye, which is the bliss of solitude"; where the soul seeks it as a perpetual and necessary refreshment to the sources of activity and intuition; where all the other sacred ideas of our nature, the idea of good, the idea of perfection, the idea of truth, are habitually contemplated through the medium of this predominant mood, so that they assume its colour, and are subject to its peculiar laws, there is little danger that the ruling passion of the whole mind will cease to direct its creative operations, or the energetic principle of love for the beautiful sink, even for a brief period, to the level of a mere notion in the understanding.

We do not deny that it is, on other accounts, dangerous for frail humanity to linger with fond attachment in the vicinity of sense. Minds of this description are especially liable to moral temptations; and upon them, more than any, it is incumbent to remember, that their mission as men, which they share with their fellow-beings, is of infinitely higher interest than their mission as artists, which they possess by rare and exclusive privilege. But it is obvious that, critically speaking, such temptations are of slight moment. Not the gross and evident passions of our nature, but the elevated and less separable desires, are the dangerous enemies which guide the poetic spirit in its attempts at self-cultivation. That delicate sense of fitness which grows with the growth of artist feelings, and strengthens with their strength, until it acquires a celerity and weight of decision hardly inferior to the correspondent judgments of conscience, is weakened by every indulgence of heterogeneous aspirations, however pure they may be, however lofty, however suitable to human nature.

We are therefore decidedly of opinion that the heights and depths of art are most within the reach of those who have received from nature the "fearful and wonderful" constitution we have described, whose poetry is a sort of magic, producing a number of impressions, too multiplied, too minute, and too diversified to allow of our tracing them to their causes, because just such was the effect, even so boundless and so bewildering, produced on their imaginations by the real appearance of Nature.

These things being so, our friends of the new school had evidently much reason to recur to the maxim laid down by Mr. Wordsworth, and to appeal from the immediate judgment of lettered or unlettered contemporaries to the decision of a more equitable posterity. How should they be popular, whose senses told them a richer and ampler tale than most men could understand, and who constantly expressed, because they constantly felt, sentiments of exquisite pleasure or pain, which most men were not permitted to experience? The public very naturally derided them as visionaries, and gibbeted *in terrorem* those inaccuracies of diction occasioned sometimes by the speed of their conceptions, sometimes by the inadequacy of language to their peculiar conditions of thought.

But it may be asked, does not this line of argument prove too much? Does it not prove that there is a barrier between these poets and all other persons so strong and immovable, that, as has been said of the Supreme Essence, we must be themselves before we can understand them in the least? Not only are they not liable to sudden and vulgar estimation, but the lapse of ages, it seems, will not consolidate their frame, nor the suffrages of the wise few produce any impression, however remote or slow matured, on the judgment of the incapacitated many.

We answer, this is not the import of our argument. Undoubtedly the true poet addresses himself, in all his conceptions, to the common nature of us all. Art is a lofty tree, and may shoot up far beyond our grasp, but its roots are in daily life and experience. Every bosom contains the elements of those complex emotions which the artist feels, and every head can, to a certain extent, go over in itself the process of their combination, so as to understand his expressions and sympathize with his state. But this requires exertion; more or less, indeed, according to the difference of occasion, but always some degree of exertion. For since the emotions of the poet, during composition, follow a regular law of association, it follows that to accompany their progress up to the harmonious prospect of the whole, and to perceive the proper dependence of every step on that which preceded, it is absolutely necessary *to start from the same point*, i.e. clearly to apprehend that leading sentiment of the poet's mind, by their conformity to which the host of suggestions are arranged.

Now this requisite exertion is not willingly made by the large majority of readers! For very many, therefore, it has become *morally* impossible to attain the author's point of vision, on account of their habits, or their prejudices, or their circumstances; but it is never physically impossible, because nature has placed in every man the simple elements, of which art is the sublimation. Since then this demand on the reader for activity, when he wants to peruse his author in a luxurious passiveness, is the very thing that moves his bile, it is obvious that those writers will be always most popular who require the least degree of exertion. Hence, whatever is mixed up with art, and appears under its semblance, is always more favorably regarded than art free and unalloyed. Hence, half the fashionable poems in the world are mere rhetoric, and half the remainder are, perhaps, not liked by the generality for their substantial merits. Hence, likewise, of the really pure compositions, those are most universally agreeable which take for their primary subject the usual passions of the heart, and deal with them in a simple state, without applying the transforming powers of high imagination. Love, friendship, ambition, religion &c., are matters of daily experience even amongst unimaginative tempers. The forces of association, therefore, are ready to work in these directions, and little effort of will is necessary to follow the artist.

For the same reason, such subjects often excite a partial power of composition, which is no sign of a truly poetic organization. We are very far from wishing to depreciate this class of poems, whose influence is so extensive, and communicates so refined a pleasure. We contend only that the facility with which its impressions are communicated is no proof of its elevation as a form of art, but rather the contrary.

What, then, some may be ready to exclaim, is the pleasure derived by most men, from Shakespeare, or Dante, or Homer, entirely false and factitious? If these are really masters of their art, must not the energy required of the ordinary intelligences that come in contact with their mighty genius, be the greatest possible? How comes it then, that they are popular? Shall we not say, after all, that the difference is in the power of the author, not in the tenor of his meditations? Those eminent spirits find no difficulty in conveying to common apprehensions their lofty sense and profound observation of Nature. They keep no aristocratic state, apart from the sentiments of society at large; they speak to the hearts of all, and by the magnetic force of their conceptions, elevate inferior intellects into a higher and purer atmosphere.

The truth contained in this observation is undoubtedly important; geniuses of the most universal order, and assigned by destiny to the most propitious era of a nation's literary development, have a clearer and a larger access to the minds of their compatriots than can ever open to those who are circumscribed by less fortunate circumstances. In the youthful periods of any literature there is an expansive and communicative tendency in mind which produces unreservedness of communion, and reciprocity of vigor between different orders of intelligence.

Without abandoning the ground which has always been defended by the partizans of Mr. Wordsworth, who declare with perfect truth, that the number of real admirers of what is really admirable in Shakespeare and Milton is much fewer than the number of apparent admirers might lead one to imagine, we may safely assert that the intense thoughts set in circulation by those "orbs of song" and their noble satellites "in great Eliza's golden time," did not fail to awaken a proportionable intensity of the nature of numberless auditors. Some might feel feebly, some strongly; the effect would vary according to the character of the recipient; but upon none was the stirring influence entirely unimpressive. The knowledge and power thus imbibed became a part of national existence; it was ours as Englishmen; and amid the flux of generations and customs we retain unimpaired this privilege of intercourse with greatness.

But the age in which we live comes late in our national progress. That first raciness and juvenile vigor of literature, when nature "wantoned as in her prime, and played at will her virgin fancies" is gone, never to return. Since that day we have undergone a period of degradation. "Every handicraftsman has worn the mark of Poesy." It would be tedious to repeat the tale so often related of the French contagion and the heresies of the Popian school.

With the close of the last century came an era of reaction, an era of painful struggle to bring our over-civilised condition of thought into union with the fresh productive spirit that brightened the morning of our literature. But repentance is unlike innocence; the laborious endeavor to restore has more complicated methods of action than the freedom of untainted nature. Those different powers of poetic disposition, the energies of Sensitive, of Reflective, of Passionate Emotion, which in former times were intermingled, and derived from mutual support and extensive empire over the feelings of men, were now restrained within separate spheres of agency. The whole system no longer worked harmoniously, and by intrinsic harmony acquired external freedom; but there arose a violent and unusual action in the several component functions, each for itself, all striving to reproduce the regular power which the whole had once enjoyed.

Hence the melancholy which so evidently characterises the spirit of modern poetry; hence that return of the mind upon itself and the habit of seeking relief in idiosyncrasies rather than community of interest. In the old times the poetic impulse went along with the general impulse of the nation; in these it is a reaction against it, a check acting for conservation against a propulsion towards change.

We have indeed seen it urged in some of our fashionable publications. that the diffusion of poetry must be in the direct ratio of the diffusion of machinery, because a highly civilized people must have new objects of interest, and thus a new field will be open to description. But this notable argument forgets that against this *objective* amelioration may be set the decrease of *subjective* power, arising from a prevalence of social activity, and a continual absorption of the higher feelings into the palpable interests of ordinary life. The French Revolution may be a finer theme than the war of Troy; but it does not so evidently follow that Homer is to find his superior.

Our inference, therefore, from this change in the relative position of artists to the rest of the community is, that modern poetry in proportion to its depth and truth is likely to have little immediate authority over public opinion. Admirers it will have, sects subsequently it will form; and these strong under-currents will in time sensibly affect the principal stream. Those writers whose genius, though great, is not strictly and essentially poetic, become mediators between the votaries of art and the careless cravers for excitement. Art herself, less manifestly glorious than in her periods of undisputed supremacy, retains her essential prerogatives, and forgets not to raise up chosen spirits who may minister to her state and vindicate her title.

One of the faithful Islâm, a poet in the truest and highest sense, we are anxious to present to our readers. He has yet written little and published less; but in these "preludes of a loftier strain" we recognize the inspiring god. Mr. Tennyson belongs decidedly to the class we have already described as Poets of Sensation. He sees all the forms of nature with the "eruditus oculus," and his ear has a fairy fineness. There is a strange earnestness in his worship of beauty which throws a charm over his impassioned song, more easily felt than described, and not to be escaped by those who have once felt it. We think he has more definiteness and soundness of general conception than the late Mr. Keats and is much more free from blemishes of diction and hasty capriccios of fancy. He has also this advantage over that poet and his friend Shelley, that he comes before the public unconnected with any political party or peculiar system of opinions. Nevertheless, true to the theory we have stated, we believe his participation in their characteristic excellences is sufficient to secure him a share of their unpopularity.

The volume of "Poems, chiefly Lyrical," does not contain above 154 pages; but it shews us much more of the character of its parent mind, than many books we have known of much larger compass and more boastful pretensions. The features of original genius are clearly and strongly marked. The author imitates nobody; we recognise the spirit of his age, but not the individual form of this or that writer. His thoughts bear no more resemblance to Byron or Scott, Shelley or Coleridge, than to Homer or Calderon, Ferdusi or Calidas.

We have remarked five distinctive excellencies of his own manner. First, his luxuriance of imagination, and at the same time his control over it. Secondly his power of embodying himself in ideal characters, or rather moods of character, with such extreme accuracy of adjustment, that the circumstances of the narration seem to have a natural correspondence with the predominant feeling, and, as it were, to be evolved from it by assimilative force. Thirdly, his vivid, picturesque delineation of objects, and the peculiar skill with which he holds all of them fused, to borrow a metaphor from science, in a medium of strong emotion. Fourthly, the variety of his lyrical measures, and exquisite modulation of harmonious words and cadences to the swell and fall of the feelings expressed. Fifthly, the elevated habits of thought, implied in these compositions, and imparting a mellow soberness of tone, more impressive, to our minds, than if the author had drawn up a set of opinions in verse, and sought to instruct the understanding rather than to communicate the love of beauty to the heart.

We shall proceed to give our readers some specimens in illustration of these remarks, and, if possible, we will give them entire; for no poet can be fairly judged of by fragments, least of all, a poet like Mr. Tennyson, whose mind conceives nothing isolated, nothing abrupt, but every part with reference to some other part, and in subservience to the idea of the whole.

Recollections of the Arabian Nights!—What a delightful, en-

dearing title! How we pity those to whom it calls up no remi-
niscence of early enjoyment, no sentiment of kindliness as towards
one who sings a song they have loved, or mentions with affection
a departed friend! But let nobody expect a multifarious enumera-
tion of Viziers, Barmecides, Fireworshippers, and Cadis; trees
that sing, horses that fly, and Goules that eat rice-pudding!

Our author knows what he is about; he has, with great judgment, selected our old acquaintance, "the good Haroun Alraschid," as the most prominent object of our childish interest, and
with him has called up one of those luxurious garden scenes, the
account of which, in plain prose used to make our mouth water
for sherbet, since luckily we were too young to think much about
Zobeide! We think this poem will be the favourite among Mr.
Tennyson's admirers; perhaps upon the whole it is our own; at
least we find ourselves recurring to it oftener than to any other,
and every time we read it, we feel the freshness of its beauty increase, and are inclined to exclaim with Madame de Sévigné, "à
force d'être ancien, il m'est nouveau." But let us draw the curtain.
[*The poem is reprinted here.*]

Criticism will sound but poorly after this; yet we cannot give
silent votes. The first stanza, we beg leave to observe, places us
at once in the position of feeling, which the poem requires. The
scene is before us, around us; we cannot mistake its localities, or
blind ourselves to its colours. That happy ductility of childhood
returns for the moment; "true Mussulmans are we, and sworn,"
and yet there is a latent knowledge, which heightens the pleasure,
that to our change from really childish thought we owe the
capacities by which we enjoy the recollection.

As the poem proceeds, all is in perfect keeping. There is a
solemn distinctness in every image, a majesty of slow motion in
every cadence, that aids the illusion of thought, and steadies its
contemplation of the complete picture. Originality of observation
seems to cost nothing to our author's liberal genius; he lavishes
images of exquisite accuracy and elaborate splendour, as a common
writer throws about metaphorical truisms, and exhausted tropes.
Amidst all the varied luxuriance of the sensations described, we
are never permitted to lose sight of the idea which gives unity to

this variety, and by the recurrence of which, as a sort of mysterious influence, at the close of every stanza, the mind is wrought
up, with consummate art, to the final disclosure. This poem is a
perfect gallery of pictures; and the concise boldness, with which
in a few words an object is clearly painted, is sometimes (see the
6th stanza) majestic as Milton, sometimes (see the 12th) sublime
as Aeschylus.

We have not, however, so far forgot our vocation as critics, that
we would leave without notice the slight faults which adhere to
this precious work. In the 8th stanza, we doubt the propriety of
using the bold compound "black-green," at least in such close
vicinity to "gold-green"; nor is it perfectly clear by the term,
although indicated by the context, that "diamond plots" relates
to shape rather than colour. We are perhaps very stupid, but
"vivid stars unrayed" does not convey to us a very precise notion.
"*Rosaries* of scented thorn," in the 10th stanza is, we believe, an
entirely unauthorized use of the word. Would our author translate
"*biferique rosaria Paesti*"—"And *rosaries* of Paestum, twice in
bloom"?

To the beautiful 13th stanze we are sorry to find any objection:
but even the bewitching loveliness of that "Persian girl" shall
not prevent our performing the rigid duty we have undertaken,
and we must hint to Mr. Tennyson that "redolent" is no synonyme
for "fragrant." Bees may be redolent of honey; spring may be
"redolent of youth and love"; but the absolute use of the word
has, we fear, neither in Latin nor English any better authority
than the monastic epitaph on Fair Rosamond: *Hic jacet in tombâ
Rosa Mundi, non Rosa Munda, non redolet, sed olet, quae redolere
solet.*"

We are disposed to agree with Mr. Coleridge when he says "no
adequate compensation can be made for the mischief a writer
does by confounding the distinct senses of words." At the same
time our feelings in this instance rebel strongly in behalf of
"redolent"; for the melody of this passage, as it stands, is beyond
the possibility of improvement, and unless he should chance to
light upon a word very nearly resembling this in consonants and

vowels, we can hardly quarrel with Mr. Tennyson if, in spite of our judgment, he retains the offender in his service.

Our next specimen is of a totally different character, but not less complete, we think, in its kind. Have we among our readers any who delight in the heroic poems of Old England, the inimitable ballads? Any to whom Sir Patrick Spens, and Clym of the Clough, and Glorious Robin are consecrated names? Any who sigh with disgust at the miserable abortions of simpleness mistaken for simplicity, or florid weakness substituted for plain energy which they may often have seen dignified with the title of Modern Ballads.

Let such draw near and read *The Ballad of Oriana*. We know no more happy seizure of the antique spirit in the whole compass of our literature; yet there is no foolish self-desertion, no attempt at obliterating the present, but everywhere a full discrimination of how much ought to be yielded and how much retained. The author is well aware that the art of one generation cannot *become* that of another by any will or skill; but the artist may transfer the spirit of the past, making it a temporary form for his own spirit, and so effect, by idealizing power, a new and legitimate combination. If we were asked to name among the real antiques that which bears greatest resemblance to this gem, we should refer to the ballad of *Fair Helen of Kirkconnel Lea* in the *Minstrelsy of the Scottish Border*. It is a resemblance of mood, not of execution. They are both highly wrought lyrical expressions of pathos; and it is very remarkable with what intuitive art every expression and cadence in *Fair Helen* is accorded to the main feeling.

The characters that distinguish the language of our *lyrical* from that of our *epic* ballads have never yet been examined with the accuracy they deserve. But, beyond question, the class of poems which in point of harmonious combination *Oriana* most resembles, is the Italian. Just thus the meditative tenderness of Dante and Petrarch is embodied in the clear, searching notes of Tuscan song. These mighty masters produce two-thirds of their effect by *sound*. Not that they sacrifice sense to sound, but that sound conveys their meaning where words would not. There are innumerable shades of fine emotion in the human heart, especially when the senses are keen and vigilant, which are too subtle and too rapid to admit of corresponding phrases. The understanding takes no definite note of them; but then can they leave signatures in language? Yet they exist; in plenitude of being and beauty they exist; and in music they find a medium through which they pass from heart to heart. The tone becomes the sign of the feeling; and they reciprocally suggest each other.

Analogous to this suggestive power may be reckoned, perhaps, in a sister art, the effects of Venetian colouring. Titian explains by tints, as Petrarch by tones. Words would not have done the business of the one, nor any groupings or narration by form, that of the other. But, shame upon us! we are going back to our metaphysics, when that "sweet, meek face" is waiting to be admitted. [*The poem is reprinted here.*]

We have heard it objected to this poem that the name occurs once too often in every stanza. We have taken the plea into our judicial consideration, and the result is that we overrule it and pronounce that the proportion of the melodious cadences to the pathetic parts of the narration could not be diminished without materially affecting the rich lyrical impression of the ballad.

For what is the author's intention? To gratify our curiosity with a strange adventure? To shake our nerves with a painful story? Very far from it. Tears indeed may "blind our sight" as we read; but they are "blissful tears." The strong musical delight prevails over every painful feeling and mingles them all up in its deep swell until they attain a composure of exalted sorrow, a mood in which the latest repose of agitation becomes visible, and the influence of beauty spreads like light over the surface of the mind.

The last line, with its dreamy wildness, reveals the design of the whole. It is transferred, if we mistake not, from an old ballad (a freedom of immemorial usage with ballad-mongers, as our readers doubtless know) but the merit lies in the abrupt application of it to the leading sentiment so as to flash upon us in a few little words a world of meaning, and to consecrate the passion that was beyond cure or hope by resigning it to the accordance of inanimate Nature, who, like man, has her tempests and occasions of horror, but august in their largeness of operation, awful by their dependence on a fixed and perpetual necessity.

We must give one more extract, and we are almost tempted to choose by lot among many that crowd on our recollection, and solicit our preference with such witchery as it is not easy to withstand. The poems towards the middle of the volume seem to have been written at an earlier period than the rest. They display more unrestrained fancy and are less evidently proportioned to their ruling ideas than those which we think of later date. Yet in the *Ode to Memory*—the only one which we have the poet's authority for referring to early life—there is a majesty of expression, united to a truth of thought, which almost confounds our preconceived distinctions.

The *Confessions of a Second-rate, Sensitive Mind* are full of deep insight into human nature, and into those particular trials which are sure to beset men who think and feel for themselves at this epoch of social development. The title is perhaps ill chosen. Not only has it an appearance of quaintness which has no sufficient reason, but it seems to us incorrect. The mood portrayed in this poem, unless the admirable skill of delineation has deceived us, is rather the clouded season of a strong mind than the habitual condition of one feeble and "second-rate." Ordinary tempers build up fortresses of opinion on one side or another; they will see only what they choose to see. The distant glimpse of such an agony as is here brought out to view is sufficient to keep them for ever in illusions, voluntarily raised at first, but soon trusted in with full reliance as inseparable parts of self.

Mr. Tennyson's mode of "rating" is different from ours. He may esteem none worthy of the first order who has not attained a complete universality of thought, and such trustful reliance on a principle of repose which lies beyond the war of conflicting opinions, that the grand ideas, *"qui planent sans cesse au dessus de l'humanité,"* cease to affect him with bewildering impulses of hope and fear. We have not space to enter further into this topic;

but we should not despair of convincing Mr. Tennyson that such a position of intellect would not be the most elevated, nor even the most conducive to perfection of art.

.   .   .   .

The *Sea Fairies* is another strange title; but those who turn to it with the very natural curiosity of discovering who these new births of mythology may be, will be unpardonable if they do not linger over it with higher feelings. A stretch of lyrical power is here exhibited which we did not think the English language had possessed. The proud swell of verse as the harp tones "run up the ridged sea," and the soft and melancholy lapse as the sounds die along the widening space of water, are instances of that right imitation which is becoming to art, but which in the hands of the unskilful, or the affecters of easy popularity, is often converted into a degrading mimicry, detrimental to the best interests of the imagination.

A considerable portion of this book is taken up with a very singular and very beautiful class of poems on which the author has evidently bestowed much thought and elaboration. We allude to the female characters, every trait of which presumes an uncommon degree of observation and reflection. Mr. Tennyson's way of proceeding seems to be this. He collects the most striking phenomena of individual minds until he arrives at some leading fact, which allows him to lay down an axiom or law; and then, working on the law thus attained, he clearly discerns the tendency of what new particulars his invention suggests, and is enabled to impress an individual freshness and unity on ideal combinations. These expressions of character are brief and coherent; nothing extraneous to the dominant fact is admitted, nothing illustrative of it, and, as it were, growing out of it, is rejected. They are like summaries of mighty dramas. We do not say that this method admits of such large luxuriance of power as that of our real dramatists; but we contend that it is a new species of poetry, a graft of the lyric on the dramatic, and Mr. Tennyson deserves the laurel of an inventor, an enlarger of our modes of knowledge and power.

We must hasten to make our election; so, passing by the "airy, fairy Lilian," who "clasps her hands" in vain to retain us; the "stately flower" of matronly fortitude, "revered Isabel"; Madeline, with her voluptuous alternation of smile and frown; Mariana, last, but oh not least—we swear by the memory of Shakespeare, to whom a monument of observant love has been raised by simply expanding all the latent meanings and beauties contained in one stray thought of his genius—we shall fix on a lovely, albeit somewhat mysterious lady, who has fairly taken our "heart from out our breast." [*Here follows* "Adeline."]

Is not this beautiful? When this Poet dies, will not the Graces and the Loves mourn over him, "*fortunatâque favilla nascentur violae*"? How original is the imagery, and how delicate! How wonderful the new world thus created for us, the region between real and unreal! The gardens of Armida were but poorly musical compared with the roses and lillies that bloom around thee, thou faint smiler, Adeline, on whom the glory of imagination reposes, endowing all thou lookest on with sudden and mysterious life. We could expatiate on the deep meaning of this poem, but it is time to twitch our critical mantles; and, as our trade is not that of mere enthusiasm, we shall take our leave with an objection (perhaps a cavil) to the language of cowslips, which we think too ambiguously spoken of for a subject on which nobody, except Mr. Tennyson, can have any information. The "ringing bluebell," too, if it be not a pun, suggests one, and might probably be altered to advantage.

One word more before we have done, and it shall be a word of praise. The language of this book, with one or two rare exceptions, is thorough and sterling English. A little more respect, perhaps, was due to the "*jus et norma loquendi*"; but we are inclined to consider as venial a fault arising from generous enthusiasm for the principles of sound analogy, and for that Saxon element, which constituted the intrinsic freedom and nervousness of our native tongue. We see no signs in what Mr. Tennyson has written of the Quixotic spirit which has led some persons to desire the reduction of English to a single form, by excluding nearly the whole of Latin and Roman derivatives. Ours is necessarily a compound language; as such alone it can flourish and increase; nor will the

author of the poems we have extracted be likely to barter for a
barren appearance of symmetrical structure that fertility of expression and variety of harmony which "the speech that Shakespeare spoke" derived from the sources of southern phraseology.

In presenting this young poet to the public as one not studious
of instant popularity, nor likely to obtain it, we may be thought
to play the part of a fashionable lady who deludes her refractory
mate into doing what she chooses by pretending to wish the exact
contrary; or of a cunning pedagogue who practises a similar
manoeuvre on some self-willed Flibbertigibbet of the school-
room. But the supposition would do us wrong. We have spoken in
good faith, commending this volume to feeling hearts and imaginative tempers, not to the stupid readers, or the voracious readers,
or the malignant readers, or the readers after dinner!

We confess, indeed, we never knew an instance in which the
theoretical abjurers of popularity have shewn themselves very
reluctant to admit its actual advances. So much virtue is not,
perhaps, in human nature; and if the world should take a fancy
to buy these poems, in order to be revenged on the *Englishman's
Magazine*, who knows whether even we might not disappoint its
malice by a cheerful adaptation of our theory to "existing circumstances"?

Rinehart Editions